Retired?

What's Next

Michael Bivona

iUniverse, Inc.
Bloomington

Retired? What's Next

iUniverse books may be ordered through booksellers or by contacting:

iUniverse
1663 Liberty Drive
Bloomington, IN 47403
www.iuniverse.com
1-800-Authors (1-800-288-4677)

ISBN: 978-1-4620-8307-7 (sc)
ISBN: 978-1-4620-8308-4 (hc)
ISBN: 978-1-4620-8309-1 (e)

Library of Congress Control Number: 2011963516

Printed in the United States of America

iUniverse rev. date: 2/20/2012

I would like to dedicate this book to my dear brother,
Victor Bivona, 1925-2011,
whose memory I will always cherish.

Contents

Prologue – Retired? What's Next?

When fortunate enough to arrive at that point in time where a decision must be made about retiring, almost everyone becomes overwhelmed with uncertainty and anxiety. Some perplexing questions that surface include the following: Is the time right? Can I afford to support my lifestyle with retirement income? And, what will I do with my spare time?

The reason I became interested in writing *Retired? What's Next?* is that I also faced all of the above uncertainties and the resulting anxiety that followed. I didn't realize how prevalent and unsettling these pre-retirement concerns were until I was personally faced with them. What piqued my curiosity was a New Year's Eve party on December 31, 1999, hosted by DJ and dancer extraordinaire, Mac Torres. The party was held at the Knights of Columbus Hall in Oyster Bay, Long Island, New York. There were about 100 dancers in attendance, mostly revelers who were in love with ballroom dancing and were a part of the dancing community of Long Island.

My wife Barbara and I were seated at a table with eight other people. Six of them were our dancing buddies who were retired; the other couple, Joe and Jill, were new acquaintances who were reaching retirement age. As the evening and festivities pleasantly moved on toward the magic hour, our new friends asked us how we were enjoying our retirements. The ages of the retired folks at the table were sixty to seventy-five. Barbara and I were in our early sixties, two couples were about seventy years old, and the oldest couple was around seventy-five. The questions Joe and Jill asked were all of the aforementioned, in addition to, "How much time do you spend with your spouse? And what does it do to your relationship?"

Not only was it the night before the long awaited year 2000; it was also my wife's birthday. Again, Barbara was missing out on a personal birthday party, but was content that the whole world was celebrating her end-of-the-year celebration. With all the excitement, as much as we tried, we couldn't get a meaningful dialogue going with our new friends, as the noise level and the festivities kept interfering with our conversations. By the time the evening ended, I had decided that writing a book about retirement might be a good idea and would keep me busy during my golden years. I enjoy writing and when I began this endeavor, I had already completed three books: *Business Infrastructure in a Computer Environment*, published in 2000, *Dancing Around the World with Mike and Barbara Bivona*, 2009, and *Was That Me? Turning Points in my Life*, 2010. I thought that adding another book to my collection about such a universally important subject would keep my fingers busy pounding the keyboards, which has gone from an amusing pastime to a passion. So, at age 66, I decided to keep a diary for the year 2000 and extract from it experiences that my beautiful wife and I were fortunate enough to live through at that wonderful stage of our lives, which would, I hoped, be of interest to people contemplating retirement. I decided to use the diary as a guide and reference to the daily events in our lives. Unfortunately, my plans for writing the book were postponed until 2010, as I was pleasantly distracted by traveling, dance lessons, dancing, playing golf, writing other books, charitable endeavors, and just having a good time. In the meantime, I read some books on the subject of retirement and found that most of the authors indulged in lecturing the readers on the right things to do, in their opinion, prior to the happy event and during retirement. I thought that writing about the subject from our experiences would put an interesting spin on the topic, although there may be times that I will express my opinion on subjects when I think it is appropriate.

Acknowledgments

I would like to thank my many ballroom dancing friends for their love, enthusiasm, and camaraderie, especially when considering the different reasons they love to dance, which makes dancing with people that have such diverse passions all the more exciting. Some of our friends think it's a great way to exercise while smiling. Others enjoy the sport and the competition, while others consider it a good way to meet people in a friendly environment, or an excellent way to build individual confidence, or an effective way to keep one's brain sharp. It has been proven that "Dancing makes people smarter," as attested to by world-renowned scholar and expert on American Social Dancing, Stanford University Professor Richard Powers in his article, "Use it or lose it: Dancing Makes You Smarter." With his permission, the article appears in a later chapter.

It's our many friends, such as June and Misha Rudolph and Ellie and Sal Guarneri, that keep us fascinated and in love with ballroom dancing. We met the fabulous international dancers June and Misha over 15 years ago at Dan Maloney's DanceSport Ballroom in Delray Beach, Florida. It was their love of dancing and their dedication to promoting ballroom dancing that encouraged us to continue with this wonderful art form. Misha has voluntarily helped fellow dancers with their problems on the dance floor and has encouraged many new dancers to continue, even when they were frustrated with the discipline and ready to quit. June competed in Buenos Aires, Argentina at the 2008 World Champion Pro/Am (Professional/Amateur) competition with her professional dance instructor, Thomas Del Flore, of Delray Beach Florida. They placed third in that worldwide competition in three categories: Pro/Am International Standard Championship for ages 50 to 70, Pro/Am International Standard Gold Championship for ages 50 to 70, and International Standard Gold Open Scholarship, which was open to all ages. Each of the categories required performing five dances: Viennese Waltz, Quickstep, International Tango, International Slow Waltz, and International Foxtrot. What a wonderful accomplishment for a senior citizen and her young, handsome professional dance partner.

We met Ellie and Sal at Kismet Hall in New Hyde Park, Long Island, New York, about 16-years ago. They were single at the time and were introduced to each other by mutual dance friends. They became dance partners and, several years later, life partners. Today, at age 85, Sal is still dancing with all the vim, vigor, and passion of a younger man. He and Ellie do a Peabody dance routine in sweetheart position (facing in the same direction) that captures everyone's attention on the dance floor. It never fails; all the dancers stop to watch their performance with utter admiration and lots of envy. In life, there are times when *six degrees of separation* crosses one's path. With me and Sal, it was when we met at the Kismet Dance Hall in Long Island and had a **kismet moment.** He seemed very familiar to me; I kept searching my mind trying to figure out when our paths had crossed. I finally approached him and asked if I looked familiar. He said, "Somewhat, but I'm not sure." So we searched our pasts and discovered we had many things in common. We both came from the East New York section of Brooklyn, and had lived only a few blocks from each other, he also went to the same high school as my older brother Vic and my sisters Anne and Rosaria. Then it hit home, we both worked for a company 50-years ago named Appeal Printing, in Manhattan, New York City, at the same time. He was, in fact, my supervisor—my idol. I was in my mid-teens at the time and looked up to him as an older brother and authority figure. When I told him he accidentally locked me in the warehouse overnight, he knew exactly who I was, but he didn't recall if the lock-up was an accident or on purpose.

It was near the end of the day and he had sent me down to the warehouse, which was in the basement of the building we worked in, to get some boxes for the following day's shipments of our annual calendars. As I had trouble finding the sizes he requested, I remained in the basement-warehouse for quite some time and while in the midst of my search, the lights went out. I immediately made my way to the exit and found that the door was locked. I pounded and yelled for what seemed to be an eternity, but to no avail. I was alone in a dark basement with no chance of getting out until morning. There was still some daylight remaining; noticing a fire axe on the wall, I immediately placed it in my hands and was ready to break the door down when I realized that if someone called the police, I would have a difficult time explaining my presence in the warehouse with an axe breaking the door down to get out. I would probably spend the night in jail waiting for someone to verify my story. As I was only 16 years old at the time, explaining to my father why I was away from home overnight with a jail story attached was another major concern. Unfortunately, in those days telephones were a luxury and only placed in very select locations, our warehouse not being one of them. Today I would whip out my cell phone and the story would end there. So, there I was, no cell phone, the light switch to the warehouse located outside the area, and me all alone in a cold, damp, smelly place. I thought things couldn't get any worse until I tried to get some sleep. I found a box large enough to accommodate my young body, crawled in, and had a very restless night's sleep trying to ignore the squealing and scratching of the night critters. I didn't look to see what was making all the creepy noises, but kept quite still, hoping that they wouldn't discover my intrusion into their domain. After a long and sleepless night, daylight came. My hero Sal opened the door and was surprised to see me in a position ready to pounce on him. He said, "You shouldn't be in here; you'll get into a lot of trouble when the boss finds out." In a rage, I told him my tale of woe, which sent him into a roaring laughter; he put his arm around my young shoulder and said, "Calm down, come, I'll buy you a hearty breakfast at the corner diner and I'll pay you an extra day's wages, after all you were on the premises looking for the boxes I sent you down for. By the way, did you find the boxes?" He also gave me the day off and a note to give to my father explaining the incredible story of my night out.

I would also like to thank my boating friends, some of whom I've known since the purchase of my first boat, an 18-foot runabout, in 1965. Many have remained our friends over the years; others have been added to our boating community along the way. The camaraderie, excitement, commonality, and love for boating are shared in our travels of the waterways to familiar or new destinations, creating a bond between sailors that is hard to explain to landlubbers. I would also like to thank my father-in-law Charley Selden, who introduced me to boating over 40-years ago when we lived in Brooklyn, New York, and sailed the Bergen Beach and Coney Island waters. Our most recent seafaring friends, Greg and Mattie Genovese, are to be congratulated for their passion and adventurous boating spirit. Their conduct as seamen and their pure purpose and love of boating, for all the right reasons, are inspiring and raise the level of the sport for everyone that shares their love of the sea. Their favorite pastime is to "gunk hole," which is done by anchoring at safe harbors overnight enjoying the scenery, sunset, sunrise, and delicious meals whipped up by his wife, **Admiral Mattie.** They do this very often with their children and seven grandchildren, rotating the brood to make sure that there is ample room on board and enough quality time for everyone. We often raft (attach) our 42-foot boat to their 48-foot yacht and join them in relaxing and enjoying incredible nautical surroundings. The gals cook up a storm and socialize while the guys swim, row our small dinghies around, fish a little, and entertain the kids.

Lastly, my beautiful wife Barbara deserves special thanks. I was fortunate to share the year 2000 with her. Her critiques, proofreading, patience, and encouragement throughout this endeavor and my other writings, always brings enjoyment to me and solidifies our 40-plus years of blissful marriage.

Chapter One – Developing Retirement Plans

Retirement in the 21ˢᵗ century is without a doubt complicated and in many cases illusory. People look forward to retirement as that time of life where they are free to do all the fun things that were unobtainable or rare while employed and raising a family. It's visualized as "Our time of life," free from the responsibilities that were required when earning a living and guiding one's children to a place in life where they were safely on their own. When looking at our circumstances and those of our retired friends, we readily determined that devoting all of one's time to the betterment of one's self is not always a reality easily attained. Money, health, and personal obligations usually dictate how much time can be spent in fulfilling all or part of our retirement expectations.

Availability of money can certainly put restrictions on retirement plans, but the lack of it shouldn't stop people from pursuing many of their dreams, perhaps on a different level than anticipated. Some examples are housing and hobbies. Many retirees remain in the homes where they raised their families. Others decide to downsize and escape the financial and physical responsibilities of maintaining a larger, more expensive residence. Some people relocate to other states, while many remain in areas that they are familiar with in downsized dwellings. Whatever their choices, there are an abundance of real estate options in price ranges that can fit everyone's budget, even if the outcome is short of what their expectations were when dreaming about their golden years.

Tennis and golf enthusiasts dream of a time when they can spend most of their free moments playing and perfecting their games. The main considerations during retirement are how much will it cost, and where are the best places to play. Again, reality surpasses dreams. We are all guilty of envisioning the perfect game on the perfect court or fairway. But the reality is dictated by the size of our pockets, where we live, and our health. Fortunately, in the United States, the variety and price ranges of venues to play are astounding. At the top of the financial apex are country clubs and renowned sites, such as the crown tennis facility in the world, the Polo Club in Boca Raton, Florida, and the celebrated golf site, Pebble Beach Resort in Pebble Beach, California. Facilities such as these require large membership fees and hundreds of dollars a day for playtime. On the other hand, there are less expensive sites that are in abundance throughout the country at prices as low as ten dollars a day at county and city facilities, and at reasonable prices at less expensive country clubs. Locating the right places to play can be determined by accessing "Golf Courses or Tennis Courts" in a geographical location of choice on the Internet. The information usually details the various fees for playing and the rules and regulation of the particular facility for guests. It's advisable to take lessons before trying to play either sport, as inexperienced players can be a hazard to themselves and others. The cost of private lessons usually runs from $50 to $100 an hour per person. Group lessons are also available at a much reduced rate at private clubs and municipal facilities. One of my favorite golf courses is the North Shore Veterans' Course in Northport, Long Island, New York. The fees for playing the 9-hole course starts at $16 for walking and $26 with a cart.

Many people, like myself, dream of the time when enjoying the sun while fishing from a boat is the only responsibility facing them. Loafing, drinking a beer, and teasing the ocean's occupants with delicious bait, such as worms or squid, are considered the *mother of all dreams*. The cost of fishing can range from inexpensive to very pricey. The least expensive methods are surf fishing from a beach or dropping a line from designated safe piers or bridges. The cost is the price of a rod and reel and bait. Some municipal piers rent equipment and charge a minimal price for the use of their facilities. A popular way to spend a day in the sun is group fishing on charter boats. The costs can range from $20 to $50 a person, which includes bait and equipment rentals, for a full-day or half-day trip. Renting charter deep sea fishing boats, for a half or full day can be expensive and can cost hundreds of dollars a day for the boat and the use of a skipper, first mate, and the required fishing equipment. Fishing has become a recreation of choice for many disabled wheelchair people. Some municipal piers are lined with wheelchaired fishermen enjoying the sun while telling great fish stories about reeling in **the big one.**

An alternative to renting a boat or pier fishing is to own a boat and fishing in the privacy of a comfortable, familiar place. Boats can range from small rowboats to mega yachts. In our case, we started with an 18-foot runabout Crestliner four-passenger, open cockpit, powered by a 60-horsepower Johnson outboard motor. We eventually upgraded to a 28-foot cabin Chris-Craft, a 35-foot double cabin Chris-Craft, and our current boat in retirement, a 42-foot double cabin Christ-Craft. From the day I went boat-picnicking-fishing on my father-in-law Charley's 28-foot, "Rube Goldberg" boat *No Yak* (No Talking), I was hooked on boating and fishing. The reason I use Goldberg as a reference is because Charley's craft was put together with plumbing pipes. He was a plumber by trade and was adept at using spare parts from his various jobs to keep his boat running and shipshape. His shift lever for his inboard engine was several lengths of pipe that would move the gears from forward to neutral and reverse. Handrails were made out of various lengths of brass and steel pipes; even his footrest under the driver's seat was concocted from pipes. His surreal vessel, which was painted mustard yellow, took us to many islands in Broad Channel and Coney Island in the Borough of Brooklyn, New York, for delightful days of swimming, fishing, and picnicking. The cost of running the boat was quite minimal thanks to Charley's ingenuity.

Almost every woman's dream is to dance with Fred Astaire, Gene Kelly, or even the great Latin romantic Valentino. Being that the dream is not readily attainable, their next choice by default is their husband or significant other. Most men do not share the same passion as their mates for artsy endeavors. They would rather stay at home watching sports channels, playing cards, mowing the lawn, or doing other manly tasks. With perseverance, girls usually gently coerce their mates into joining them in a dance lesson or two to see if it's something that they might both enjoy doing. It's surprising how many men become the dominant person once they decide that dancing is a great pastime. They are attracted to the sport because it provides good exercise, can be very competitive, is a social event that allows switching of partners to dance, and gives everyone a chance to show off, especially with younger women. Like any other sport, lessons should be taken before entering the arena or in this case the dance floor. It's important to know dance floor etiquette, which I discuss in detail in a later chapter, and the importance of allowing other dancers to move around the dance floor without interference. An integral part of dance lessons is to teach the proper movements that everyone should be making on the floor to allow for smooth, uninterrupted dancing. Private dance lessons can run from $50 to $125 an hour per person or couple. The lessons could be at a dance studio or in someone's home, depending on the arrangements that are most comfortable for the student and instructor. Group lessons can start at $10-per-person and higher, depending on the number of students in the class. The more students taking lessons, the less the hourly cost per person, and vice versa. Many dance venues give free lessons before general dancing begins, which gives students an opportunity to practice what they have learned without worrying about looking foolish or being embarrassed as there are many other students practicing and in many cases helping each other with their recently learned routines.

Vacationing is probably the most dreamed of retirement aspiration. Throughout most people's working years, they compile a *Bucket List*, either mentally, or as Barbara and I did, by writing each wish down and hoping that we would live long enough to experience most of our desires before we *kick the bucket*. During our pre-retirement years, time was always of the essence. We seemed to find time to take our children to their extracurricular fun activities, but never seemed to have enough time to satisfy all of our traveling and vacation desires. The cost of traveling today can be relatively inexpensive. Auto trips to national parks such as the Grand Canyon, Brice Canyon, Zion, and Yellowstone are many retirees' favorite destinations. Local state parks are also visited by millions of people each year who stay at the parks' campgrounds or local motels or rent trailers to satisfy their desires and budgets. Sailing the oceans today has also become a popular pastime for senior citizens. Remaining on a ship without worrying about lugging luggage around and eating good food in familiar surroundings has become a very attractive way for people, especially those with limited energy, to travel in comfort. It's surprising how many wheelchaired people have chosen this method of vacationing for the comfort it offers without the physical and mental stress that moving around on land invariably requires. Of course the cost of these vacations can run from inexpensive $100 overnight trips, to voyages around the globe on world-class vessels costing tens of thousands of dollars, on ships such as the new, 5,200-passenger ocean liner *Allure of the Seas.* The list of places and methods of travel are endless and depends on cost and what's on one's *"list of things to do before I die."*

Many people today have had to postpone their retirement expectations because they fall into the 21st century's new phenomenon of being caretakers of multiple family generational members. *Webster's Dictionary* in 2006 added a new term, "Sandwich Generation." These are people that find themselves supporting their children and parents, or their grandchildren and parents, or even their children and grandchildren and in many cases all three generations. The financial strain on the caregivers dictates that they not only postpone the *fun time in their lives,* but that they also must adjust their quality of life as well. In addition to being a part of the "Sandwich Generation," they are also becoming members of the "Mataroq Generation" (Money and Time are Running out Quickly). For this generation of caregivers, vacationing takes the form of backyard barbeques, short road trips, flat-screened television sets, and frequent visits to parents, who hopefully live in Florida where the caring can be combined with some nice sun-related activities like swimming, fishing, boating, or lounging around in the sun in warm weather.

Volunteering for charitable, religious, artistic, scholastic, and any number of other not-for-profit organizations, has become a favorite pastime that many people enjoy in their senior years. These activities don't require cash contributions, just a person's time and energy. Some preferred volunteer services that friends of mine are active in include working as docents at museums, ushers at legitimate theaters, and hospital helpers in the form of patient entertainment and social services, and joining in church activities. The list of volunteer work for good causes is endless, but can be a gratifying experience for retired seniors as it gives them something to occupy their time in a meaningful way.

The important thing to consider is that you have to have something to retire to. Before retiring, it's wise to begin building bridges to things you are passionate about so that when the time comes, you have a choice of which bridges you can comfortably take into the next phase of your life.

Chapter Two – The Beginning of a New Millennium – Year 2000

It might be appropriate to begin my story with some history of the important worldwide events that happened in the year 2000. The first sentence on January 1, 2000 in my diary began with "So where's the **Y2K** computer crash that was predicted by so many **Propeller Heads**?" The **Year 2000 problem** (also known as the **Y2K Problem**, the **Millennium Bug**, the **Y2K Bug**, or simply **Y2K**), was a crisis for both digital and non-digital computer-related documentation and data storage situations due to the practice of abbreviating a four-digit year with two digits. It was believed that without corrective action, existing systems would break down when the abbreviated year 99 concluded and the year 00 ascended. The experts claimed that the reason there were no major failures throughout the globe was due to the preparations taken by responsible individuals and governments. Other gurus claimed that Y2K was a scam perpetrated on the computer population by manufacturers to get them to replace their computers and related equipment with newer, problem-proof ones. The end result was that equipment users around the world replaced or upgraded their hi-tech babies by spending **billions if not over a trillion dollars** to make sure that their computer equipment didn't crash at the appointed moment.

From my own experience, nothing happened to my equipment. I had a fifteen-year-old Epson computer that continued to operate, a ten-year-old HP Pentium that continued to operate, and a brand new HP Pentium III, which I purchased in anticipation of the crash; all operated as well as they did before the phantom event. I was associated with Manchester Technologies at the time; our main product was building and enhancing personal computers. During the panic period, our sales skyrocketed. After the main event, our position was that the reason our customers' computers didn't crash was because of our proactive sales force that alerted them to the impending nightmare. We convinced the end-user that replacement equipment was the best preventative action that they could take, and with few exceptions, they took our advice.

On the same first day of the New Year, a headline in the *New York Times* stated, "Stocks End the Year on an up note." It went on to report, "In a week with relatively little news other than fears of Y2K, the Dow Jones industrial average broke two records last week—the second coming on the final day of trading. The Dow closed Friday at 11,497, giving it a 25 percent return for the year. The return is considered above average under most standards—and continues the streak of returns above 20 percent for the Dow—but it pales in comparison to the astounding finish for the NASDAQ composite index and its host of technology companies.

"The NASDAQ ended the year at a record 4,069.29, an astounding return of nearly 86 percent. The index's 1999 return is the largest ever for a U.S. stock index." Life was good, crime had fallen, stocks had soared, and the Treasury was actually running a surplus. All we had to worry about was whether there were bugs in our computers that would bring the world's electronic babies crashing down at precisely midnight on December 31, 1999.

By January 14, 2000, the Dow peaked at 11,723. NASDAQ followed when it hit its all-time high of 5,132.52. By the end of the year, the indices bottomed at 10,788 for the Dow and an astonishing drop for NASDAQ to 2,470.52. It was the beginning of every investor's nightmare. In 2001, the NASDAQ lost an additional 21.05%, going from 2,470.52 to 1,950.40. It continued to crumble in 2002, when it bottomed out at 1,108.49—a 78.4% drop from its all-time high of 5,132.52. The Dow Jones Industrial Average followed, ending at 10,021 in 2001 and an unpredicted drop to 8,341 in 2002, for a 28.85% drop from its peak of 11,723.

The decrease in stock value from the 2000 crash is estimated to have been in excess of 8 trillion dollars. Needless to say, the impact on people contemplating retirement was devastating. Many postponed their plans, while others had to come out of retirement and return to the workforce—if they could find employment. Some of the causes of the crash that **experts(?)** have determined were:

- **Corporate corruption.** Many companies fraudulently inflated their profits and used accounting loopholes to hide debt. Corporate officers enjoyed outrageous stock options that diluted company stock.
- **Overvalued stocks.** Many companies that had large losses with no hope of turning a profit reported profits and market capitalization of over a billion dollars.
- **Day traders and momentum investors.** The advent of the Internet enabled online trading as an inexpensive way to play the stock market. This revolution led to millions of new investors and traders entering the markets with little or no experience.
- **Conflict of Interest between Research Firm Analysts and Investment Bankers.** It was a common practice for the research departments of investment banks to give favorable ratings on securities for which their clients sought to raise money. Many companies received favorable ratings, even though they were actually having financial problems.

One would think that after suffering over 8 trillion dollars of devalued assets in the stock market worldwide, after the Crash of 2000, that people would have learned some sort of lesson and shy away from investing in corporate America. But greed and unrealistic dreams seem to overcome good sense when getting rich fast in the stock market is concerned. Here we are in the year 2010 witnessing investors pouring money back into the stock market, which recently crashed in the Panic of 2008 that probably equaled if not exceeded the loss of wealth witnessed by the former Panic Crash between 2000 and 2002.

Crowding the headlines of January 1, 2000 on page one of every newspaper in the world was the announcement that the man who was responsible for bringing democracy to Russia with open elections, President Boris N. Yeltsin, resigned his office, "Asking his people and the world for forgiveness for his mistakes and failures and for dashing the hopes of his people for an open democratic society." In his place, Prime Minister Vladimir V. Putin took over as acting president, and a short time after as President of Russia. Putin summarized Yeltsin's contribution to the dissolution and democratization of the Soviet Union and the Eastern Bloc in a eulogy at Yeltsin's funeral on April 25, 2007 where he was put to rest at age 76. He said:

> Yeltsin's presidency has inscribed him forever in Russian and in world history.... A new democratic Russia was born during his time, a free, open, and peaceful country, a state in which the power truly does belong to the people.... The first President of Russia's strength consisted in the mass support of the Russian citizens for his ideas and aspirations. Thanks to the will and direct initiative of President Boris Yeltsin, a new constitution, one that declared human rights a supreme value, was adopted. It gave people the opportunity to freely express their thoughts, to freely choose the leaders in Russia, and to realize their creative and entrepreneurial plans. The new constitution permitted us to begin building a truly effective Federation.... We knew him as a brave, warmhearted, spiritual person. He was an upstanding and courageous national leader. He was always very honest and frank while defending his positions.... He assumed full responsibility for everything he supported, for everything he aspired to, and for everything he tried to do, and did so for the sake of Russia, and for the sake of millions of Russians. He invariably took upon himself what he felt in his heart, which was all the trials and tribulations of Russia, and his peoples' difficulties and problems.

Well, what more can one ask for? January 1, 2000 was the beginning of a new millennium, the beginning of the world's investors' aspirations becoming a reality, where they could all become wealthy in the sky-rocketing stock markets; the Y2K event didn't collapse governments or bring down tall buildings, and the Soviet Union was dissolved with a second elected president taking office, removing our greatest fears of an atomic confrontation with that power. Our President Bill Clinton had the Monica Lewinsky affair behind him, avoiding impeachment by a narrow margin, and was going to leave his successor George W. Bush with a balanced budget. Even the crime rate in the United States was at its lowest peak in decades. What a promising beginning for any new year. What could possibly go wrong?

Well, whatever could go wrong went wrong! As mentioned previously, the bottom dropped out from under the stock markets around the world and would continue doing so for two additional agonizing years, wiping out peoples' fortunes and investments, and setting the stage for a worldwide recession and uncontrolled government deficits, which are still impacting countries in the year 2010, at this writing. There was one other historical event worth mentioning that occurred in the year 2000. The presidential election between George W. Bush, the son of former President George H. W. Bush, and Albert Gore, Jr., former Vice President of the United States under Bill Clinton, ended in a stalemate. The deciding electoral votes were determined by many recounts of Florida's ballots, which at one point gave George W. Bush a mere 177-vote lead. The issue was brought before the U.S. Supreme Court, and for the first time in American history the court would be instrumental in determining who the President of the United States would be. They issued a ruling that stopped the recounting in Florida, thereby giving G.W. Bush the presidency. His brother, Jeb Bush, who was the governor of Florida at the time, thought that the ruling was a fair and just one.

Chapter Three – Our Family

A little history of my family will show that we have a lot in common with most readers. When I began my diary in the year 2000, my wife Barbara, was 63-years of age: she was born in Brownsville, Brooklyn, New York and lived in that neighborhood for the first 20-years of her life. When we met, she was living in the renowned former Brooklyn Dodgers' section of Brooklyn on Flatbush Avenue, on the first floor of a relatively new high-rise building. It is said that the most important things in finding the right place to live are "**location, location, location.**" Well, she certainly found the **right** place to live; it was two blocks from Brooklyn's pride and joy, Prospect Park, where we spent many leisurely summer afternoons rowing on the gigantic lake, walking through beautiful Technicolor gardens and picnicking around, lunch basket, blanket, and wine in hand, on the spacious grass areas. Just one block from her apartment was the Rutland Road subway train station where she caught the train to Manhattan each morning to begin her workday. She was employed as a secretary and financial manager at Rugoff Theaters and subsequently at an advertising firm that specialized in theater advertising. The only downside to the "L-shaped" apartment was the subway train approaching the Rutland Road Station that ran alongside the rooms and mercilessly vibrated the whole unit, which consisted of a small kitchen, a very small dining room, a nice-sized living room, a small alcove bedroom, and a very modern but small bathroom. Barbara attended Brooklyn College, majoring in astronomy with a minor in geology. While in attendance she wrote for various news publications. My beautiful wife-to-be was also an accomplished pianist and a passionate guitarist when we met.

We were introduced to each other at the offices of Rugoff Theaters, which was located at 1270 Avenue of the Americas, in Manhattan, where she was employed as a financial manager at Rugoff Theaters' home office. The building was adjacent to Radio City Music Hall and a part of the Rockefeller Plaza Center Complex. Her boss, Mr. Rugoff, was one of the first to present art movies in New York City, and showed great first-run exclusive movies such as *GIGI*, James Bond movies, and many Japanese art films, some of which played in two theaters simultaneously, which was an experiment in theater presentation in the 1950s. His 15-movie houses, which included some of the first multiplex theaters in the metropolitan area, kept Barbara busy keeping track of their financial records. My job as an auditor with a certified public accounting firm was to review Barbara's work, and review I did. It became my favorite place to work, as I was captivated by her winning smile and charming character. We spent many lunch hours watching people ice skating in the winter at the Rockefeller Ice Skating Rink, which was around the corner from her office, shopping at Saks Fifth Avenue Department Store, which was a couple of blocks away, and at the underground mall that ran beneath Rockefeller Plaza. On payday, which was Friday of every week, when we had some extra *shekels,* we would hang around the bar at the Rainbow Room in the NBC building across from Radio City Music Hall, and literally rub shoulders with fellow New Yorkers who were packed around the smoke-filled bar four deep, and enjoying every moment of the discomfort. At that magical time of our lives, we also spent many enjoyable evenings dining on Restaurant Row, which is on 46th Street, between 7th and 8th Avenues, devouring the *cuisine* at the French, Italian, Spanish, and Russian restaurants, and attending many Broadway shows for free thanks to Barbara's connections in the entertainment industry. What a magical time to be in our mid-twenties, working in the heart of Manhattan and in love with the time, place, and energy of the most exciting city in the world, and **passionately in love with each other.**

When I put pencil to paper in my year 2000 diary at the turn of the century, I was 65-years young. I was born in the East New York section of Brooklyn, and spent my formative years at several different residences throughout the borough. At the age of 18, I joined the United States Air Force in anticipation of my presence shortening the Korean War. My most memorable days were the two years spent in Japan as a Communication Specialist. I was fortunate to spend my last year in Tokyo, as a liaison at the Imperial Palace overseeing the Japanese personnel who were using communication equipment that was the property of the United States. After completing my four years in the service of the United States, I attended Long Island University, located in downtown Brooklyn, New York, majoring in accounting with a minor in economics. After completing my tour of duty at the university, I worked for a certified public accounting firm in Manhattan, New York, and was fortunate to be assigned to their Rugoff Theater account. That is where I met my soul mate and life partner, Barbara Selden. A couple of years later, we were married and moved from Barbara's apartment in Brooklyn to Menlo Park in New Jersey, where, with the help of Barbara's good cooking and her scholastic drilling skills, I passed the New York State Certified Public Accounting examinations. In short order we were back in the Empire State relocating to Dix Hills on Long Island, where we still reside with no plans of moving.

After a few years of marriage we were blessed with our son Stephen Paul, and a little over a year later we were also blessed with our daughter, Laurie Jo, who completed our family unit. In time I started my own accounting firm and eventually had offices in Melville and then Massapequa, Long Island, practicing under the name of Bivona, Ambrico and Dlugacz, Certified Public Accountants. After 25-years in the accounting business, I retired from the profession and became a part owner of Manchester Technologies, which was located in Hauppauge, Long Island. The 12-years I spent with the computer enhancement company went by quickly, and at age 63, when our organization became a public company trading on NASDAQ, I was able to retire on a fulltime basis.

The first important day for us in the new millennium was our grandson Ian Charles Bivona's first birthday, which was on January 4.

He was born to Stephen and Donna on the beautiful island of Oahu, Hawaii. Steve and Donna were in the United States Army and working at Schofield Barracks when their new bundle of joy arrived. We visited them the prior year and were pleasantly surprised when they told us that they were expecting a little boy. We were overjoyed to hear the news as it gave us a reason to again visit the magical island that was the birthplace of our new grandson. It also fit in with our plans for traveling as much as we could afford during our retirement. Visiting our kids would be our third trip to Hawaii and we couldn't wait to celebrate the blessed event with them.

Chapter Four – Making Our Bucket List a Reality

Traveling

Our first trip to the **Islands of Paradise** was on our 25th anniversary when we took a cruise ship that had ports of call on the islands of Maui (Kahului), Kauai (Nawiliwili), and Oahu (Honolulu) and the Big Island of Hawaii. We sailed from Honolulu on the 625-foot, 1000-passenger vintage ship, *S.S. Independence*, for a seven-day voyage to the most idyllic ensemble of islands in the world.

On the first night out at sea we witnessed a once-in-a-life-time sight. At a safe distance, the vessel slowed to an almost dead-stop while we absorbed and inhaled the magical view and offensive gas odors of the surreal, bright red steaming lava flowing from the Kilauea (spewing) Volcano on the Big Island of Hawaii. The red fire slowly integrated and became an integral part of the surrounding water, turning the aqua-green water into a dark red steam bath. The flashes from the passengers' cameras became deafening and the brightness of their lights interfered with the viewing of the natural wonder. The captain of the vessel made an announcement requesting that the guests refrain from using their flash features so that their shipmates could enjoy one of the true **natural** wonders of the world. First thing the next morning, we boarded a bus and were on our way to visit the amazing volcanic site from a land perspective. The volcano is 4,091 feet above sea level, and is the most active volcano in the world with 45 eruptions in the 20th century. Strangely, it is flanked and dwarfed by the world's largest snow-capped active volcano, Mauna Loa, which is 13,677 feet above sea level and 56,000 feet high from its base. This giant has had 33 eruptions in its recorded history, the last one in 1984 when its molten lava almost reached the city of Hilo.

Barbara, who is a devout amateur geologist, went berserk when we disembarked the bus. She ran to the cordoned-off restricted area at light speed, and began taking rapid-fire pictures as if she were photographing a miraculous happening, which to her it was. Her most cherished pictures till this day are the ones she took of the bubbly hot lava with smoke and gases spewing from its crest making its inevitable journey down the hill to its final destination in the sea below. In time, the lava recycles itself and becomes once again a part of the real estate of the Big Island of Hawaii at an estimated rate of one foot per annum.

The Kilauea Volcano is the home of the volcano goddess Pele of ancient Hawaiian legend. There are several lava formations named after her, including Pele's Tears (small droplets of lava that cool the air and retain their teardrop shapes) and Pele's Hair (thin, brittle strands of volcanic glass that often form during the explosions that accompany the lava flow as it enters the ocean). In Hawaiian mythology, Kilauea is where most of the conflict between Pele and the rain god, Kamapua'a, took place. Since it was the residence of Pele, Kamapua'a, jealous of Pele's ability to make lava spout from the ground, covered it with the fronds of the fern, which caused Pele to choke from the inverted smoke. Pele emerged, realizing that each could threaten the other with destruction; the gods decided to call their fight a draw and divided the island between them: Kamapua'a got the windward northeastern side of the island and Pele got the drier, Kona leeward side.

On our journey back to the ship, we stopped at another remarkable site, the Kalapana Black Sand Beach, which was formed as a result of volcanic remnants since before recorded times. The scene was unreal and resembled scenes from horror movies. We were given half an hour to relax on the coarse black sand, which had the most obnoxious odor; none of our group of 30_tourists accepted the challenge. The dark sand didn't stop other bathers and sun worshipers from relaxing and enjoying the smelly environment, as there were well over a hundred people spread out, some on blankets, others on the black sand, all enjoying the dark strange-looking environment. Many swimmers were in the turquoise-blue water totally oblivious of how strange the whole scene appeared to our group.

Our last stop on the Big Island was Captain Cook's Memorial in Kealakekua Bay to pay homage to the great sea captain who was the first Westerner to discover the Hawaiian Islands. The obelisk lies a short distance from where he was killed in a battle with hostile natives. His sailing master was the much-maligned Captain William Bligh of the infamous ship *Bounty,* whose crew chose to stay with the beautiful women and easy life of the island of Tahiti rather than return to the hardship of a sailor's life on board the *Bounty.* It was Bligh that Captain Cook sent ashore to fetch fresh water and food for the crew, thereby making Bligh the first European to set foot on Hawaiian soil. Cook's men also enjoyed the readily available sexual favors of the local girls and the easy life of living among its bountiful beauty. He would have probably had the same mutinous results as Bligh had the local natives been friendlier; unfortunately for him, they were war-like and actually provoked fights with the intruders, which eventually resulted in the death of Cook and many of his men.

On board the ship, we enjoyed dining with our many new friends while devouring the cuisine that included a variety of fresh local fish. We indulged ourselves with *mahi mahi,* swordfish, and lobsters, plus a variety of delicious meat selections and an assortment of tasty desserts. After dinner we would withdraw to the nightclub for big band music and dancing. There was a ten-piece band dressed in flowered, rainbow-colored shirts complemented with bright white pants, playing Hawaiian and lots of ballroom dance music. We were fortunate that most of the people in the nightclub were not serious dancers, so we had the dance floor pretty much to ourselves. We requested Fox Trots, Cha-Chas, and Mambos that the orchestra leader played within minutes of our requests, which had us dancing till the wee hours of the morning. A fun and memorable evening was a ukulele contest for men; we had to wear hula skirts minus tops and were required to learn the instrument and hula dance so we could perform for our shipmates. The results were hilarious; the most amusing part of the exhibitions were our bouncing flabby bellies and hairy chests. I not only had trouble learning to play the small ukulele but had lots of difficulty wriggling my hips without looking like someone from outer space trying to adjust to earth's gravity. Many of the guys did a pretty professional imitation of hula girls, except, that is, for their hairy legs and chests; some of the guy-hulas sported beards that seemed to match their hula skirts, which resulted in a comical, belly-laughing performance. The ladies had a great time poking fun at their husbands and the other wannabe hula girls. Playing our ukuleles and singing "We Are Going to a Hukilau" started out disjointed, but about halfway through the song everyone seemed to get their harmony together and the end result was quite impressive as we sang "We Are Going to a Hukilau, a Huki, Huki, Huki, Huki, Hukilau."

The following day we sighted humpback whale pods while passing between the islands of Maui County. The sight of hundreds of humongous creatures breaking the turquoise-blue sea water in choreographed harmony is certainly one of the most spectacular ocean wonders of the world. The whales migrate approximately 3,500 miles from Alaskan waters each autumn, spending the winter months mating and birthing in the beautiful warm waters off the island of Maui. It's a shame that these mammals are facing possible extinction due to increased levels of pollution, high-speed commercial vessels, and military sonar testing, all of which have diminished their population over the years. They are considered an endangered species and are protected by the world's governments; hopefully, awareness of their plight might result in reestablishing their rightful place on earth. We spent a few hours swimming and sunbathing on the pristine soft white sand of Maui's beach, while mentally swaying in harmony with the palm trees' soft coordinated responses to the mild breeze coming from the sea. An unexpected treat was the conch soup and fritters that were provided by the ever-pleasant native attendants. It was fascinating watching them dive and retrieve the conch shells. They quickly extracted the delicious conch and in short order made exotic-tasting soup and fritters that everyone devoured with lots of favorable mmmmms and ahhhhhs. It was difficult leaving the heavenly beauty of the island to return to our ship; surely there is no other place on earth to compare with its natural beauty and bountiful resources—so I thought. That is, until we visited the Island of Kauai, which is considered the tropical centerpiece of Hawaii.

It is carpeted with lush greenery, covered with flowers of every color, and has visible fresh fruit growing in abundance. There was an ever-present comforting cool mist, which we were in dire need of that day, as it gave us relief from the hot rays of the ever-present sun. Kauai is the oldest of the Hawaiian Islands; it was here that Captain Cook gave the islands their first Western name, Sandwich Islands. It was named after his sponsor the Earl of Sandwich who invented the sandwich as we know it today. He was an avid card player and, to keep the players at the card table instead of the food bar, he concocted the sandwich to ensure uninterrupted gambling. We spent the better part of the day exploring the island and visiting Waimea Canyon, which is the largest canyon in the Pacific. It measures ten miles long, one mile wide and is more than 3,500 feet deep. It was carved thousands of years ago by rivers and floods that flowed from Mt. Waialeale's summit. It's not as large as the Grand Canyon in Arizona, but certainly rivals its beauty and complexity. The lines of the canyon walls reveal different volcanic eruptions and lava flows that have occurred over the centuries, which from certain points look like the colors of a rainbow. The canyon is in Koke'e State Park, which encompasses endless acres of land, with 45 miles of trails that run through it and nearby swamps. The island is certainly a place to add to our *Bucket List* for a future visit of a week so we could spend time exploring the trails and campsites while staying at the rustic Hale Koa Cabins that are located in the park.

Our last stop was the Spouting Horn. This natural wonder occurs when water rushes under a lava shelf and bursts through a small opening on the surface. Every wave produces another spray, frequently 50 feet into the air. The phenomenon is especially exciting at sunset, when the spray becomes incandescent with the colors of the rainbow. There are signs warning viewers to stay behind the cordon ropes, as injuries and even fatalities have resulted to people that wandered close to the blowhole. Legend has it that the coast was guarded by a large *mo'o* (lizard) that ate anyone who tried to fish or swim in the area. One day, a native named Liko entered the water to explore the ocean's treasures, when the *mo'o* attacked him; he swam under the lava shelf and escaped through the hole. The *mo'o* followed him but got stuck and couldn't free himself. The groaning from the blowhole is his cry from hunger and pain as he remains trapped under the rocks for eternity. I love Hawaiian legends, they seem to be steeped in mystique that captures and stretches the imagination. Many years ago there was a much larger blowhole called the Kukuiula Seaplume adjacent to the Spouting Horn. It shot water 200 feet into the air. However, as the salt spray damaged a nearby field of sugar cane, which no longer exists, the hole was blasted away in the early part of the 20th century. Imagine trying to destroy such a natural wonder today; every environmentalist in the world would be up in arms. The island has such diverse beauty that over 60 featured movie films have been shot there, such as the majestic scenes of the Manawaiopuna Falls in *Jurassic Park,* the Wailua River in Elvis Presley's *Blue Hawaii,* and the Anahola Mountains, which were used as the backdrop in the *Raiders of the Lost Ark.* Unfortunately, we again had to drag ourselves from another island in paradise as the sun began to disappear in the sky, and returning to our home on the sea before nightfall became an unpleasant reality.

Our last night was a formal dress evening. Out came my black tuxedo, starched collared shirt, bow tie, suspenders, and a sash wrapped around my waist, which gave me the feeling of being prepared for mummification. The dinner was spectacular. I chose once again freshly caught *mahi mahi* (dolphin, not the playful ones with long snouts, but the blue-finned type). Watching the tuxedoed waiters singing Hawaiian songs while serving our meal was amusing; the only distinguishing differences between their dress and the tuxedoed guests were that the waiters wore white gloves and were singing. Aside from those two differences, we all looked alike, which made socializing at times a little difficult, especially when I asked a guest where some of the amenities on the ship were, thinking that he was a waiter. After dinner, I returned to my cabin to take off the uncomfortable tuxedo and put on more comfortable attire that would allow me to dance the evening away with some comfort and ease. We spent the evening dancing to the wonderful music of the live band, which went out of their way to play our requests for ballroom dance music.

At that time it was customary for many cruise vessels to have different themed midnight buffets every evening. Barbara's favorite has always been the chocolate nights, which so happened to be the theme on the last day of our cruise. Nowadays cruise ships have replaced the chocolate sculptures and goodies with ice ones complemented with small desserts. But that evening, we feasted on chocolate birds, flowers, miniature tigers, and an assortment of other little critters. I found it difficult biting into a chocolate canary, but Barbara had no trouble devouring her favorite desserts; I thought she would eat herself into heavenly chocolate oblivion. Cruise ships today wisely have done away with these daily evening buffets as they resulted in an unnecessary waste of food and added needlessly to the expense of cruising. Today, most ships have just one night of pigging out with a buffet style extravaganza, which helps alleviate the guilty feeling that most people have when eating a late unnecessary fourth meal consisting of mountains of sweets.

We docked in Honolulu at the same pier that we departed from on the heavily populated island. It's easy to understand why more than half the people in Hawaii live on this island in paradise; it not only has some of the most beautiful beaches in the world, but it is also a metropolis of the first order, with cultural and educational facilities readily available. It even boasts the world's largest wind generator (20-stories high with 400-foot blades), which is employed to create electricity for a good part of the island. We headed straight to the Sheraton Waikiki Hotel, which is located on the main beach on Kalakaua Avenue, and has commanding views of Diamond Head Mountain, Honolulu, and Waikiki Beach. Our plans were to spend the remaining few days of our vacation exploring the sophisticated clubs and some of the world-renowned local sights.

To get our land legs back, we decided to spend the first day walking along the main street, Kalakaua Avenue, and exploring the shops and Waikiki Beach. As luck would have it, we immediately stumbled onto the Waikiki Town Center. The name is deceiving; I thought it was a visitor's center, but it wasn't. It was a shopping mall with about 50 vendors, restaurants, and lots of tourists. Barbara was ecstatic; it was just what she needed after spending a week on board a ship with limited shopping, aside from souvenirs and T-shirts. Our first stop was an outside vendor displaying oysters. For a price we were invited to buy one that might, miraculously, contain a pearl. Barbara got lucky and bought one that had a mini-pearl enclosed. She immediately made plans to have it set in a ring, which the vendor's cousin, located at the next booth, just happened to have at a much discounted price. During our walk, I noticed everyone seemed to be as lucky as she, they all won pearls with their purchases, but not many chose to use the cousin's services to mount their new-found treasures. The center was dominated by a gorgeous fountain in an open courtyard with shops surrounding it having local names like Red Dirt Tees, Quicksilver Boardrider's Club, and Chin Lan. For the most part, the shops sold Hawaiian souvenirs and clothing. It didn't take long before I coaxed Barbara out of the small shopping center and, wouldn't you know it, right next door was the International Marketplace with 130 carts, shops, and artisan stands. It seemed that I wasn't going to have a good day, as shopping isn't one of my favorite pastimes, unless it has something to do with golf or boating. I must say, the local craftspeople were very friendly and volunteered tales of their heritage, especially if they were **real Hawaiians** (unbroken racial lineage), which they are very proud of. We took some nice photos of a small cascading waterfall from under a century-old banyan tree. The large eccentric tree was fascinating; the twists and turns of its branches and the bulges in its trunk were an anomaly, as if the creator couldn't make up its mind in which direction the tree should travel. Its distortions make the tree one of nature's special works of art. Another unusual attraction was the Swiss Family Robinson-style tree house, which was the original home of one of the locals, Donn the Beachcomber.

We previously made a mental note to visit the Royal Hawaiian Hotel, known worldwide as the Pink Palace, which is located on the beach side of the main street. The entire outside façade of this enormous hotel is bright pink, which illuminates the beach and sky when the sun sets in the evening. A pink color theme prevails throughout the hotel, right down to the plush beach towels. As guests of its sister, the

Sheraton Hotel, we had dining and beach privileges, so we brought along our swimsuits and decided to spend an afternoon on its private, pristine beach. Upon entering the hotel, native girls dressed in colorful skirts greeted us with beautiful multicolored leis and pieces of banana bread. The overwhelming pink-vaulted ceilings blended in with the huge Art Deco arched mirrors in the public areas and over the shops, which matched the pink outfits that the staff wore. We were escorted to dressing rooms where we could change into our swimsuits; we then proceeded to the beach, where bronze suntanned boys secured pink chaise lounges, pink and tan striped umbrellas, and pink beach towels for our pleasure. The pink Pacific gem, which was built in 1927 on Waikiki Beach, has to be experienced to be believed. A BBQ of ribs was being prepared, which spread its delightful aroma throughout the beach, while music filled the air with soft exotic Hawaiian songs coming from a live, four-piece Polynesian band, who were accompanied by two gorgeous tan, black-haired, barefooted, shapely hula girls moving their hips and arms to the rhythm of the music.

We ordered Mai Tai drinks from the open-air Mai Tai Bar, where it is boasted that the drink originated. Small handouts were delivered with the drinks listing its ingredients:

> One ounce of dark rum
> One ounce of light rum
> One ounce of orange Curacao
> Two ounces of orange juice
> One-half ounce of lime
> A dash of Orgeat
> A dash of simple syrup
>
> Combine all of the ingredients, in the order listed, into an old fashioned-style glass and pour over shaved ice. Stir with a swizzle stick. Garnish with a slice of pineapple and a cherry, and then drink slowly.

We decided to order the concoction in a pineapple with a small pink umbrella on top, which certainly enhanced the drink and made it a truly Hawaiian experience. It was easy to settle in and enjoy the food from the BBQ; spareribs and roasted pork strips with pineapple trimmings, while sucking in the fresh air and the hypnotic aroma coming from the BBQ pits. Watching the four to six-foot afternoon waves beating on the sandy shore and then gently retreating, leaving foamy bubbles as a reminder of their visit, quickly opened my heart to the magic of Hawaii as being one of my favorite places on earth.

We replenished our Mai Tai drinks and relaxed for the rest of the afternoon, enjoying hula exhibitions by gorgeous Hawaiian girls and ukulele serenading by handsome, young, colorfully dressed Hawaiian men. We stayed until sundown, which is an experience not to be missed. The sky turned bright red with rainbows dancing in the sky and bouncing off the ocean, as the sun inched out of sight into the horizon to the moans and sighs of the viewing spectators. We returned to our hotel exhausted from the pleasures of the day and went directly to our room for a glorious night's sleep.

Rising early in the morning to the bright Hawaiian sunlight, we decided to follow the aroma that was coming from the exotic tropical breakfast buffet being served at the open air rooftop restaurant, which was located several stories below our terrace. It was surprising to see the variety of Japanese food presented: miso soup, rice, and even sushi were scattered throughout the maze of goodies. Looking around and noticing the diners explained why; about two-thirds of the guests were Japanese enjoying sushi with all the trimming as a breakfast. It was difficult while looking around the dining room and city to believe that the Japanese lost World War II. It seemed that what they couldn't conquer during the hostilities they succeeded in conquering during peace time, as the sushi bars and menus at restaurants throughout the islands were written in English and Japanese, and not particularly in that order. Japanese food has always been one of Barbara's favorite indulgences and that morning was no exception. She couldn't stop raving about how wonderful the delicacies were. Although I also love Japanese food, having it for breakfast didn't interest me, so I satisfied myself with cereal, eggs, and plenty of Hawaiian pineapple, which I couldn't seem to get enough of as the sweetness of the Hawaiian fruit is without equal.

We picked up a walking map of the area and decided to walk in the direction of the Diamond Head Crater, which was a short distance from our hotel and is a part of the Kapiolani Park Complex. The 500-acre park was created by King Kalakaua in the late 19th century and is home to the famous Kodak Hula Show, the world-renowned 42-acre Honolulu Zoo, and the Waikiki Shell Amphitheater. It boasts tennis courts, a soccer field, an archery range, and a three-mile joggers' trail, but the most spectacular jewel is its beach with the historic Diamond Head Crater in the background. We brought beach-mats with us and leisurely spread them under a shady palm-treed picnic beach area and spent the better part of an hour sipping our coffee and absorbing the heavenly beauty of nature's gifts to the island and its inhabitants.

The respite gave me time to read the fascinating history of the Diamond Head Crater, as follows:

> It's considered one of the most famous dormant volcanic craters in the world, located on the southeast coast of Oahu at the end of Waikiki Beach, overlooking the sparkling rippled blue Pacific Ocean. It was originally named Laeahi by the ancient Hawaiians. The name meant "Brow of the tuna," looking at the silhouette of the crater from Waikiki the resemblance becomes quite evident. The current name was given to the crater by British sailors in the early 19th century. When they first saw the crater from their ships, the calcite crystals in the lava rock appeared to glimmer in the sunlight. They mistakenly thought that there were diamonds in the soil, and hence the name Diamond Head was born. The crater has been extinct for over 150,000 years. It's 3,520 feet in diameter with a 760-foot summit.

Here is what makes it one of the most unusual craters in the world:

> When the United States annexed Hawaii in 1898, its harbor defense became one of the government's main concerns. A major defense fort, Fort Ruger, occupied

the crater. A battery of cannons was located within the crater, providing complete concealment and protection from invading enemies. An observation deck was constructed at the summit in 1910 to provide target sightings. A four-level underground complex, built within the walls of the crater and a command post was carved into the mountain. Its 580-foot tunnel, which was dug through the crater wall, provided easy access to the fort and its confines. With the advent of radar, the observation deck and underground complex became obsolete and was abandoned, but evidence of the command post is still present along the Diamond Head Trail. The trail is paved almost its entire length, but is very steep in spots and quite dangerous. There are two sets of stairs, one 99 steps and the other 76 steps. There is also a 225-foot unlit tunnel that must be traversed very carefully to avoid serious accidents. A hike up the mountain is classified as easy to moderate in exertion, but is certainly worth the breathtaking, unparalleled view of the entire west side of the island, from Waikiki to Koki Head.

The history was fascinating to read, and even though walking up to the crater was considered easy, we decided to have a relaxing day and just hang around the lower part of the mountain.

We followed the sound of the island music and arrived at the Kodak Hula Show, where we were greeted by beautifully dressed young girls in hula skirts, with colorful leis around their necks and multi-flowered tiaras neatly placed on top of their long, black, shiny hair. They greeted us with *alohas* and exchanged their leis, which were so beautifully displayed around their necks, over our heads and onto our shoulders. This was ceremoniously done while wriggling their hips and waving their arms to the rhythm of the wavy tropical music coming from a ukulele combo. The Kodak Hula Show has been a Hawaiian tradition since 1937. The fabulous outdoor spectacular is an historical look at the island through the beauty of the hula dance performed by Hawaiian natives. The show that day consisted of a cast of 40 entertainers from the Royal Hawaiian Glee Club. The dancers were dressed in traditional skirts made of green Ti leaves, coconut-shell bras, and fragrant flowered leis decorating their hair. Performances were conducted at the Shell Amphitheater and were probably the most synchronized, harmonious, and beautifully choreographed dances that I have ever seen. The music seemed to be coming from within the dancers as they moved around the stage performing soft, flowing sensual motions in harmony with one and other and the music. I must say that Hawaiian dancing and music is an integral part of why so many people love the beautiful islands, and why I became so captivated with the magic of it all.

After the show we moseyed over to the world-renowned 42-acre Honolulu Zoo. We were immediately drawn to the unique African Savannah, which had lions, giraffes, zebras, elephants, and other natural habitat creatures wandering around as if they were in an African jungle. What sets the zoo apart from others is that it features moonlight tours so that visitors can enjoy the wildlife animals that normally sleep by day, such as skunks, toads, snow leopards, raccoons, possums, hedgehogs, fireflies, and badgers. To make a visit to the zoo more interesting, they have overnight camping where participants bring their own camping equipment and set up for the evening in designated areas very close to the savannah. Supervised feeding of the animals is also allowed. I heard one young girl that spent an evening with her family in the park talking about how she visited the hippo den and fed an apple to a four-thousand-pound resident. She saw that I was interested in her adventure and excitedly told me of being escorted by the zookeeper to a hyena's home at feeding time and helping him feed its hungry family. I asked her what her most memorable experience was and she said, "Trying to avoid the toads at night that seemed to be all over the walking paths and were attracted to everyone's flashlights." Her happiest experience was when Pizza King delivered pizzas, soda, garlic nuggets, and doughnuts. It is certainly not an unpleasant way to spend a night-out with the family.

We returned to our hotel for a nap, which was becoming a necessary, every-day event due to our excessive walking and the soothing sea air that seemed to relax us down to our core, making us numbly sleepy.

We visited our hotel concierge, Jackson, and asked him if there were any good dancing venues close by. He suggested the Hilton Hawaiian Village Beach Resort and the Pink Palace. We asked him to make reservations at the Hilton for dinner and whatever entertainment that was available for the evening, and to do the same for the Pink Palace for the following evening. We headed to our room and immediately visited dreamland for a well-deserved nap; we were so exhausted that we didn't even whisper our usual pre-slumber niceties to each other.

We arrived at the Hilton Hawaiian Hotel just in time to hear the loud horn-like sounds from conch shells announcing the end of daylight and the beginning of the lighting of torches ceremony throughout the tropical area, to the beat of island drums, singing, and fireworks. We were again greeted by beautiful young daughters of Hawaii, who pleasantly placed leis around our necks while gyrating their voluptuous hips to the rhythm of the native drums. It was certainly a great way to put us in the mood for an enjoyable evening, especially when their second act was to put Mai Tai drinks in our hands. We were seated facing the man-made, enormous Duke Kahanemoku Lagoon, and were startled to see a large canoe with about a dozen Hawaiian fisherman land on the Great Lawn in front of us, which signaled the start of the night's *luau* extravaganza. The Hawaiian fishermen began to mingle with the guests, inviting them to learn and dance the *Hukilau*, a traditional song and dance that tells about fishermen and their catch of the day. It was so spontaneous and exciting that we actually started imitating the men doing the *Hukilau* dance while trying to catch and sing the words to the "Hukilau Song," which was originally written by an American, Jack Owens, in 1948. I think it went something like this:

> What a wonderful day for fishing in the old Hawaiian way, where the Hukilau nets are swishing down in Old Laie Bay. Oh we're going to a Hukilau, and huki-huki-huki-huki Hukilau. Everybody loves a Hukilau, where the laulau is the kaukau at the big luau. We throw our nets out into the sea, and all the ama-ama come a-swimming to me. Oh we're going to a Hukilau, a huki-huki-huki-huki- Hukilau.

What a great time we had imitating fishermen casting their nets upon the sea and then retrieving them with the catch of the day. We enacted this to the rhythm of the "Hukilau Song" as we swayed our hips and arms, trying to imitate the Hawaiian men's motions. After settling down from the fishing activity, we were escorted to the *imu* (underground oven), while we were still in motion, to see the ceremonial removal of the cooked pig from the *imu* and its preparation for the forthcoming feast. The luau menu included *kalua* pig, *poi*, *iomi-iomi* salmon, and cold selections, such as island-style macaroni salad and seasonal fruit. Other hot items included grilled *huli-huli* chicken, *mahi-mahi* with macadamia nuts, creamed spinach, rice, taro, and sweet rolls. Desserts included macadamia nut cream pie, coconut cake, and guava cake. To add insult to injury, where our diets were concerned, Mai Tais were included in the price of the feast. We tried to be very selective in our choice of food, but between the two of us, we couldn't help sampling everything on the menu.

We needed the long walk back to our hotel to work off the heavy meal and the delicious potent drinks that we consumed. We swore that we would never again devour such large quantities of food and beverages, and decided that the next day we would avoid any place that had elaborate or tempting food selections. So we spent the next day hanging around the hotel's swimming pool and working out at the gym, hopefully working off some of the calories we forced into our bodies, so unwillingly, the night before. We visited our concierge, Jackson, who reminded us that the dress code at the Pink Palace was not casual and that we had an eight o'clock reservation for dinner and dancing that evening.

We dressed accordingly, wearing our most comfortable shoes for some serious dancing. Entering the large dining hall was a throwback to the WWII era. A large 17-piece band, its members dressed in tuxedoes, resembled scenes from some of John Wayne's war movies, especially when seeing the many naval officers throughout the hall sporting their white dress uniforms. The venue has been a naval hangout since the beginning of WWII and, evidently, continues to be a favorite with the sailors stationed in Hawaii. We danced, danced, and danced around the ballroom and on the enormous outside terrace overlooking the

Pacific Ocean, which reflected the distant flames of night torches, which not only kept the mosquitoes away, but provided a very romantic setting for slow dancing. The side views from the terrace of Waikiki Beach's glowing nightlights added to the ambiance and mood of the evening. I was surprised at the number of people, especially sailors that were not only dancing acceptable smooth ballroom dancing and swing, but were also quite good at Latin Mambo, Cha-Cha, and Merengue. We had a special treat that evening: Martin Denny was in the audience and was asked to play some of his poplar music, which he did without hesitation and a big smile on his face. He played the piano to perfection, entertaining us with "A Taste of Honey," "The Enchanted Sea," *and* "Ebb Tide." Unfortunately he didn't have members of his band with him; if he had, we would have heard some of his exotic Hawaiian music. His writing and performances with unusual percussion instruments brought life back to many old standards such as "Flamingo" and "Sayonara." We ended the evening with a conga line dance, where the guests lined up in back of each other and moved around the floor to the music of "Locomotion." Somehow I found myself at the head of the line leading 100-plus guests to the beat of the drums, singing the words "do the locomotion" while moving our arms back and forth, imitating a locomotive train gone awry. The conga line dance ended our evening and our 25th "Anniversary Waltz" with the heavenly islands of Hawaii.

We promised ourselves that we would return to Hawaii and continue our love affair with the glorious islands, but we knew that the possibility was remote as there were so many other places on our *Bucket List* that we would have to explore before returning to the islands of our dreams. But providence decided that we would again visit Hawaii. Our son Stephen and daughter-in-law Donna were both officers serving in the United States Army, and after spending two years in Korea, they were fortunate to be assigned to Schofield Barracks on the Island of Oahu, which was just a short ride from Waikiki Beach. As married officers they had a choice of living on the military base or receiving a housing allowance, which allowed them to live in their own home off-base. They chose to live in the residential community of Waialua on the north shore of Oahu, but wouldn't tell us anything else about the location, as they wanted to surprise us. All they would say is that we would have our own room with a private bathroom for our convenience. So being that we were going to live among the natives for a couple of weeks, we decided to do some in-depth research about the customs of the friendly Hawaiians.

Aloha, Aloha, Aloha, is a word that is heard every minute of every day when traveling through the islands. What better way to understand the natives than to understand the meaning of the mysterious-sounding greeting. The word conjures up all sorts of beautiful images, such as hula girls dancing, waves embracing pristine beaches, palm trees swaying in soft breezes, colorful dresses and shirts, and flowers of every description in bloom year round lending their fragrances to receptive breaths of fresh air. The word *Aloha* has come down through the ages and doesn't have one meaning, but a combination of meanings that describe its use, as follows:

> **A**-means welcome, what I have you may have, come share with me.
> **L**-comes from the Hawaiian word *loko maikai* which means, what I have said comes from my heart and good intentions.
> **O**-comes from the Hawaiian word *oluolu,* meaning happy, this is part of our heritage—a happy people, happy doing for others.
> **H**-comes from the word *haahaa,* meaning humility and meekness; we welcome you; we do things for you because we are happy doing it and are very humble to serve.
> **A**-means all of these expressions mean *Aloha* and should only be used when you feel them in your heart.

Well, the above poetic revelation certainly explained the pleasant attitude of the Hawaiians that we met on our first trip. It certainly would give us all the more reason to use the word with a lot more understanding and humility when we return to the islands.

Another familiar custom is the *shaka,* which is a hand movement that translates to "hang loose, everything is cool bruddah." It is done using the thumb and pinky of your hand and doing a little wriggle. It's a friendly gesture and is done with good intentions, similar to your saying 'have a good day' while tipping your hat. It's believed that the traditional *shaka* originated in ancient times when a great chief lost his three middle fingers in an accident. Thereafter, he would greet his subjects by waving the altered hand at them. They, in turn, not to show any disrespect, would respond in the same manner.

Another tradition that is practiced throughout the islands is the ceremony of *Luau.* It has significance far beyond it being a BBQ. A *Luau* means "good food and drink, music and dance, conviviality and fun, usually set against a background of a blazing tropical sunset." To the ancient Hawaiians it was all this and more, since *Luaus* were also occasions to thank the gods for good fortune and to ask for future blessings. Among the ancients, their gods were involved in every earthly activity, ruling over birth, marriage, death, war, seasons, sports, skills, and indeed, all daily happenings. Major events in the life of a village were commemorated with a communal feast, which was originally called an *ahaaina* but in time became known as a *Luau.* It was only natural that these celebrations should be dedicated to a particular god, or gods, who held primary influence over the event. For instance, a feast celebrating the gathering of crops would be especially sacred to "Lono," the harvest god. The gods had their favorite *Luau* foods; *Kalua* pig, baked in an underground oven called an *imu,* and chicken were traditional offerings. No *Luau* would be complete without the Hawaiian staff of life, *taro,* which is the tender young leaf of the plant called *Luau,* from which the current name of the feast is derived. It is lavishly cooked with coconut cream and its roots pounded into *poi.*

With a better understanding of Hawaiian customs, we were ready to journey part way around the world to visit our children, and hopefully spend some time enjoying the camaraderie of the friendly natives. I looked up the kids' new home, Waialua, and found that there were lots of recreational activities to keep us busy: fishing, sailing, scuba diving, swimming, surfing, and many other water sports to suit our fancy. The kids remained secretive and mysterious about the details of where they lived. The only thing we could get out of them was, "We want to surprise you." When we arrived at their home we were certainly surprised. They occupied a three-bedroom two-level house, with a 200-foot backyard leading to the most gorgeous beach in the world. My heart doubled its pace when I saw the magnificent view. After unpacking, I had stretched out on the hammock hanging from the ceiling of their terrace facing the ocean, while nursing a tropical drink, when my son Steve asked me: "Dad, did I do the right thing in renting this house instead of living on the base at Schofield Barracks, which is a lot less expensive?" My answer was spontaneous; I said, "Steve, if I were your age I couldn't think of a more beautiful place on this planet that I would rather be than right here, on this hammock, looking at this ocean." He then said, "Dad, we have another surprise for you." At that moment, I heard Barbara let out a scream from inside the house where she was hugging Donna, as she yelled, "You're pregnant!" That said it all; we hugged and kissed, our first grandchild was on its way. It was one of the happiest moments in my life. My baby boy's wife was having a baby boy.

Steve decided to have a cookout on the beach that afternoon. They invited some of their army buddies and neighbors for the feast. Steve has always been a great chef and especially enjoys doing BBQs. About 12 of their friends arrived to the smell of hotdogs, burgers, and spareribs roasting on their open oversized pit. I couldn't believe the whole scene; it was dreamlike. We came to see our children, who were in the military and had just returned from tours of duty in Korea. We were expecting to see them in the drab surroundings of a military base, but instead, here we were on a beach in their backyard, enjoying the surf, tropical fruit drinks, spareribs, and the camaraderie of their friends—what an exquisite turn of events from what we expected. The food had a special flavor, which was enhanced by the smell of fresh sea air, the pale blue sky with an ensemble of various-shaped clouds, the sound of the waves caressing the sandy beach, pleasant military and native company, and of course, my pregnant daughter-in-law. I thought that I had died and gone to heaven. After our feast, as if rehearsed, everyone donned their swimsuits and ran pell-mell into the delicious turquoise-blue surf screaming and howling at the pleasure of the water cooling their bodies. While we were swimming and horsing around, we were joined by a neighbor's two Labrador retrievers, who couldn't resist an opportunity to join in the excitement and add to the splashing and clamor. The setting of the sun was another spectacular event. It made the sky look as if it were fire-bright red and orange, blending in with the clouds and then, very gently, but quickly, disappearing out of sight beyond the horizon. Steve lit a camp fire and we started toasting marshmallows as we sang. One of the guys magically produced a guitar and began playing Hawaiian songs, including, "Tiny Bubbles (tiny bubbles), in the wine (in the wine), makes me happy (makes me happy) . . ." What a memorable way to end our first day in Hawaii with our lovely children, their jovial friends, and the serendipitous surrounding of nature's landscape beaming with perfection.

Waking to the sounds of waves hitting the beach, and the urge of rushing to take a swim was too much to resist. I ran as quickly as I could and dove, head first, into the breaking surf, with my eyes wide open so I wouldn't miss any underwater marine sights. After swimming underwater and coming up for air when needed, I decided that it was time for an oversized breakfast. When I exited the water, my eyes burning from the salt and my lungs consuming the fresh sea air in short bursts, I again thought that I must have died and was in heaven. Steve, who is one of the best chefs in the world, whipped up my favorite blueberry pancakes for breakfast, which we quickly devoured and washed down with the sweetest pineapple juice and the most delicious Hawaiian Kona coffee this side of heaven. He then asked what we would like to do for the day. We decided to visit downtown Honolulu and hang around the beach area. That is just what we did on our first trip to paradise; we made lots of beach visits, we drank many gallons of Kona coffee, and ate pineapples till they were coming out of our ears.

Our second visit to Hawaii ended with lots of hugs and kisses from our children, and many handshakes and nose rubs from their neighbors, who seemed to have adopted us into their island culture. They assured us that if we returned to Hawaii a third time we would be considered honorary citizens and would be given Hawaiian names. We couldn't wait to return to see our first grandchild the following year and possibly being christened with Hawaiian names.

Needless to say, we began planning our trip back to Hawaii as soon as we returned to New York. We had seven months before returning and Barbara figured with our existing American Express frequent flier remaining miles balance, that by the time we were ready to depart, we might have enough miles to fly free. As usual, she was right, so we exchanged our frequent flier miles for two coach seats and then upgraded them to first class for an additional fee, which would certainly make the 12-hour flight a lot more comfortable. We also heard from our dancing friends that there was a great dancing venue right at Waikiki Beach called the Palladium Dance Hall, which is located at the Ali Wai Country Club. So we booked rooms at the Hyatt Regency Hotel on Kalakaua Avenue, which is across the street from the breakwater at Waikiki Beach, and a short distance from the International Marketplace, Waikiki Aquarium, Honolulu Zoo, Kapiolani Park, and, most importantly, the Palladium Dance hall.

With the "blink of an eye," it was January, and we were on our nonstop flight from JFK Airport to Honolulu, Hawaii, or so we thought. We boarded our American Airlines' plane and settled in for the takeoff, but there was a mechanical problem and we had to exit the plane and wait several hours for a replacement. Fortunately, as first-class passengers, we had the use of the Admiral's Club Lounge, which made life a little more tolerable as we had access to comfortable seats, finger food, cold drinks, coffee, newspapers, private toilets, and several television sets. We boarded the next plane and were informed that it didn't have the fuel capacity to take us nonstop to Hawaii; we would have to land in Los Angeles to refuel. To make a very long story short, our 12-hour flight took 16 uncomfortable hours. When we landed in Honolulu we were exhausted and totally annoyed at the whole experience; what else could possibly go wrong? We soon found out. I can't explain the gruesome feeling I had while waiting for our luggage at the carousel. There was no baggage left on the arrival conveyor. There we were, standing by the carousel, flat footed, totally exhausted from the long flight, and not knowing what to do next. We went to the American Airlines' office and waited in line with about twenty other people. Some of the travelers in line were frantic, as they had to catch connecting flights out of Honolulu and were totally baffled as to what to do without their luggage. We finally filled out the appropriate forms and explained our dilemma to a very sympathetic young lady, who assured us that our luggage was safe and would be found within a few days. Ugh! I couldn't imagine being without our personal belongings for that period of time. What was most upsetting, however, was that we had lots of presents for our new grandson in the baggage.

Seeing beautiful Waikiki Beach again had a calming effect on me and eased my frustration, somewhat. Seeing the Hyatt Regency's two 40-story towers also recycled my anger and made me a little more comfortable. The final comforting scene was the three-story, open-air atrium with orchids, palm trees, and cascading waterfalls, plus, to Barbara's delight, more than 60 upscale oceanfront shops surrounding the atrium. We had been using the Hyatt Regency in Washington D.C. on our car trips to Florida in the winter months, and were card-holding members of the chain, which gave us another welcome surprise: a free room upgrade, which included breakfast. Our suite was on the 38th floor and was very spacious with an opening onto a fully furnished balcony facing the ocean, and a view to die for.

A nice feature was a pillow-top mattress draped beneath earth-toned duvets and fine linens. The oversized bathroom featured granite countertops and was stocked with Portico toiletries, which Barbara wasted no time in adding to her international collection. There was also a laptop-sized safe, which accommodated my computer easily, with room to spare. We were exhausted from the day's mishaps and jet lag, so we immediately jumped into bed to get some much-needed sleep and to get rid of some of the stress that we were carrying around.

Thank God we woke up to a whole new sunny day, with a much-relieved attitude, and were famished. The breakfast buffet was still open, so we showered and made a beeline straight to the dining hall. What a pleasant surprise! The buffet was endless, with an overwhelming smell of pineapple and bacon filling the room. I didn't waste any time getting an omelet with mushrooms and ham, and a large glass of pineapple juice. Barbara went to the Japanese food section and came back with an assortment of sushi, and two large glasses of pineapple juice. The Hawaiian Kona coffee was delicious beyond words and, after drinking a whole pot between us, the day began to get brighter and our anxiety began to level off. If we were lucky, our luggage would be waiting for us in our room after we had breakfast. Another pleasant experience was our waitress; a beautiful tan-skinned, bright *wahine* (girl) named Lois. She brought sunshine into the room and lighted our table when her colorful, flowered red and white dress appeared before us. She asked, in a soft bubbly voice, if there was anything she could get us? I couldn't take my eyes off the plumeria flower inserted on the top of her ear. Barbara also couldn't stop admiring it and we told Lois so several times. Our day started to perk up a bit after the wholesome breakfast and meeting the beautiful Hawaiian flower, Lois. We had no luck with our baggage arriving, so we prepared for the 45-minute drive in our rented Buick Regal to see our new grandson Ian Charles, with only a couple of presents that we had packed in our carry-on luggage.

There he was our seven-pound, nine-day old bundle of chubby joy. We couldn't stop kissing Donna and Ian Charles Bivona, while telling them how happy we were with the new addition to our family. Steve, our little baby, all six-foot-two of him, was smiling so hard I thought that his smile was going to continue around to the back of his head. We spent the day holding, cuddling, and kissing Ian Charles' small body until it was time to change his diaper. At that point, I turned him over to the girls, who seemed to get a special delight out of changing diapers "the right way," whatever that means. Steve prepared another of his wonderful BBQs that we so enjoyed eating, on their expansive lawn, on our last visit. Cherishing the food and absorbing the sight of the waves, capturing sand and replacing it in different locations along the beach, rounded out a perfect moment for me and my lovely family. We were anxious to return to our hotel to see if any of our baggage had been recovered, which made the return drive seem a lot longer than the morning trip. No luck, no luggage. We asked the kids to join us for breakfast at the hotel the next morning, and to spend the day with us enjoying the hotel's amenities, which included a great rooftop pool, a gym-spa, and ample lounge chairs scattered sparingly around the tropical pool area. We decided to buy some swimsuits so we could at least enjoy the pool when the children arrived. The hotel had a nice beach store, so we didn't have any difficulty finding suits that were very tropical looking, with lots of flowers and colorful designs.

The kids arrived for a late breakfast buffet at the outdoor Terrace Grill, which overlooked the ocean and Diamond Head Mountain. They were thrilled to be out of their house and at a place that felt like vacationland. It was just what the doctor ordered for them after spending several weeks isolated while preparing for and giving birth to our little bundle of joy. Barbara and I couldn't get over how delicious the Hawaiian Kona coffee tasted. The kids were already Kona fans, but said that they thought the brew at breakfast was exceptionally good; I think the salt water air and the view had a lot to do with its taste. We spent the day hanging around the rooftop pool, which was bordered by two spa tubs that were caressed by the gentle sea air coming from Waikiki Beach. I took advantage of the hotel's diversified cardiovascular exercise equipment, in their state-of-the-art gym. Exercising has become part of my new lifestyle since my open-heart surgery in 1993, so I was looking forward to using their sophisticated equipment. We told the kids that we would watch the package (Ian Charles), if they got the urge to wander around on their own. Before I could get the last word out of my mouth, they were gone. What a pleasure it was to be babysitting again; we hadn't had that pleasure for over 20 years and enjoyed every moment of it. We told the new parents to take their time and not to hurry back; they returned in the late afternoon, which was perfect, as it gave us a good part of the day to play with and show off our new baby to the other hotel guests. We decided to have dinner at one of the local Japanese restaurants and had a choice of several along the main strip. It was a new experience for us to be spending time not only with our children but with their child, who required lots of attention and soft soothing sways to keep him happy. After dinner, they left and we returned to our room anticipating finding our baggage, but no such luck. Numerous telephone calls to the airline were to no avail. They reassured us that, in time, they would locate and forward our luggage to us, but we just didn't believe them. We knew our baggage was somewhere in "Davey Jones' Locker," and that our personal belongings were probably being sold somewhere on the black market.

Our telephone rang early the next morning and, lo and behold, our luggage had arrived. It was brought up to our room, and I had had an overwhelming urge to hug and kiss the suitcases on sight. We examined all the bags and found that everything was intact, just slightly jostled around due to their long journey to God knows where and back. I wondered, where does lost luggage go? Is it left at the airport? Is it left on the airplane in some dark corner? Is it put on the wrong airplane? Is it put on the wrong conveyor carousel? Is it put aside and looked into for possible theft? There are so many possibilities; I decided to just be content with the fact that ours was returned to us without any loss. We headed for our children's home with lots of presents for our new baby and a couple of niceties for our kids.

We had a leisurely lunch on their terrace while enjoying the peaceful surroundings of the swaying palm trees and the hypnotizing sounds of the ocean being reduced to small waves and teasing the beachfront of our children's home. Donna suggested that, being that we were fascinated by the aroma of pineapple in the air, we should go to the source and pay a visit to the Dole Plantation Pineapple Museum, which was only a few miles from the small town of Wahiawa. Upon entering the plantation, we were immediately drawn to the world's largest maze. It had eight rest stations in an area occupying more than two acres with a path in excess of three miles. It contained over 11,000 colorful Hawaiian plants, including hibiscus, heliconia, croton, panax, and pineapple. The center of the maze was in the shape of a huge pineapple, made up of croton with a crown of agapanthus (blue lilies). There was an ongoing contest for adventurers to search for the eight secret stations on their way to solving the mystery of the labyrinth. In each station there was a maze card directing participants to possible paths to the next station; hopefully, the cards and the adventurers' abilities would lead them to the exit. The winner for the day had their name placed on the entrance and received a special prize, usually pineapple related. The best time recorded was about seven minutes, while the average was between 45 minutes to one hour. We all entered at the same time and eventually took our own paths through the network. Steve exited in about 15 minutes, with Donna right behind him. Barbara exited in about 25 minutes, and I was dead last at 45 minutes. So much for my accounting background, it certainly didn't help that day. I got so lost I couldn't believe it. How can an accountant get lost in a maze when it's such an integral part of his life? Oh well, it was lots of fun, although slightly embarrassing for me, especially the ribbing I took when I exited and found everyone pretending to be asleep. We then took a two-mile open bus tour around the plantation that showcased the legacy of the pineapple and its impact on Hawaiian agriculture. There were several acres of diversified farming, including specimens of lychee, banana, mango, papaya, cacao, and coffee. Along the route, we were treated to views of the Koolau Waianae mountain ranges that monopolized the background and added to the overall splendor of the plantation.

A brochure at the Center explained the purpose of its one-of-a-kind museum: "The plantation blends the traditional elements of Hawaii's plantation life and the early pineapple industry with the new breed of diversified agriculture currently being grown on the North Shore of Oahu. It is dedicated to perpetuating the agricultural heritage of Hawaii and its place in history, and the progress of the islands and its people. The founder, James D. Dole, came to Hawaii in 1899, after graduating from Harvard University with $1,200. He single handedly began the pineapple industry in Hawaii with 60 acres of rich red dirt on the site of today's Dole Plantation." In addition to learning about the wide variety of fruits, vegetables, Hawaiian plants, and tropical flora, we participated in pineapple planting. We also learned how to pick the fruit, as well as how to safely and properly slice it for consumption. The museum center began as a fruit stand on the 60-acre plantation in 1950, and has become a first-class museum telling the story of how the pineapple impacted Hawaii and its people. The plantation store featured "Made in Hawaii" items, including a variety of wares, pineapple-themed baked goods, snacks, Waialua chocolates, and delicious Waialua coffee. Antique tables, baskets, and traditional wooden bins displayed items reflecting Hawaii's plantation stores of days gone by. The objective was to present a traditional marketplace, a country store, and a series of building facades reminiscent of the town of Haleiwa on Oahu's North Shore. We had a late lunch in their restaurant that featured a "Crown of Hawaii" menu and enjoyed their Teri Chicken, Kalua Pig, Mahi sandwiches, salads featuring ingredients from the plantation and, of course, our drink of choice, freshly made pineapple juice.

We spent the rest of our visit playing with our new grandson, swimming at their beach, visiting the Pearl Harbor Museum, the sunken battleship Arizona, and many of the dance venues along the main strip in Honolulu. We spent several evenings ballroom dancing at the 10,000 square-foot dance hall in the Ali Wai Country Club, showing off some of our American Style dance routines to the locales, who were mostly International Style dancers. I discuss the difference between the two styles of dancing later on in the dancing section of this book. Saying goodbye to our children and the newest addition to our family was heart wrenching, but as all good things finally come to an end, our dream vacation also ended with smiles and tears visiting our faces simultaneously.

One other favorite vacation worth mentioning was a themed cruise on the *Mississippi Queen* Paddlewheel to New Orleans' Mardi Gras. The journey began while I was sorting through our mail. A colorful brochure stood out from the other documents; it was a vacation invitation from the Delta Steamboat Company requesting our presence on one of their Mississippi River cruises. The one that caught my eye was a theme cruise featuring Big Bands, such as Guy Lombardo's Royal Canadians and Les Elgart and his Manhattan Swing Orchestra. The cruise coincided with the annual New Orleans Mardi Gras and the 500th Centennial of the Discovery of America by the Italian explorer Christopher Columbus, which was the main theme of the festival. Well, there it was: Barbara's childhood dream of traveling down the Mississippi River with Tom Sawyer and Huck Finn on a paddlewheel boat, and my dream of going to the Mardi Gras festival in New Orleans. Both of our dreams of sailing on a Showboat (like the one in the great musical of that name) with Big Band music, and my passion and infatuation with collecting books on the Age of Discovery, especially concerning the great navigator, Christopher Columbus, were all in one package, with Mardi Gras thrown in as a bonus. Barbara and I couldn't believe that so many of the items on our *Bucket List* could be realized on one vacation. We figured that we could take a riverboat trip on the *Mississippi Queen* Paddlewheel for seven days, which began and ended in New Orleans, and then extend our trip to include six days in a centrally located hotel around Bourbon Street, so we could really get into the Mardi

Gras spirit. We spent a previous vacation in New Orleans many years ago, but not at festival time—although it does seem that every day in New Orleans is a festival. We were familiar with the layout of the area and what would be the most advantageous location for our stay. On our prior visit to the city, we stayed at the Royal Sonesta Hotel in the Bourbon Street area, but the people and traffic noise made the stay less desirable then we hoped for. We did have occasion to enjoy a great dinner in an upscale restaurant at the 17-floor Hotel Monteleone in the French Quarter off of Bourbon Street, which was located in a less noisy location than the other hotel, especially in the rooms on the upper floors. It also boasted a rooftop swimming pool with spectacular views of the French Quarter and the historic city. With this information in mind, we called our travel agent, Barbara, at Liberty Travel and told her what our plans were and asked her to put together a travel package for us. Considering that the trip would be quite extensive and somewhat complicated, we decided to leave all the arrangements and details in her experienced hands. Our decision turned out to be a wise one; within a week, she laid out our itinerary, including all the sightseeing that we planned plus some extra goodies, like attending a Grand Mardi Gras Ball.

We flew American Airlines to New Orleans, and that's when the fun began. Our luggage didn't appear on the arrival carousel; the sinking feeling in my stomach got worse when we were the only passengers left waiting for our baggage to appear. After wasting a couple of hours with representatives of the Steamship Company and American Airlines, and filling out numerous forms describing our missing property, we left the airport and took a taxicab to the New Orleans Port where our ship was docked. The cab driver got lost in a downpour that restricted his visibility. I brought to his attention that what seemed to be the buildings of the city were behind us; he said, "Sorry, my mistake" and then turned his cab around in the right direction. We finally got to the embarkation point just as the rain stopped. There was a small crowd of people on the dock in a covered area enjoying the music provided by a small combo band, while imbibing drinks provided by several waitresses from the ship. I immediately had a scotch and water, which was my drink of choice in those days, and before I knew it, down went several more, but to no avail. I was so hyper from the loss of our luggage and the possibility of going on a two-week vacation with little or no clothes, which was exacerbated by our getting lost on the way to the ship, that I was convinced that the whole journey was going to turn out to be a disaster. Barbara, although upset, tried to calm me down. She wasn't overly concerned, as the prospect of buying a new wardrobe for the trip didn't seem to be an unhappy event for her. My mind formed prayers, hoping that the representative of the steamship company, who remained behind at the airline terminal, would locate our baggage. Until then, we just had to make the best of a combination of unfortunate events. We boarded the paddlewheel and checked with the ship's coordinator, who informed us that due to our misfortune, they were upgrading our room at no charge, to a full suite. Well, maybe things were starting to turn around; in time, my drinks did their job, and I calmed down quite a bit, returning to my optimistic, fun-loving self.

We went to dinner and felt the boat moving away from the dock, which brought back the helpless feeling that one gets when unpleasant things happen that are out of their control; where was our luggage and what could happen next? How would we replace all of our personal belongings? The delicious French cuisine that evening tempered my feeling of anxiety, somewhat, but sharing a bottle of wine with Barbara was more effective. We hurried back to our cabin, opened the door, and miracles of all miracles, our baggage was staring at us. I lifted a piece, and panic returned; the luggage was weightless. Now we had our bags, but there was nothing in them. Unbeknownst to us, our cabin steward had unpacked our bags and put our belongings in the dressers and closet. We both collapsed on the queen-size bed and just remained silent and motionless for about 15 minutes. We regained our composure, freshened up, and journeyed to the lounge area for orientation and to meet our fellow passengers. When retiring for the evening, we both agreed that we should put the day behind us and erase the mishaps from our minds. Hopefully, we would continue with our wonderful vacation with no further unhappy incidences. Mark Twain aptly said, "The face of the river, in time, becomes a wonderful book... not one to be read once and thrown aside, for it has a new story to tell every day." Well, we were hoping for a new story when we woke up the following morning.

And a new story it was. The sun peeked through our partially opened drapes; fresh Mississippi River air forced its way into our senses, while a whiff of bacon and eggs floating by got our attention, so we quickly dressed and hastened to the place creating the aroma. I would have been content to just sit on one of the outside chaise lounges and breathe in the fresh air and intoxicating aroma from the food being prepared for our morning meal. What a wonderful beginning to a new day. After breakfast, the first mate took some of us on a guided tour of the *Mississippi Queen*. His dissertation was robotic, but precise as to the history and specifications of the paddlewheel. He said: "The boat was built in 1976 in celebration of the bicentennial and, when built, was the largest steamboat in existence. It is 382 feet long, 68 feet wide, weighing 3,364 tons, has 208 staterooms accommodating 422 passengers with a complement of over 100 crew members and staff. The red circular paddlewheel itself weighs 70 tons; located forward of it, at the stern of the boat, is the largest steam driven calliope on the river, boasting 44 pipes, whose music is magical and can be heard for five miles, when announcing the majestic ship's presence on the river. The décor of the boat is Americana, with floral wallpaper and matching fabric, beveled mirrors, crystal chandeliers, and polished brass railings. The staircases are red carpeted with ornate wooden hand rails; chairs and accessories are in the Victorian style. The Grand Saloon is the center of activity and is used as a showroom and gathering place; its dance floor is large enough to accommodate the swinging dancers on the ship."

My favorite place, the wheelhouse, was forward; what a thrill it was to steer the ship—with the captain's permission of course, and under his watchful eyes. He let me navigate an easy part of the river for about five minutes. "The steamboats were finer than anything on shore—like palaces." Mark Twain was right when he wrote those words in his book *Life on the Mississippi*. I was navigating a palace down the waterway, with images of the great river flowing through my mind from the Broadway musical *Showboat*. I was humming the river's song, "Old Man River," and, for a few minutes, I became a riverboat captain transporting my passengers and cargo to the far-away towns along the majestic river during the heyday of the paddlewheel boats.

We spent a relaxing and friendly day traveling on the majestic river, making friends, and just enjoying the homey feeling that is so prevalent on small river boats. A big difference compared to cruising on a large ocean liner is that the staff of the river boats were all American, not what we experienced when traveling on larger vessels, where most of the crew members and staff were usually foreigners with difficult names to remember. It didn't take us long to get used to the odiferous surroundings in the air of deep Southern fried cooking and the comforting feeling of the sun resting on my body as I enjoyed reading some of Mark Twain's adventures, while spread out on a chaise lounge, in the open air at the stern of the boat, lulled by the rhythm of the bright red paddlewheel and dozing into dreamland between paragraphs. The ship's small combo band of six, including two pianists, played music on and off all day. Their sounds floating through the air, mixing with the heavenly aroma of our next meal, gave me the feeling of being at a carnival. Dinner was a cholesterol nightmare; Barbara and I ordered the same food: Southern fried chicken, tons of biscuits, candied beans, and, for dessert, Shoo Fly Pie. It took many turns around the boat to try to alleviate the guilt of overeating before we came to terms with the fact that we were on vacation and an occasional "pig out" wasn't going to kill us, at least not right away.

We followed the sound of music to the Grand Saloon, where Les Elgart's Manhattan Swing Orchestra had guests busy on the dance floor doing a Cha-Cha. It was surprising how many single ladies were in attendance, but the cruise operators evidently anticipated this and provided male hosts to dance and talk with the girls throughout the evening. Between sessions, the ship's smaller band entertained us with light jazz and singing from their female vocalists. We danced until the wee hours and returned to our upgraded suite, content that the forgettable mishaps we experienced were being replaced by "happy times." We decided to save our complimentary champagne for another time, but the temptation of the chocolates resting on our bed was too much to resist, so we munched while listening to the smooth-lazy-soft-piped-in-music, and concluded a relaxing, pleasant day on the

Mississippi River as we entered from the beginning of a dream vacation into our evening's dreamland.

We were awakened the next morning by the ship's deafening steam whistle, toot-toot-toot, which announced to the town of Natchez and everyone else within listening range that we were coming to town to explore its beauty and meet the local folks. One of the ship's pianists joined in on the calliope and began harmonizing with the whistle's tooting. We again followed the scent of bacon and eggs and, after indulging in a hearty, but not so healthy breakfast; we disembarked and stepped onto the hospitable soil of Natchez. A committee of the town's people and a small brass band greeted us to their historic antebellum town. We planned on spending time exploring the town and visiting at least one of the plantations that were located in and around the quaint settlement. The area of the town dates back to the 8th century, when the Natchez Indians were masters of that part of the country. Built on the site of an ancient Indian village, it takes its name from that tribe. Around 1730, after several wars, the French defeated the inhabitants and dispersed the Native Americans, keeping many as slaves. Today, most of the remaining Natchez tribe has integrated with the Chickasaw, Creek, and Cherokee Indians, and are mainly in Oklahoma within the Cherokee and Creek nations, quite a distance from their ancestral lands. The town boasts a population of about 18,000 people including some Natchez Indians, who are the descendants of French slaves. It is probably one of the oldest cities in North America; it is elegant, well preserved, and a showcase for antebellum homes and magnificent plantations. Walking through the town was a throwback to pre-Civil War times, especially when viewing areas where town folks were dressed in period costumes, I'm sure for the benefit of tourists such as myself, who were totally captivated by the charade. Like many Southern towns, the fragrance of flowers, particularly magnolias, freely occupied the air to the enjoyment of its recipients. We couldn't avoid walking into Stanton Hall Plantation, which occupies a full block in the town. It was built between 1851–1857 for Frederick Stanton, a cotton broker, who went to great lengths to import building materials from Europe, such as moldings, marble fireplace mantles, wrought ironworks, and a great deal of the furnishings, some of which are still intact and displayed throughout the mansion. The entrance immediately impresses visitors with its 17-foot-high ceiling and 72-foot-long hallway. The parlor displayed gilded French mirrors and the fireplaces and mantles throughout were stunning in color and glaze. While exploring the mansion, the smell of buttered biscuits caught our attention; we were pleased to learn that the mansion, which became a National Historic Landmark in 1974, had its own restaurant, The Carriage House. The stately gardens were inviting and spending a few minutes enjoying the colorful flowers and topiary, while sitting on a bench, was refreshing and tranquil. The compelling "call of the biscuits" finally overcame us and we went with haste to the place where the hypnotic aroma was being created. We had our favorite foods: biscuits with gravy, fried chicken legs, toasty fries, berry ice tea, and more biscuits. The steamboat's whistle, toot-toot-toot, announced that it was time for us to return. The following is a picture of the beautiful lady:

When we returned to our cabin, neatly placed on our bunk were written instructions and competition rules for the dance contest that was to be held that evening. There was also fabric laid out for us to make costumes for the Mardi Gras party, which was to be held on the last day of our cruise, while heading back for the live New Orleans' festival. Much to do and so little time to do it in! We were novice dancers at that time and were embarrassed to enter a dance contest, especially having seen some pretty good dancers on the floor the night before. The competition rules were trophies for first, second, and third place in Cha-Cha, Rumba, Foxtrot, Waltz, and Swing, and a special trophy for best overall dancers. No professionals, dance hosts, or crew members were allowed to enter the contest. We only knew the basics to all the dances except for Swing, which we had taken some lessons in over the past year. So we reluctantly entered the Swing contest just to get into the spirit of things.

The music from Les Elgart's Band could be heard throughout the boat. We followed his sound to the Grand Saloon, where many of the passengers were warming up their dance routines in preparation of the competition. We were both intimidated by the better dancers showing their skills on the dance floor and were inclined to withdraw from the event, but we gathered our courage and picked up our numbers 25 and pinned them onto each other's clothing. It didn't take long for us to realize that we made the right decision in entering the competition, which resulted in our meeting new friends at a very rapid pace. Before the main event, everyone on the dance floor had a great time moving and jumping around to the sound of the band, while changing partners, on cue, from the boat's dance master, which also enhanced our becoming friendly with many of the passengers. The various dance competitions had from 15 to 20 couples in each category ranging from beginners to somewhat good dancers, but absolutely no top-notch dancers, which made the atmosphere a lot less tense for us. The judges included some dance hosts and different ranks of crew members; all in all, they did a commendable job in judging the contestants. It seemed that everyone won a prize, including us for coming in third place in Swing dancing. The evening felt more like a jamboree than a dance competition, and the atmosphere was relaxed and jovial without the stress that usually accompanies dance competitions. We ended the evening as champions and retired to our cabin after wishing our many new friends a "fond farewell until the morrow."

We were again awaken by the toot-toot-toot of the steam whistle, reminding us that today we had a mock race with the Mississippi Queen's older sister, *Delta Queen*, which was the undisputed current paddlewheel champion on the river. The Delta Queen was born in 1927, weighed 1,650 tons, is 285 feet long and 60 feet wide, and carries 200 passengers and 80 crew members. She is quite a small ship compared to her younger sister, which is 3,364 tons, 383 feet in length, 68 feet in width, and carries 422 passengers with over 100 crew members. But, the Delta was a feisty ship and had won the symbolic "Golden Antlers," which she proudly displayed below her pilot house attesting to the fact that she is the fastest steamboat on the Mississippi River (based on her pilot's expertise and having won its last annual encounter). The history of the Golden Antlers dates back to 1963 when the steamships, *Belle of Louisville* and the *Cincinnati Delta Queen*, ran their first race. It was a 14-mile battle up and down the Ohio River on the first Wednesday in May before the Kentucky Derby. Over the years, the race has been drawing as much attention from the locals as the Derby race. Since then, the boats race against each other every year prior to the Kentucky Derby, for the bragging rights of "fastest boat on the river," and for the coveted Golden Antlers. The antlers are from an elk and are sprayed gold, signifying the sleekness and speed of the animal and the purity of gold. Our race with the champion began at "Dead Man's Bend" and ended at "Washout Bayou." These names conjured up all kinds of images; various stories have come down through the years and have been repeated so often that they are accepted as fact. According to Jeffery, our ship's historian, one of the more popular myths is the following:

> Over 150-years ago, during the heyday of the rootin' tootin' steamboat era, the river landings were lawless and violent places to live. The most popular of these roughhouse places was the Natchez-Under-the-Hill Landing, located just below the bluffs overlooking the river at Natchez, Mississippi. There were brawls and knife fights daily; so violent was the neighborhood that the local police would not venture down Silver Street,

which stretched from the top of the bluffs down to the river's edge. It was a busy stop for steamboats and a hangout for cutthroats, thieves, mustached gamblers, and ladies of the night. With all that violence, there were always dead bodies that had to be disposed of, and the river was a convenient repository. The bodies would float down to the bend in the river and accumulate there. Many of the corpses that were retrieved still had knives protruding from their decaying bodies, hence the name "Dead Man's Bend."

The crew members spent the morning decorating our boat with banners, and placed noise makers throughout the vessel for our use to add some sound to the festivities. The male crew members dressed in period costumes; many were mustached gamblers, gentlemen of the day, or other unsavory-looking characters. The girls wore riverboat attire from that era, which included frills on their beautifully colored dresses, fancy hats, and pom-poms for the cheerleaders. The calliope played continuous music, including some songs of Stephen Foster, such as "Oh' Susanna," "Nelly was a Lady," "Nelly Bly," "Old Folks at Home," "My Old Kentucky Home," and of course, "De Camp Town Races." The *Delta Queen* pulled alongside us and blew her challenging whistle loud and clear, "toot-toot-toot." Our response was a spontaneous, "toot-toot-toot." Back and forth they went with the whistle blowing and music playing from their respective calliopes, battling each other for the supremacy of the air and waterway. In addition to the *Delta's* jazz band playing on her bow, the passengers on board seemed to be having a post-victory celebration—a little prematurely for our taste, so we also started singing, howling, and making all sorts of loud sounds with our noisemakers trying to drown out the boisterous celebration of their anticipated victory.

The whistle blast from the *Delta* signaled the start of the race; being the smaller and lighter of the two vessels, she was off and running ahead of us with ease. We struggled for what seemed to be an eternity to get our heavier craft ahead, but to no avail; even though our boat had more powerful engines, we had trouble keeping up with the little lady.

The little mistress moved ahead; its pilot evidently had more experience than ours, and found more of the slow water (slack water), which allows a boat to move with less resistance and, therefore, more speed. Near the end of the race, our boat's engines began to show their strength and started pulling up to her older sister; inch by inch we finally caught up, but it was too late. The *Delta* seemed to become jet propelled as we approached and crossed the finish line ahead of us by several boat lengths. She would retain her title as queen of the Mississippi and hold on to her "Golden Antlers" until challenged again by a faster boat. The celebration noise became louder from her majesty as she sped away, whistle blowing and calliope singing, while the passengers swayed to the jazz band's rhythmic sounds, waving goodbye to our losing vessel. Her bright red paddlewheel churned and splashed water far and high as the boat picked up steam and disappeared around the bend and out of sight.

We were greeted by brass bands and the local citizenry when we visited Vicksburg, Mississippi and Baton Rouge, Louisiana. Although we enjoyed the food and history of both places, our minds were on our last stop, New Orleans. During the week, Guy Lombardo's Royal Canadians replaced Les Elgart's band. We couldn't be more excited as he was a Long Island, New York resident and while alive, conducted the world-renowned New Years Eve orchestra that played at the dropping of the ball in New York City at midnight. In preparation of our visiting the "City of Sin," we prepared our costumes for the Mardi Gras Ball that we were having on the last day of our voyage. Barbara created an outfit that looked like a large salmon: pinkish sequins, with drawings that resembled fish scales. The strange thing about it was her head sticking out from the fish's mouth and her little feet protruding from the fish's tail, but overall her walking fish was quite effective. I took the easy road and made a toga from a white sheet and wore a Roman laurel wreath painted gold on my head, which I put together with some of the material supplied by the crew. The ball was visually bizarre; there was a variety of fish, many men and women dressed in togas, (but not as good as mine), mustached gamblers all over the place, and lots of girls dressed as ladies-of-the-night. We danced and sang the night away to the sweet music of Guy Lombardo's band, which wasn't an easy task, especially if your costume was bulky like Barbara's. Her fish's stomach kept getting in the way of our dancing close, and my toga had the habit of sliding off my shoulder showing my hairy chest. But, all in all, the evening was delightful, especially the laughs at seeing such strange creatures jumping around trying to dance without tripping on themselves or their partners. We raised our champagne glasses to the music of Guy Lombardo's Royal Canadians, and ended the evening singing "Auld Lang Syne." To help us with the words we were given an envelope marked "Don't Open till Midnight." An English version was written in large clear letters, so we could all enjoy singing the whole song. The words were somewhat bastardized from a poem written by Robert Burns in 1788. Here is the rendition that we sang:

> Should old acquaintance be forgot, and never brought to mind?
> Should old acquaintance be forgot, and auld lang syne?
> For auld lang syne, my dear, for auld lang syne.
> We'll take a cup of kindness yet, for auld lang syne.
> And surely you'll buy your pint cup! And I'll buy mine!
> And we'll take a cup of kindness yet, for auld lang syne.
> We two have run about the slopes, and picked the daisies find.
> But we've wandered many a weary foot, since auld lang syne.
> We two have paddled in the stream, from morning sun till dine.
> But seas between us broad have roared since auld lang syne.
> And there's a hand my trusty friend! And give us a hand of thine!
> And we'll take a right good-will draught, for auld lang syne.
> We'll take a cup of kindness yet, for auld lang syne.

We woke up the next morning in New Orleans and spent a week celebrating Mardi Gras with other exuberant revelers. Other vacations that we were fortunate to enjoy and remove, one by one, from our *Bucket List,* were visits to our National Parks: Yellowstone, Grand Canyon, Bryce, Zion, Yosemite, Red Wood Forest, and Mount Rushmore. We have traveled and spent time in Italy, (four times), France, England, Greece, Switzerland, Argentina, Nova Scotia, Alaska, and Niagara Falls, Quebec, and Montreal, in Canada. We have sailed to the Caribbean several times, visiting her many islands along the way; we've sailed the Mediterranean visiting Greece and its treasured islands of Santorini and Mykonos; Kusadasi and Istanbul in Turkey; Venice, Sicily and Sardinia, Italy. We have also sailed from England to the Baltic Countries visiting Norway, Sweden, Denmark, Estonia, Finland and Russia; we have sailed and visited the Islands of Hawaii, as mentioned previously. We have sailed on our own boats to Montauk Point, Long island; Martha's Vineyard, Nantucket, New Bedford, Plymouth, and Cape Code in Massachusetts; Block Island, Newport and Narragansett Bay and surrounding islands, in Rhode Island; and Essex, East Norwich, Cedar, and the Thimble islands of Connecticut.

Before concluding our travel stories, I would like to mention one other place that we visit almost on a yearly basis when driving from New York to Florida, and occasionally on our return trips, and that is the Smithsonian Museums in Washington, D.C. The reason that it's an advantageous place for seniors is that visiting the various locations requires time, and the one thing that we are constantly looking for are places to occupy our time and hopefully enrich our lives. So what better place to spend some quality time than in the capital of our country, where there are no entrances fees at any of the museums. A bonus is to visit in the springtime when colorful cherry blossoms change the concrete background of the buildings into a picturesque pink painting. We have also found it to be the perfect place to spend quality time with our children and grandchildren while visiting the Air and Space Museum, the exotic Castle, which is the administrative offices of the Institution and a good starting place, and the many other incredible places of interest. One of the most attractive features is when we visit with my son and his family in Virginia; six of us enter the museums of our choice in D.C. free of any charges.

A little history about the Smithsonian Institution will shed some light on the complexity and uniqueness of the organization. It was funded from a fluke bequest to the United States by the British scientist James Smithson (1764–1829), who had never visited our new democracy. In his will, he stipulated that should his nephew die without heirs, the Smithson estate would go to the government of the United States to create an "Establishment for the increase and diffusion of Knowledge among men." After his nephew died without heirs in 1835, President Andrew Jackson informed Congress of the bequest, which amounted to a little over $500,000 (about $11,000,000 in current value). The money was invested in shaky state bonds, which quickly defaulted. After years of heated debates in Congress (so what's new?), the Massachusetts Representative (and former President) John Quincy Adams successfully argued that the lost funds plus interest should be restored and used for its original purpose. Congress finally accepted the legacy as intended and pledged the faith and support of the United States to the charitable trust.

In the meantime, the United States Exploring Expedition of the U.S. Navy circumnavigated the globe between 1838 and 1842 and returned with thousands of animal specimens, 50,000 various plants, diverse shells and minerals, tropical birds, jars of seawater, and ethnographic artifacts from the South Pacific. In addition, several military and civilian surveys of the American West, including the Mexican Boundary Survey and Pacific Railroad Surveys, assembled many Native American artifacts and natural history specimens, which they brought to the Capital. So within the first 50 years of our independence, the new democracy was on its way to developing what would become the largest museum complex in the world. The big question was what to do with all that stuff? Our government and private donors decided to begin a building program in the capital to house the collections that were pouring in from the new nation's expansion programs, resulting in the institution currently employing over 6,000 federal employees, and in its latest budget request, after considering the income from the original endowment, contributions, and profits from its retail operations, the federal government was asked to contribute an additional $800 million to allow the institution to continue to pay for the salaries, excellent upkeep of over 136 million items in its collections at 19 museums, its zoo, and its nine research facilities. The facilities are located in Washington, D.C., New York City, Virginia, and Panama, and are associated with 168 other affiliate museums from around the world. It also publishes the monthly *Smithsonian* and bimonthly *Air & Space* magazines; quite an accomplishment in less than 200 years.

The National Zoological Park, also referred to as the National Zoo, is part of the Smithsonian complex, which is located in the Capital, is also worth a visit by seniors, and will be especially exciting and memorable if children and grandchildren can share the experience, as we were fortunate enough to do. A great treat is the "Snore and Roar" event that is sponsored by the "Friends of the National Zoo" (FONZ) a non-profit membership organization. The event allows individuals and families to spend a night at the zoo, in sleeping bags inside of tents. A late-night flashlight tour of the zoo and a two-hour exploration of an animal house or exhibit area are led by a zookeeper as part of the experience. The program is offered between the months of June and September each year. What a great way to spend some quality time with the family while enjoying the outdoor lives of our animal friends. On our visit to the zoo, we couldn't enjoy seeing all of the hundreds of animals that are meticulously housed there, but we did get to see *Mei Xiang* and *Tian Tian*, the two panda residents *(Mei Xiang* gave birth to *Tai Shan* in 2005). We also had the opportunity to walk the Asia Trail, which has a series of habitats for seven Asian species, including sloth bears, red pandas, and clouded leopards. Another thrill we enjoyed with our children, no grandchildren allowed, was the "Brew at the Zoo" beer sampling from the microbreweries located at the zoo; it worked wonders in cooling us off on the hot day that we visited.

It is a beautiful, free-of-charge urban family park with something new to discover at every twist and turn throughout the animal kingdom. The zoo has a long history of innovation and leadership in the care of wild animal exhibitions that also includes educational and scientific programs, both on-site and around the world. Some of the popular programs are:

- **Woo at the Zoo** – A Valentine's Day talk by some of the zoo's animal experts discussing the fascinating, and often quirky, world of animal dating, mating, and reproductive habits.
- **Earth Day – Party for the Planet** – A celebration of Earth Day, where guests can find out about simple daily actions they can take to enjoy a more environmentally friendly lifestyle.
- **Easter Monday** – Easter Monday has been a Washington-area multicultural tradition for many years. There is a variety of family activities, entertainment, and special opportunities to learn more about animals. The celebration began in response to the inability of African Americans to participate in the annual Easter Egg Roll held on the White House lawn prior to Dwight Eisenhower's presidency.
- **Zoofari** – A casual evening of gourmet foods, fine wines, entertainment, and dancing under the stars. Each year, thousands of attendees enjoy delicacies prepared by master chefs from a hundred of the D.C. area's finest restaurants.
- **Zoolights** – The National Zoo's annual winter celebration. Guests can walk through the zoo when it is covered with thousands of sparkling, environmentally friendly lights and animated exhibits, attend special keeper talks, and enjoy live entertainment.

Dancing

Barbara and I have always been fascinated by people who get on a dance floor and dance to whatever music was being played, whether it was Latin, Smooth, or just Social Dancing. They seemed to dance with confidence and style and had an air about them that said, "There isn't anything else that I would rather be doing." We always seemed to enjoy whatever little dancing we did at weddings and social events, but never got the hang of doing routines that made sense or would make us feel that we had accomplished anything resembling other good dancers. So when we got close to retirement, we decided to give dancing a chance and started looking for a reputable dance instructor who would help us begin our new journey. Finding a qualified, honest dance studio or instructor was a challenge. Many dance studios, but not all, try to sign new students to long-term contracts costing thousands of dollars, and when the training begins, the instructors teach more than one dance at the same time. One of the major problems with long-term contracts, which can run up to one year, is that if the students aren't happy with their progress or instructors, they are obliged to continue under the terms of their contract, resulting in many cases of students quitting and losing their money. So it's important that if dancing is in the future for retirees, that they sign with a reputable dance studio or instructor and arrange to learn one dance at a time on a **pay-as-you-go basis**. To save money and experiment to see if dancing is something that a person is interested in, there are many dance halls that give free group lessons before general dancing begins. The prices of entrance to these facilities are usually in the 10 to 15 dollar range and often include refreshments, dessert, and in some instance a light meal.

We decided to take our first lessons at Swing Street Studio, which was owned and operated by the talented Elektra Underhill. Our arrangement was that we would take a couple of Swing dance lessons and if we were pleased, we would continue until we were happy with our performance. Well, that was the beginning of a life-long relationship with Elektra and the local dance community, of which she seemed to be the *prima donna*. In time, we would become an integral part of that community and our lifestyles would be, more or less, directed by the activities and events within our dancing society. It took some time for me to get over my macho persona and accept the constructive criticism that was a part of the learning experience. But in time, with Elektra and Barbara's patience, I learned to behave myself and progress and love every step of the journey.

Our dance group had review sessions twice a week at the studio, which allowed us to practice the routines we learned and switch partners to get the feeling of how others interpreted what they had learned. We also planned our social dancing excursions at various dance halls together and traveled to dance exhibitions and shows as a family. The uniqueness of belonging to a group where everyone has the same common passion of being happy while expressing themselves in dance is a life-changing experience and should certainly be tried by everyone with a desire to fill in the spare time that retirees find they have in abundance when they begin their journey into their **Golden Years.**

One of the first disciplines that we learned was how to conduct ourselves when moving around the dance floor. It is imperative that dancers understand that their conduct on the floor affects others and, if not properly practiced, can result in unnecessary disruptions in the flow of dancing and in many cases the safety of fellow dancers. A popular diagram of the **Line of Direction** that should be adhered to follows with the permission of its artist, Ray Gerring:

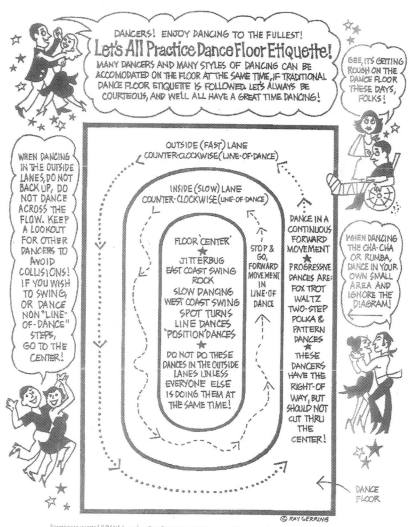

There are many terms and expressions that are peculiar to dancing, and without some explanation of their meanings, it would be difficult to navigate within the dance community comfortably. The following are some common terms and phrases that are found in the unique dance vocabulary:

- **Amateur Dancer:** A person who dances for pleasure and does not seek financial gain.
- **Professional Dancer:** A dancer who teaches, performs, or competes for financial gain and, therefore, is not eligible to compete as an amateur.
- **Social Dancing:** Ballroom, Latin, Swing, and Nightclub dances that are done for enjoyment and relaxation and are not meant for show or competition.
- **Slow Dancing:** A general term meant for dancing to very slow romantic music, improvising moves, with a very close hold. No lessons are required, as there are no formulated steps or patterns involved.
- **General Dancing:** Usually done at dance halls and between dance performances in competition dancing when the floor is available to the audience for social dancing.
- **Line Dancing:** Can be performed with or without a partner. Dancers form a line and repeat sets of patterns to the chosen music. Some of the more popular line dances are: Country Western, Disco, Cha-Chas, Waltzes, and even Polkas. Probably one of the most popular line dances on the east coast is Zorba. The dance comes from the unforgettable movie *Zorba the Greek,* starring Anthony Quinn. He performed the dance as a single and then was joined by his friend to make it a duet. In Greece, the dance is usually done by men in a line formation. Oddly, in the United States, the dance is performed by women with very few men participating. In this country, a man dancing with other men is not considered macho, but in Europe and South America it is very common.
- **Mixers:** Women form a line and men pick the first person in the line as a dance partner; they dance once around

the floor and she is then returned to the end of the line; the male then proceeds to his next partner at the head of the line. This continues until the dancing is over, which is usually 10 minutes. Mixers are usually done to Foxtrots and Waltzes and are very popular where there are single people at a dance event.

- **Formation Dancing:** Formation dancing allows dancers to show off their techniques in addition to their ability to move as a team. Teams are composed of 4, 6, 8 or more couples that perform dance routines in Tango, Cha-Cha, or any combination of other dances. A popular format is a potpourri routine, which often mixes dances in the same category, e.g., International Latin formations or International Standard formations. The latter format is used during the competitions of ballroom formations teams in such places as the world-renowned British Dance Championships at the Tower Ballroom in Blackpool, England.

- **American Style:** This type of ballroom dancing evolved from social dancing and is now a fully recognized competitive style of dancing. The smooth style allows dancers to be in open or closed positions, allowing for a beautiful "Fred & Ginger" style of dancing. There are nine American style dances divided into two groups, Smooth and Rhythm.

- **Smooth Style** consists of Foxtrot, Waltz, Tango, and Viennese Waltz.

- **Rhythm Style** consists of Cha-Cha, Rumba, East Coast Swing, Bolero, and Mambo.

- **International Style:** In this type of ballroom dancing, couples remain in closed dance positions throughout the standard dances. Many of the steps and routines are similar to American Style dancing, but are performed in closed positions for the standard dances and open and closed positions in the Latin dances. The 10 International Style dances are also divided into two categories, Standard and Latin.

- **Standard International Style** dancing consists of Slow Foxtrot, Waltz, Tango, Viennese Waltz, and Quickstep.
- **Latin International Style** dancing consists of Cha-Cha, Samba, Rumba, Paso Doble, and Jive.
- **Argentine Tango** and the above ballroom International and American Tangos use very different techniques and vocabularies, which is confusing considering they are all called tangos. In Argentine Tango, the body's center moves first, and then the feet reach to support the move. In ballroom Tango, the body is set in motion across the floor through the flexing of the lower joints (ankles, knees, and hips) while the feet are delayed. Then the feet move to catch up to the body, resulting in a snatching or striking action that reflects the staccato nature of the style of music. The Argentine Tango steps are more gliding, but can vary in timing, speed, and character and follow no single rhythm. The dance is led and followed at a level of individual steps; variations can occur from one step to the next. This allows the dancers to vary the dance from moment to moment to match the music, fast or slow, and to match their mood. Improvisation and attitude are the essence of this dance. For the novice dancer, the difference between the three dances boils down to the following points. The International Style is rigid and requires precise moves in preordained routines and lacks any semblance of passion. The American Style is a little softer in motion and appearance with some passion being displayed, but the dancers all perform the same routines with variations in their styling. The Argentine Tango is a down-and-dirty dance. It was the original tango and came out of the brothels of Argentina. The essence of the dance is flirtation and seduction, and does not rely on any particular syllabus to obtain its goal, just romantic passion and the dancers' abilities to execute their objective. Both the American and International Tangos are refined offshoots of the original Argentine Tango.
- **Showcase Dancing:** These exhibitions can be performed by professionals or amateurs or a combination of both. One

of the more popular types is performed by a Professional/ Amateur (Pro/Am) couple, usually a teacher and student that team up and compete against other Pro/Am dancers.

- **Medalist System:** This is a uniform method of testing used by dance schools to measure a student's progress. It offers structure in dance programs and gives students a standardized method of measuring their development.
- **Bronze Level:** This is the first level of the Medalist System and consists of specific basic dance concepts and movements. This level is represented in dance competitions and allows performers to compete within their level of expertise.
- **Silver Level:** The second level in the system allows dancers to use continuity (open steps) in the American Style Waltz and Foxtrot. It also allows dancers to compete with others on their own level and to be judged accordingly. International Style Silver dancing has its own requirements that are similar to American but conform to their own particular standards.
- **Gold Level:** This is the highest level in the Medalist System, representing the most advanced figures and dance concepts. The dancers are held to a higher standard and are expected to have mastered the bronze and silver dance level routines and syllabuses. As an example of the athletes that dance at this level, the professional dancers on Dancing with the Stars, are all Gold Level dancers and it certainly shows in their performances.

As an example of the pleasure that we received during our journey within the dancing community, I would like to relate an experience we had that was the highlight of our dancing memories. Our story began with an advertisement appearing in the catalogue "Bridge to the Tango," published by Daniel Trenner of West Medford, Massachusetts. The picture of Tango dancers and the description of their trip to Buenos Aires, Argentina took my breath away. The adventure was for eleven days of intensive studying and training with instructors whose ages ranged from early twenties to late seventies. The experiences and memories of the older instructors ranged from the beginning of the 20th century when Tango was in its infancy and danced mostly in brothels, through the reign of the infamous dictator Juan Peron and his popular wife Evita. The younger instructors were far removed from the hard times and challenges that their elders experienced and were mostly interested in the rapture and passion of their profession as Tango aficionados and instructors. The brochure explained the purpose of the tour and the descriptions of the instructors and their backgrounds. It also included some exciting favorable comments from former students who went on the tour, which added to the flavor, expectation, and romance that occupied my mind at that time.

I showed Barbara the travel brochure, and, after her excitement wore off, we reviewed the itinerary inch by inch. She didn't know that I had already booked the trip, and the more we delved into the details the more excited she became. Famous Tango dancers, such as Gustavo Naveira, Olga Besio, and Omar Vega were listed as mentors and instructors. Even Tango dancers we had seen, so many years ago, in the *Tango Argentino* Broadway show were part of the professional group that would be our instructors on the tour.

When I told Barbara that I had already booked the trip as a birthday present for her, she didn't say a word; she thought I was joking, as I so often do. When I convinced her that it was for real, the hugs and kisses that followed are still felt by me when we dance the Tango. What a surprise birthday present for her, and what a chance for us to really get the feel of the Tango in the country where the passionate dance originated. I had booked a March tour, which is summer/early fall in Buenos Aires, so we had to prepare the proper clothing for that time of year. We also had to arrange for air transportation and research the best exchange rate for the U.S. dollar. Exchange rates can be very tricky; there can be a difference of 10 to 20 percent if the right choices aren't made. Many travelers use their hotels or exchange stores to convert their dollars to local currency, which can be a very costly mistake. We found that our Citibank ATM card was the fastest and least expensive way to convert dollars. There are many Citibank outlets in Buenos Aires with no lines, no forms to fill out, and no passport problems; you can just walk into the bank as you would in the United States, go to the

ATM machine, insert your card, enter your password, and, behold, the local currency is in your hand at a very favorable exchange rate.

Our tour had an optional airfare on coach with not much of a discount. The flight was 10 hours long, and considering that we had to be at the airport two hours prior to takeoff, we decided to explore flying business or first-class so we could use the special lounges that are provided for those classes. Of course, the extra comforts of flying in upper classes were also an inducement to upgrade our flight. American Airlines was the primary airline going to Argentina; its price for first-class was more than the tour price. So we opted for business class, which worked out to be a couple of hundred dollars more per person than coach. As luck would have it, the airline was running a special for our time slot, which included the use of their Admiral's Club first-class lounge. This turned out to be a blessing in disguise. Foreign flights required that passengers check in two hours prior to the scheduled takeoffs. Our plane was delayed for an additional hour, which meant killing three hours at the airport. What a difference having the use of the upper-class lounge made, as they served free coffee, Danish pastries, nuts, and pretzels and also had comfortable, large spacious seats, with no crowding, plenty of reading material, private rest rooms, several television sets, and finger sandwiches. Not a bad way to spend three hours. Since then, whenever possible, we try to fly business or first-class if the airline's lounge is included in the price.

We left for Buenos Aires from Miami International Airport in Florida. Luckily, we were wintering in sunny Florida at that time, which made it convenient for us to take an airport limousine from Boca Raton, where we were staying, to the airport, without worrying about parking or the safety of leaving our car for two weeks at the airport garage. Business class on our ten-hour trip was exceptionally more enjoyable than our experiences with coach; there was more than adequate room for our carry-on bags in the overhead compartments and an area for hanging clothes or storing golf bags. After settling in, we were offered champagne, wine, refreshments, and finger snacks. The seats were spacious and reclined completely for sleeping, and were almost as comfortable as our bed at home. This was especially important as our flight left around midnight for a scheduled arrival at

10:00 A.M. By the time we boarded and got organized, a good night's sleep was a welcome friend.

While resting on my comfortable seat/lounge, I took the opportunity to read about the history of Argentina and to see if there were any places of interest that we might include in our sightseeing. I purchased the *Lonely Planet City Guide to Buenos Aires,* by Wayne Bernhardson. While at home, we did extensive research on the Internet about Buenos Aires, so reading the information in the travel guide was easy and familiar to us. Although Argentina dates back to 1536, when the Spanish explorer Pedro de Mendoza made camp in Buenos Aires, the romantic history of the country actually began at the turn of the 20th century with the introduction of Tango dancing and a singer/writer named Carlos Gardel. To appreciate the passion that the people have for the Argentine Tango, a brief history about the dance and its first and foremost hero, Carlos Gardel, is in order.

The Tango originated in the streets around the capital of Argentina, Buenos Aires, about 1890, and was considered a vulgar dance practiced in houses of ill repute and other unsavory places. It combined the gaucho's (cowboy) verse with Spanish and Italian music. Carlos Gardel was also considered to have been born and nurtured in the streets, but not in Argentina. He was born to a single mother, Berthe Gardel, in Toulouse, France, in or around 1890. Today, being a single mother carries very little social stigma, and in many cases, women travel that journey by choice, preferring not to be tied to a permanent partner, while enjoying the experience of motherhood. But in the late 19th century, Berthe and her young son were a disgrace to her family and community. When Carlos was three or four years of age, Berthe's lover paid for her and her son to relocate to Argentina. They arrived in the capital alone and abandoned, and were immediately destined to live in the poor neighborhoods of Buenos Aires. So we have the arrival of the Tango and Carlos at the same time, late in the 19th century, and the same place, Buenos Aires. These two forces were to become engaged in one of the most passionate dances of all time. The dance began in the lowest of places, brothels and tenements, and eventually found its way into homes of the rich and famous. Around the world it travelled—New York, Paris, and Italy—making music, inspiring dancers, and finally the grand finale; acceptance of its passion in motion pictures with the likes of Rudolf Valentino the great Latin Lover.

In Argentina today wherever Tango music is heard, a picture or the sound of Carlos' voice is in close proximity. He has become almost mystical. When he died in an unfortunate plane crash in June 1935, it is said that a Cuban woman committed suicide in Havana, while a woman in New York and another in Puerto Rico tried to poison themselves, all over the same man whom they had never met but whose voice and music they were enamored with. Below is a picture of Carlos Gardel playing the romantic hero opposite Mona Maris in the 1934 movie *Cuesta Abajo:*

Gardel with Mona Maris in the film "Cuesta Abajo", Paramount 1934

Our plane arrived at the Aeropuerto Internaconal Minisro Pistarini de Ezeiza, simply known as Ezeiza (EZE), Buenos Aires, at 10:00 A.M., exactly on time and with no unusual surprises. The airport was located only 29 miles from our hotel, the Continental on San Roque Boulevard, downtown, in Old Buenos Aires. Our luggage arrived at the airport unharmed, which was another pleasant surprise so we didn't waste any time boarding a shuttle bus to our hotel. We were surprised at how light the traffic in the city was considering that its population is approximately three million residents. It appeared that most of the motorists obeyed the traffic laws so there were no traffic tie-ups. We arrived at our hotel promptly and, considering that it was rated as a four-star hotel, we got another surprise, but this time an unpleasant one. We learned that foreign hotels are not rated the same as in the United States. Although the hotel was not up to the standard we expected, it was located in a great part of the city, and only two blocks from Avenida Florida Boulevard, which boasts every type of retail store imaginable: leather goods, women and men's designer clothing shops, shoe stores, etc. Also, the Boulevard had every type of restaurant that exists: Italian, Spanish, American, French, South American, Russian, etc.

Although the hotel was old, it was clean and quaint; our suite had a large bedroom and separate sitting room, serviced by window air conditioners. In the early afternoon, our group leader, Jeff Anderson, welcomed us at the reception area near the hotel's lobby. After the orientation and personal introductions, he put together a group to have lunch at an Argentine restaurant, which was located on the famous Boulevard. After lunch, he said he would introduce us to the local shoemaker, who was an expert at making soft, comfortable dance shoes to order. After having a heavy lunch of delicious Argentine steaks with all the fattening trimmings, we moseyed over to the shoemaker's shop. We negotiated with the pleasant craftsman for dancing shoes for me and Barbara. We got a kick out of watching him make the shoes that we ordered, which were made of the finest soft Argentinean leather, almost tissue-like to the touch. Needless to say, we wore our new shoes at every dancing opportunity; our happy feet enjoyed the feel of the soft tissue-like leather caressing them, as they didn't require a break-in period. Hearing Tango music while walking along the busy streets was absolutely enchanting; people just stopped and began dancing whenever their fancy dictated. Of course, Barbara and I also enjoyed a few impromptu Tango steps while we waited for our shoes to be created and on our walk back to the hotel.

Our hotel was only a short walk to San Telmo, another historic area in Buenos Aires. It is one of the oldest neighborhoods in the city, and was one of the wealthiest areas until yellow fever took its toll on the unfortunate residents in the late 19th century. The wealthy abandoned their dwellings and the area became a haven for scoundrels and the poor immigrants of that era. Still unspoiled by the rampant modernization that was going on all over Buenos Aires, San Telmo is now an artist's quarter, where bohemians can find large spaces to rent at low rates, very much like Greenwich Village, New York, right after WWII, when our GIs found inexpensive lifestyles while attending the local universities and practicing their artistic skills. It was in San Telmo in the late eighteen hundreds that the Tango was born in the brothels and houses of ill repute, and it was in the neighborhoods like this, in Buenos Aires, that Carlos Gardel grew up and turned the Tango into the nation's and then the world's most popular music and seductive dance. Most of the Buenos Aires' nightlife is concentrated in this district, as well as some of the most interesting restaurants and bars. Street dancing was also done in this neighborhood and again, Barbara and I took advantage of the great music that we heard to practice some of our new Tango steps.

Considering the location of these wonderful places and their close proximity to our hotel and the "Confiteria Ideal" (Tango Club), where we would spend most of our time being taught the Tango and listening to great lecturers, the fact that the hotel didn't meet American four-star standards became less important. We spent very little time in the hotel, and only used our room to get some much-needed sleep after long days at the dance sessions and *milongas* (dance halls). Fortunately, the hotel had a restaurant with large viewing windows looking out at the street level, which became a great comfort station for drinking delicious dark Argentinean coffee and for "people watching." It's amazing how European the people looked; the men are inclined to wear European-cut suits and the ladies dress in a very sophisticated and stylish manner. The viewing of the street activity and the beautiful Argentineans was very relaxing and became a morning ritual that we looked forward to.

On the first evening, we joined our new dancing friends in a cocktail party. The 30 people in our group came from as far away as Italy, Germany, Canada, and many parts of the United States, all anxious to learn and experience the Argentine Tango from Argentineans. Later that evening, at about 10:00 P.M., we were off to our first *milonga* at the Club Gricel. As would be the practice every evening, we were escorted by our fantastic staff instructors in a private bus. The club had a typical nightclub atmosphere and held a comfortable 200 people. There was a DJ in attendance playing a variety of music for dancing, but most of the music was Tango. There is no such thing as a "no smoking" area in the clubs in Buenos Aires, so a smoke cloud filled the place and made it very uncomfortable to see and breathe, especially since the club wasn't air conditioned, which is also the norm for that city. But, the music and dancing made up for these shortcomings. The men were all dressed in suits and wore ties, as is the custom; the women wore pretty, short-sleeved dresses and short skirts with slits down the sides, which in addition to making them look very sexy, allowed them to maneuver with ease. Considering it was early fall in Buenos Aires, there was a lot of sweating going on. It's probably one of the reasons that the *milongas* start late in the evening and continue into early morning, as it does cool down quite a bit between those hours.

The tradition at dances is that if a man wants to dance with a particular female, he makes eye contact and then nods his head. If the woman accepts, she will nod her acceptance; if she doesn't want to dance, she will turn her head away. It is customary for men to ask women to dance, even if the women are escorted by other men. Using the eye contact method takes away the embarrassment and doubt that goes along with verbally asking someone to dance and the possibility of rejection. It is really a neat way to enjoy an evening without all the uncertainties that go along with approaching a stranger and asking them to dance with the prospect of being refused. Our instructors made sure that everyone in our group had a partner to dance with. Some of us, including me, enjoyed dancing with the locals once we got the knack of "eye contact" and its meaning. The dancing routine was that three tangos would be played with about a minute intermission between each to talk and get acquainted with new partners. This allowed dancers a chance to decide whether or not to continue dancing with the chosen person. If partners decide to continue dancing, then, when the music resumes they would continue dancing in the "line of direction" (counterclockwise), being very respectful of the other dancers around them and making sure that there is no bumping. No kicks, fans, or other spacious moves are allowed on the dance floor because they could interfere or cause unnecessary collisions with other dancers. Occasionally, other dance music was played during the intermission between tangos. The students took advantage of the respite to show off their Swing, Cha-Chas, Mambos, etc. It is strange that the Argentines do not dance any other dances than the Tango and its variations, such as, Argentine Tango Waltz, and Milonga. Our night ended at about 2:00 A.M., and we left exhausted from the excitement of the new experience and the incredible amount of dancing that we had done. Many of our group stayed until closing at 5:30 A.M. God bless them!

The next morning was Saturday. We woke up at about 9:30 A.M. and rushed to enjoy a buffet breakfast, which was included in the cost of our trip. The selection included many hot and cold dishes, which we devoured to replenish our energy that had been depleted the night before. In the early afternoon, we had our first Tango lesson at one of the most picturesque salons in the city, the Confiteria Ideal, which has been featured in such movies as the 1997 *Tango Lesson,* written by and starring Sally Potter and one of our dance instructors Gustavo Naveira; the 1998 movie *Tango,* written by Carlos Saura and staring Carlos Rivarola, Cecilia Narova, and Mia Meastro; and the 1998 movie *Evita,* written by Tim Rice, Alan Parker, and Oliver Stone, starring Madonna and Antonio Banderas. The Confiteria was built in 1912 as a café-bar-nightclub and still carries the look of the turn of that century's art deco architecture, with its ancient wooden flooring, dark wood furniture, opulent marble staircase, and an ornate elevator. Some of the world's most famous people, such as Maurice Chavalier, Marie Felix, Dolores del Rio, Vittorio Gassman, Robert Duvall, and many local and foreign dignitaries have enjoyed the food and dancing at this one-of-a-kind establishment.

The emphasis on our first dance lesson was the relationship between dance partners and their responsibility towards each other. To emphasize the importance of each one knowing and respecting the other's movements, we were taught some of our partner's steps. The men danced the women's part, which required the women to do the leading. Talk about confusion, yet, it was very helpful in learning how difficult it is for a woman to dance backwards and to respond quickly to the male's lead. I learned to do *ochos* (figure eights), *cortes*, kicks, and many other sophisticated Tango steps while dancing backwards. It was certainly different than what I was used to and was very easy to confuse the different steps. It took quite a bit of practice, but the men seemed to get the routines down pretty well and translated the experience into holding and leading the ladies with a lot more consideration and appreciation for their role in the Tango. In Argentina, it's not uncommon to see people of the same gender dancing together. They are taught to dance both parts, as leaders and as followers. We did this for about two hours and then had a one-hour intimate interview session with a master teacher of Tango. Our mentor shared his joys and heartbreaks with the Tango, and related how dancing saved his sanity through troubled political times in Argentina. After the session, we had an hour of practice with our partner, the dance instructors, and other students, male and female. Dancing with a member of the same sex not only aided us in understanding the Tango, but it helped us gain important knowledge when we applied what we learned to other dances.

After the first session, members of the tour paired and enjoyed dinner at one of the local restaurants, which was followed by walking around San Telmo and enjoying the street fair that was taking place. At about 10:00 P.M., we again boarded our bus for a night at Salon El Pial, another local *milonga*; fortunately, the club was air conditioned so we were able to dance the night away in a more comfortable, cool, dance hall atmosphere. We ended our magical evening around 2:00 A.M., and again headed back to our hotel for a well-deserved night's rest; that is, except for some of our fellow students who insisted on dancing till the club closed.

After several lessons, our instructors concentrated on the meaning of improvisation in Tango dancing, which is the essence of the dance. "It is easy enough to learn many steps in the Argentine Tango, but the fun and passion of the dance is to improvise and to introduce new steps and feelings into the dance routines. To hear the music; to feel the music; to express the proper attitude; when this synergy is accomplished, then improvisation causes passion to radiate from the dancers' bodies and movements, resulting in a **dance of love.**" Dan Trenner, our tour sponsor, then interjected: "And isn't this why we traveled from around the world to Buenos Aires, to learn and experience the **dance of love?**"

The rest of our trip followed the same routine: morning buffet breakfasts, dance lessons for about four hours at different venues, lectures by master Tango dancers, an afternoon nap—time permitting—dinner at local restaurants, dancing at different *milongas* till the wee hours of the morning, and then returning to our hotel, exhausted from the day's activities.

An exceptional day was when we visited our tour leader's apartment for a private rooftop dance party at *La Cupula*, a spectacular turn-of-the-20th century penthouse. Buenos Aires is often referred to as the "Paris of the South," and the view from the penthouse roof validated that belief. We got the same feeling when we visited Paris. The views were similar and absolutely breathtaking; the church steeples, cupolas of every size and shape, and the brilliant effect of the sun's rays shining off the gold trim of many of the cupolas and steeples, were mirror images of the architecture of each city.

The party was exciting as a trio band consisting of guitar, bass, and *bandoneon* played beautiful tangos, which gave us an opportunity to meet and dance with many of our instructors, master teachers, and local dance aficionados. A buffet was set up with local finger foods and an open bar kept everyone refreshed and somewhat immune from the afternoon sun. There were several Tango exhibitions by our teachers, some local dancers, and teachers with students. The students were all given an opportunity, one couple at a time, to show off their newly acquired Tango moves. It was exciting to dance under the warm sun with our instructors, which made me feel as if I were dancing in the sky on a cloud high above the busy hustle and bustle of the city's activity. The afternoon turned into evening as we socialized and caressed our partners and our newfound friends to the sounds of Tango music. We drifted from the party and walked the enchanted streets of the magical city back to our hotel to prepare for another evening of Tango dancing at a local *milonga*; not all the students ventured out that evening, as many were exhausted from the day's excitement, drinks, and the radiant sun.

One of the places we decided to visit while in the city was Eva Peron's burial place in the Recoleta Cemetery. The cemetery is in the trendy Recoleta area of the city, where there is an artisan's market and the dwellings of the wealthy residents of Buenos Aires. The cemetery is enclosed by a high wall, but some of the high monuments and statues can be seen from the outside protruding above the wall. However, the message is clear: **Private – Privileged – Property.** Traditionally, only the wealthy and powerful aristocracies were buried at this cemetery, with Eva Peron being the exception. The remains of Eva are secured in the modest *Familia Duarte* subterranean vault, which irritates the upper class to no end. Her embalmed remains (embalming is not usual for the people of Argentina) rest there after being transported from South America to an obscure cemetery in Milan, Italy, where her husband, Juan Peron lived, and then back again to Buenos Aires to her final resting place. Her family tomb is modest, but the floral arrangements at and around the tomb are breathtakingly beautiful; fresh, colorful, and by no means humble. When entering the cemetery, one is overwhelmed by the aboveground splendor of the monuments, mausoleums, and statues, ranging from modest to grand scale mini-cathedrals. Many mini-buildings have gates and/or glass doors; their coffins and stairwells can easily be seen from outside, as if the viewers are being asked to look at the splendor within. The overall cemetery reminded me of the aboveground cemeteries in New Orleans, only on a much grander scale.

Only a few blocks from Eva's tomb, we found the resting place of her husband, President Juan Peron, in the less exclusive graveyard of Chacarita Cemetery, which is by no means as grand as his wife's resting place, but is the home of many famous people who were not of the aristocracy. The cemetery was established in 1870 to accommodate the countless victims of the yellow fever plague. It has a few tombs and statues to match the splendor of Recoleta, one of the most visited being Buenos Aires' songbird, Carlos Gardel, who is held in a near-saint status by many Argentineans who feel a quasi-religious devotion to him. Plaques from people around the world cover the base of his life-sized statue; embroidered with flowers placed by a steady procession of people paying their respect to the great Tango singer. The abundance of beautiful flowers that decorated his tomb enhanced the overall appearance of the rather dreary cemetery.

The day before our dance tour ended, we had some free time to go shopping and to walk around the nearby neighborhood; we chose to return to the leather shop to buy another pair of soft leather dancing shoes before preparing for our last dance session. Our last class and farewell *milonga* was at the Sunderland Club, where we had a cocktail party, danced with our partners, other students, instructors, our master instructors, and some of the locals. I actually danced with two male instructors and enjoyed the experience very much, even though dancing the female part was quite confusing and took some getting used to. One of our master teachers, Mingo Pugliese, and his dance partner-wife, Ester, approached us and said they liked our styling and passion for the dance. He said, "Michael, all of the teaching, demonstrations, and lectures that you were a part of mean nothing if you do not develop the proper **Attitude.** There is no dance, if you do not have the right **Attitude** when doing the Tango." He praised our attitude and told us to "Continue dancing for the love of it, and to have a happy and passionate life with the Tango as my wife and I have had for over 40 years."

The next morning, we had our farewell breakfast and said goodbye to our many new dancing friends from around the world that we shared our wonderful vacation with. We extended our stay for three additional days and accomplished all the sightseeing that we had planned. The cemetery visits to see the final resting places of Eva and Juan Peron, and Carlos Gardel will always be etched in my mind as they are etched in history because of the tragic endings to their memorable lives. We spent many hours just walking around the city, visiting neighborhoods and talking to as many locals as possible. Fortunately, Barbara has a good understanding of the Spanish language, which helped us to relax and meet people on a comfortable level.

While looking out the window of our airplane and watching the beautiful city of Buenos Aires fade from our view, Mingo Pugliese's words were still echoing in my mind: "**Attitude, Attitude and more Attitude...**" What a wonderful piece of advice for dancing the Tango and for fully enjoying life.

To give retirees an idea of what the dancing community is like and the opportunities that dancers have to join in popular dance events and to meet some of the world's famous dancers, I decided to extract from the back of my mind one of the most memorable nights that Barbara and I had at a show in the local Suburban Center in Wantagh, Long Island, New York, which was sponsored by Louis Del Prete, dance instructor and promoter extraordinaire.

Barbara and I were fortunate to have seen two shows sponsored by Louis featuring couples from *Dancing with the Stars.* We saw Karina Smirnoff and Louie Van Amstel on May 31, 2008, and the husband and wife team of Edyta Sliwinska and Alec Mazo on May 30, 2009. Needless to say, both shows were spectacular and played to full houses of over 400 dance lovers. Although the venue is small, the enthusiasm in which the audience received both events was quite large.

The exhibition that stands out in my mind is Karina and Louie's epic and passionate display of **dancing personified.** Karina and Louie go back to the year 2000, when they won the U.S. National Latin Championship, the Can-Am DanceSport Gala-Canadian open Professional Championship in International Latin, the Japan International Dancing Championship for Professional Latin, and the prestigious Emerald Ball DanceSport Championship for Open Professional Latin. That was certainly a busy and rewarding year for the new dancing partnership.

They were introduced by Louis and received a roaring welcome from the eager audience. Their first dance was Jive. The speed of the dance and the aerobic moves that they performed seemed unreal as they moved in a circle in the middle of the dance floor. Karina's short white dress and flowing legs against Louie's black suite were a contrast in perfection as they jived in unison to the beats of the fast music.

Their next dance was a romantic Rumba. They performed the "chicky-chicky-boom" to the rhythm of the music with sexy sways and *cortes*; the room heated from their sensual rubs and caresses. You could almost see the steam coming from her long white open-backed dress, which was complemented by his tight black pants and black, wide-open shirt. When watching romantic performances and getting caught up in the heat of the moment, it's easy to understand why many people prefer to call ballroom dancing an "Art Form" rather than an athletic endeavor. My opinion is that it is half of both; an athletic event when required and an "Art Form" when desired.

To continue the romantic mood, they performed a spicy Tango. The heat again radiated from their movements and filled the hall; it seemed that energy burst from her body and through her long black semi-opened shoulder dress, sparked by his shirtless tuxedo showing his chest, bordered by the jacket's velvet lapels. The smooth sways and caresses followed by quick turns and kicks clearly transmitted the essence of the dance: flirtation, chase, seduction, and then finally, conquest. It all happened before our eyes; it appeared to be a dress rehearsal of a passionate affair, which the audience approved of and confirmed with their spontaneous oohs and aahs, and then a standing ovation.

Their final dance was a Cha-Cha. They exploded onto the dance floor and went full speed ahead into the dance with arms flying and legs moving almost as fast as the speed of light. Their quick movements and acrobatic gyrations didn't resemble a conventional Cha-Cha, but then these were not conventional dancers—they were world champions and performed the dance as champions should, with moves that were far beyond ordinary. Their speed caused her yellow short sleeveless and backless dress bottom to swirl when she spun around, resembling a Hawaiian hula skirt. His open black shirt, displaying his manly chest, added to the energy of the dance.

It's commonly known that "a picture is worth a thousand words," so below are two pictures, the first of Karina and Louie followed by Edyta and Alec of their performances at the Suburban Center. While looking at the photos, one can almost feel the energy of their movements radiating from the pictures. The photos are presented below, with Louis Del Prete's permission:

After the audience calmed down from Karina and Louie's exhibition and the couple had a chance to rest, they returned for a "Question and Answer" session. The first question from the audience was directed at Karina:

"Which of the Mario's do you like best? Twenty-three-year-old R&B star Mario Barrett, from the sixth season of DWTS, or the 33-year-old television heartthrob Mario Lopez, from the third season of DWTS?"

After blushing and snickering, Karina answered: "I've been seeing Mario Lopez for some time, and there is nothing and has never been anything but a professional relationship between me and the other young Mario."

Question for Louie: "How long does it take to create the beautiful girl's outfits and the men's clothing?"

Louie answered: "The designers are given their tasks on Tuesday and they must have the outfits fitted and completed by Friday of the same week, which is a major undertaking by a staff of exceptional designers and craftspeople."

Question for Karina: "Who chooses which dances are to be performed by the couples?"

Karina answered: "ABC has a special staff of knowledgeable dance professionals that choose which couples are to perform each of the dances."

Question for Louie: "Who chooses the music for the dances that are performed on DWTS?"

Louie answered: "ABC has a special staff that chooses the music for the dances and are guided by some of the professional dancers in the choice of music that each couple will perform to. In many cases, the music is not what is usually heard when dancing to specific dances, which makes performing the dances a lot more difficult."

Question for Louie: "Is it true that the performing celebrities receive $200,000 per season and an additional bonus if they win the Mirror Ball Trophy?"

Louie answered: "That sounds about right."

Question for Karina: "Who chooses the celebrities' professional partners?"

Karina answered: "ABC chooses the partners based on a random selection with no preference to a guest's talent."

Question for Louie: "Do you create your own choreography?"

Louie answered: "Yes, I also do many of the group's choreography for the show and I'm also the Creative Director. It's very challenging to get twenty or so professionals to dance as a group, but the outcome is always a rewarding experience. When performing, I'm also responsible for the dance routines for me and my partner. Each of the professionals is required to do the arranging for their own dance routines once they are given the music and their dance assignments from ABC. So the professionals, in addition to being champion dancers, must also be proficient choreographers."

Question for Karina: "How long are the contracts between ABC and the professional dancers?"

Karina answered: "Our contracts run through 2015, but that doesn't mean that all the professionals will appear on all the shows; we are actually on standby."

Another question for Karina: "How much notice do the professionals get before they have to appear on the show?"

Karina answered: "One month."

Another question for Karina: "How much notice do the celebrities get from ABC to prepare for the show?"

Karina answered: "Two to three months."

After the question and answers session, Karina and Louie were gracious enough to remain at the center for a couple of hours to take pictures with their admirers. The line was too long, so Barbara and I decided that we would postpone the picture taking for another time. Much to the delight of the dance community, the couple remained on Long Island for a few days and conducted private and group dance lessons for the benefit of their admirers. We would catch up with Karina during her exhibition at Goldcoast Ballroom in Coconut Creek, Florida later on that year. I not only got to dance with the charming beauty, but we had our picture taken with her when we presented her with a signed copy of my book *Dancing around the World with Mike and Barbara Bivona* in which the above photos are featured. A picture of her receiving my book follows:

The intellectual and mental benefits of dancing are rarely considered by the general population. There is no doubt that dancing is considered a physical activity, so much so, that it's expected to become an Olympic event in the near future. But little has been written about the effect that dancing has on one's mental condition. I came across an article by Richard Powers, www.Vintage@Stanford.edu, world-renowned scholar and an expert on American Social Dancing that will hopefully set the stage for more people becoming aware of the intellectual advantages of dancing. With Richard Powers' permission, I'm presenting his thoughts; it's our hope that with mental enhancements thrown into the formula, more people will take up the challenge and enter the world of ballroom dancing:

"Use it or Lose It: Dancing Makes you Smarter," by Richard Powers

For hundreds of years dance manuals and other writings have lauded the health benefits of dancing, usually as physical exercise. We have also seen research on further health benefits of dancing, such as stress reduction and increased serotonin levels, with its sense of well-being. Recently we've heard of another benefit; it seems that frequent dancing apparently makes us smarter. A major study has added to the growing evidence that stimulating one's mind can ward off Alzheimer's disease and other dementia.

You've probably heard about the *New England Journal of Medicine* report on the effects of recreational activities on the mental acuity in aging. If you're not familiar with the study, here it is in a nutshell:

'The 21-year study of senior citizens, 75 and older, was led by the Albert Einstein College of Medicine in New York City, funded by the national Institute of Aging, and published in the *New England Journal of Medicine*. Their method for objectively measuring mental acuity in aging was to monitor rates of dementia, including Alzheimer's disease.

The study wanted to see if any physical or cognitive recreational activities influenced mental acuity. They discovered that some activities had a significant beneficial effect, others had none.

They studied cognitive activities such as reading books, writing for pleasure, doing crossword puzzles, playing cards, and playing musical instruments. They also studied physical activities like playing tennis, golf, swimming, bicycling, dancing, walking for exercise and doing housework.

One of the surprises of the study was that almost none of the physical activities appeared to offer any protection against dementia. There can be cardiovascular benefits of course, but the focus of this study was the mind. There was one important exception: the only physical activity to offer protection against dementia was frequent dancing. The results were:

Bicycling and swimming – 0%

Dancing frequently – 76% reduced risk of dementia

Playing golf – 0%

Reading – 35% reduced risk of dementia

Dancing without a doubt has the greatest risk reduction of any activity studied, cognitive or physical.'

Aging and Memory:

When brain cells die and synapses weaken with aging, our nouns go first, like names of people, because there's only one neural pathway connecting to that stored information. If the single neural connection to that name fades, we lose access to it. So, as we age, we learn to parallel process, to come up with synonyms to go around these roadblocks. (Or maybe we don't learn to do this, and just become a dimmer light bulb.) The key here is that more is better. Do whatever you can to create new neural paths. The opposite of this is taking the same old well-worn path over and over again, with habitual patterns of thinking.

When I was studying the creative process as a grad student at Stanford, I came across a perfect analogy to this: 'The more stepping stones there are across a creek, the easier it is to cross in your own style.' The focus of that aphorism was creative thinking, to find as many alternative paths as possible to a creative solution, but as we age, parallel processing becomes more critical. Now it's no longer a matter of style, it's a matter of survival— getting across the creek at all. Randomly dying brain cells are like stepping stones being removed one by one. Those who had only one well-worn path of stones are completely blocked when some are removed. But those who spent their lives trying different mental routes, creating a myriad of possible paths, still had several paths left. The Albert Einstein College of Medicine study shows that we need to keep as many of those paths active as we can, while also generating new paths, to maintain the complexity of our neuronal synapses. Considering the research, we immediately ask two questions: Why is dancing better than other activities for improving mental capabilities? And does this mean all kinds of dancing, or is one kind of dancing better than another?

The essence of intelligence is making decisions. And the concluding advice, when it comes to improving your mental acuity, is to involve yourself in activities which require split-second rapid-fire decisions, as opposed to rote memory (retracing the same well-worn path), or just working on your physical style.

One way to accomplish this is to learn something new. Not just dancing, but anything new. Don't worry about the probability that you'll never use it in the future. Take a class to challenge your mind. It will stimulate the connectivity of your brain by generating the need for new pathways. Difficult and even frustrating classes are better for you, as they will create a greater need for new neural pathways.

Take a dance class, which can really stimulate your mind. Dancing integrates several brain functions at once, thereby increasing connectivity. Dancing simultaneously involves kinesthetic, rational, musical, and emotional processes.

The question then is, what kind of dancing?

Let's go back to the study: bicycling, swimming, or playing golf – 0% reduced risk of dementia.

But doesn't golf require rapid-fire decision-making? No, not if you're a long-time player. You made most of the decisions when you first started playing, years ago. Now the game is mostly refining your technique. It can be good physical exercise, but the study showed it led to no improvement in mental acuity.

So taking the kinds of dance classes where you must make as many spit-second decisions as possible is the key to maintaining true intelligence and reducing dementia.

Does any kind of dancing lead to increased mental acuity? No, not all forms of dancing will produce this benefit. Not dancing, which, like golf or swimming, mostly works on style or retracing the same memorized paths? The key is the decision-making and keeping in mind that intelligence is what we use when we don't already know what to do.

We wish that 25 years ago the Albert Einstein College of Medicine thought of doing side-by-side comparisons of different kinds of dancing to find out which was better. But we can figure it out by looking at who they studied: seniors **75** and older, beginning in 1980. Those who danced in that particular population were former Roaring Twenties dancers and former Swing Era dancers, so the kind of dancing most of them continued to do in retirement was what they began when they were young: freestyle social dancing—basic Foxtrot, Swing, Waltz, and Latin.

I've been watching senior citizens dancing all of my life, from my parents (who met at a Tommy Dorsey dance), to retirement communities, to the Roseland Ballroom in New York City. I almost never see memorized sequence of patterns on the dance floor. I mostly see easygoing, fairly simple social dancing —freestyle leads and follows. But freestyle social dancing isn't that simple. It requires a lot of split-second decision-making, in both the lead and follow roles.

When it comes to preserving mental acuity, some forms of dancing are apparently better than others. When we talk of intelligence (use it or lose it), the more decision-making we can bring into our dancing, the better.

Who benefits more, women or men?

In social dancing, the follow role automatically gains a benefit by having to make hundreds of split-second decisions as to what to do next. Women don't follow, they interpret the signals their partners are giving them, which requires intelligence and decision-making, which is active, and not passive. This benefit is greatly enhanced by dancing with different partners, not always the same leader. With different dance partners, you have to adjust much more and be aware of more variables. This is great for staying smarter longer.

But men, you can also match her degree of decision-making if you choose to do so. (1) Really notice your partner and what works best for her. Notice what is comfortable for her, where she is already going, which moves are successful with her and which aren't, and constantly adapt your dancing to these observations. That's rapid-fire split-second decision-making. (2) Don't lead the same old patterns the same way each time. Challenge yourself to try new things. Make more decisions more often. And gentlemen, the huge side-benefit is that your partners will have much more fun dancing with you when you are attentive to their dancing and constantly adjust for their comfort and continuity of motion.

Dance often:

Finally, remember that this study made another suggestion: Seniors who did crossword puzzles four days a week had a significantly lower risk of dementia than those who did a puzzle once a week. So, if you can't take dance classes or go out dancing four times a week, then dance as much as you can; the more often the better."

I thought it would be appropriate to list some dancing sites that would be of interest to anyone entering and experimenting with the fun world of dancing:

- **USA Dance at** www.usadance.org, formerly the United States Amateur Ballroom Association (USABDA):

There is an annual fee of $25 for social membership in one of its local chapters. The organization is worldwide and allows members to participate in dancing events locally and around the world. Its primary goals are: "To promote amateur DanceSport as a sport both nationally and internationally and to foster its inclusion in the Olympic and Pan American games; to organize and support amateur DanceSport events globally, including national, regional and local championships; and to select the top DanceSport athletes to represent the United States in the World DanceSport Amateur Championships and the world games and to finance their participation."

It's the foremost amateur dance organization in the United States and strives to "promote social dancing as a healthful lifetime recreational activity, suitable for individuals, families, and for those who are so inclined, it's a stepping stone into competition dancing." Some of its famous former amateur members can be found performing on ABC's *Dancing With the Stars.* The following are some of the professional dancers who were once amateur members of USA Dance and now appear on that popular television show:

- Julianne Hough, www.juliannehough.net; Edyta Sliwinska, www.edytasliwinska.com; Anna Trebunskaya, www.jonahanrobertsdancer.com; Cheryl Burke, www.cherylburkedance.com; Lacey Schwimmer, www.laceymaeschwimmersworld.com; Corky Ballas, www.corky.com; Mark Ballas, www.markballas.com; Derek Hough, www.derekhough.net; Alec Mazo, www.alecmazo.com; and Brian Fortuna, www.brianortuna.com.
- **World Pro-Am DanceSport Series,** www.dancesportseries.com. This program features dance students; they hold over 70 competitions annually across the United States and encourage students on every level to participate.
- **AccessDance, www.accessdance.com.** They provide a network site that finds dance lessons and venues for students and offers information on dance organizations, competitions, merchants, and publications.

- **DanceBeat International, www.dancebeat.com.** They provide periodical highlights from competitive ballroom dancing around the world.
- **International Dance Directory,** www.dancedirectory. com. They provide a worldwide directory of dancers, with sections for locating teachers, studios and merchandise.
- **Ballroom Dancers,** www.ballroomdancers.com. They are a clearinghouse for ballroom dancing information, including worldwide dancing locations and is a dance learning center for most recognized dances.

In my neck of the woods, New York City and Long Island, there are a couple of exceptional websites and studios for dancers of all levels; they are:

- **Touch Dancing Studios,** www.touchdancing.com. Alfonso Triggiani is the director and owner of the Long Island studios. He is a renowned international dance aficionado and has his own television show, *Life Styles,* which features free dance lessons on Saturday mornings on New York City and Long Island channels.
- **Louis Del Prete,** www.louisdelprete.com. He is a dance exhibition promoter, DJ extraordinaire, and top-of-the-line dance instructor. He sponsors and DJs themed dances throughout Long Island that always include free dance lessons prior to general dancing. He has promoted dance exhibitions with world-famous dancers in New York and Florida, and is responsible for bringing some *Dancing with the Stars'* professionals to local dance halls in both states. Some of his dance exhibitions have included: Karina Smirnoff and Louie Van Amstel, Edyta Sliwinska and her husband Alec Mazo, and Karina and Dmitry Chaplin. He is currently our New York teacher.

I think that retirees should give dancing a try, preferably before retirement. A few dance lessons will determine if it's a pastime that should be continued on a more social or serious basis when time and family pressures are hopefully a thing of the past. Remember, each dance lesson builds blocks and adds to your brain's reserves, so that when blocks begin to disappear due to our natural aging process, there are hopefully ample reserves to replace the missing ones.

Sports – Boating

One way or another, we are all sports fans, whether as a participant, an avid fan whose enjoyment in life is attending sport functions, or as a couch television spectator. The lists of sporting activities are endless: golf, tennis, baseball, football, hockey, basketball, softball, fishing, boating, skiing, mountain climbing, log rolling, rodeo activity, car racing, and on and on. Of course as we age and reach retirement, many of the above sports are no longer available or advisable on a participating basis. But being an avid fan or sedentary onlooker are certainly realistic activities in our senior years. Barbara and I were lucky in that we were active boaters in our younger days and were able to continue enjoying that sport well into our retirement years.

One of our retirement dreams was to spend a month on our 42-foot Chris-Craft and cruise, if possible, to Montauk Point, Long Island; Block Island, Rhode Island; then on to Massachusetts enjoying stops at Martha's Vineyard, Nantucket, Cape Cod, and then sailing through Buzzard's Bay to New Bedford and up the Cape Cod Canal to Plymouth. After completing that semicircle, we would then head for our favorite port, Newport, Rhode Island for an extended stay and finally back to our homeport in Greenport, Long Island. What a wonderful dream come true that trip would be. To appreciate where our passion for boating comes from, a little of our history with boats is in order.

We bought our first boat, a new 18-foot Crestliner runabout, two years after we were married with money we saved to take a two-week vacation in Italy. We even took courses in Italian at Brooklyn College to prepare for our first *Bucket List* trip. We saved $2,500 and were ready, willing, and able to board a jet plane and fly to our new adventure. But fate intervened through my father-in-law Charley, who surprised us with tickets to the New York Boat Show at the Coliseum in Manhattan. We were excited to visit the show as we were slowly becoming avid sailors, thanks to my father-in-law and his 28-foot fishing boat, which we were guests on almost every weekend during the past two summers. Bypassing the mega yachts, cruisers, houseboats, and sailboats, we stopped and fell in love with an 18-foot Crestliner that was driven by a 60HP outboard Johnson motor; the price was $2,500. It didn't take long for us to decide that having a boat was an ongoing vacation and that a trip to Italy was a great idea but could be postponed for another time. So we put our vacation to Italy back on our *Bucket List*, and purchased a new 1966 Crestliner. We named our new princess *Big One* because of its small size, and knowing that some day in the future we would own a "*Bigger One.*"

The first thing we had to do was take some boating safety courses; our choice was either the United States Coast Guard Auxiliary or a private organization, the United States Power Squadron (USPS). As I had already spent four years in the United States Air Force, joining an organization connected with the Coast Guard was not an attractive option for me; so we both joined the USPS and took our first safe boating course in Seamanship. Some history about the USPS is in order to understand the importance of that non-profit organization and its impact on boating safety, and how joining such an organization can fit in nicely into one's retirement years. USPS was founded in 1914 and currently has over 45,000 members in 450 squadrons throughout the United States. Its main purpose is teaching mariners the importance of safe boating through education. The levels of courses are: Seamanship, Piloting, Plotting and Position Finding, Celestial Navigation, Cruise Planning, Engine Maintenance, Marine Electronics, Sailing, and much more. In addition to the intellectual endeavors of the organization, there is also an active social side. It is a fraternal group that encourages participation in on-the-water and on-land activities, such as cruises, rendezvous, sail races, navigation contests, and even fishing derbies. Activities ashore include meetings with marine programs and teaching classes, parties, dinner dances, picnics, field trips, and an annual "Change of Watch Ball."

We took our Seamanship course at Saint Francis College in Brooklyn, New York. We both passed the course in 1966; I was sworn in and became a member of the Brooklyn Power Squadron. Not so for Barbara, even though she took the same course and passed the same test (with higher grades than me). At that time, women were not allowed to become members; it wouldn't be until 1984 that she would become a full member with the same standing as *moi,* even though she was sworn in alongside me and probably became the first woman to be sworn into the USPS. What we noticed at the meetings and dinners that we attended were the advanced ages of many of the bridge members. Many of them had been members for over 20 years and have made the organization a major part of their lives. Barbara and I decided that the USPS would certainly be a great way to remain active in something we loved through our adult years and into retirement. What better way to spend our retirement than to be involved with a fraternal group whose main purpose is having fun while boating safely? We currently are members of the Peconic Power Squadron of Long Island and keep active with their safe boating programs and many social events.

Big One was part of our family for seven years. One of our boating friends had a 26-foot Christ- Craft cruiser named *Paper Doll* that we fell in love with after spending a day fishing aboard the beamy beauty. Barbara and I decided that it would be the perfect boat for us, being that the runabout was getting a little crowded for our growing family of four. *Paper Doll* had double bunks and could easily accommodate our two small children, Steve and Laurie, who were four and three years old at that time. In addition, it had a somewhat private V-berth at the bow of the boat for Barbara and me, which added up to a boat we could all sleep on and spend some quality time together after my grueling tax seasons, which for all intents and purposes, ended for me on the first of April each year. So the admiral (Barbara) sent me to Al Grover's Chris-Craft dealership in Freeport, Long Island, which at that time was the pleasure boating capital of New York, to find our next dream boat. He had just the boat we were looking for and it was only a few years old. So I gave him a deposit, but before we signed the contract, Al said, "Wait, I have a 1970, two-year-old, 28-foot Chris-Craft that was just traded and I think you should have a look at her, she is a beauty." Well, one look was all it took. The boat was much larger overall than the 26-footer; it's surprising how much difference two feet makes in a boat. It had lots of headroom, a nice kitchenette, a standup toilet, double bunk beds for the kids that folded down into a couch, and a nice size V-berth at the bow. What more can a soul need? The boat was $500 more than the smaller craft. I didn't waste any time in making her a member of our family by signing on the "dotted line." When I got home and told Barbara that I had bought a larger boat, she went into shock. She didn't expect me to purchase anything without her first seeing it and was annoyed that I went over our budget. All of her displeasure faded away when she boarded our new purchase *Alice B,* which was the name on the transom of the boat that was meticulously painted royal blue by its previous owner. Being that I went over budget, we decided not to spend any additional funds changing the name on the craft. Barbara immediately fell in love with the beautiful lady. Its shiny powder-blue fiberglass hull, with a white wood superstructure, a single 225HP inboard engine, a private standup toilet, a fresh water pump system, and a propane gas stove, was a far cry from what she expected after being cramped in a smaller boat for so many years. She told me from that time on I could buy any boat without asking her as she knew that it would be a perfect addition to our family. We would joke a lot about the name of the boat. As long as we owned *Alice B,* people that we met while cruising called my wife Barbara, Alice; we made a point of never correcting anyone right away and got many laughs when we explained later that Alice was not my wife's name.

Our kids were getting older and sleeping on upper and lower bunks was getting a little complicated, so we looked around for our third boat and fell in love once more (how fickle we were) with a 35-foot all-fiberglass Chris-Craft Double Cabin cruiser. We were lucky to find the exact boat that we wanted, a two-year-old 1977 35-foot Chris-Craft Double Cabin. It was a whole different kind of boat than our previous ones. It had twin 300HP engines, a 5KW generator, a toilet with a standup shower, a heat and air conditioning pump, a private master bedroom, a V-berth for Laurie with a privacy door, and a folding bed for Steve. After a family meeting, we decided to call our new family member *"Mikara,"* which is derived from the first three letters of Mike and the last three letters of Barbara. It is also sort of a play on words with the Italian word *"Mikara,"* which means in dialect, "my love."

With the availability of "LORAN C" for pleasure boats as a direction finder, we didn't waste any time in purchasing the electronic battery-operated system and putting it to good use. With its help as a navigation aide, we took our first trip on our 35-foot beauty from Long Island, N.Y. to Plymouth, Ma. What a pleasure it was to travel and arrive at planned destinations without zigzagging or getting lost. After ten wonderful boating years, we decided it was time to buy our last boat, which we planned to live on permanently when we retired, while traveling throughout the United States and the islands off of Florida.

We currently own our second *Mikara* and recently celebrated her 24th anniversary as a family member. She is a 1988 47-foot Chris-Craft, measured from bow rail to swim platform, has two 450HP engines, a 7KW generator, a master bedroom with a private head (toilet) with a nice size tub, a private guest room with a head, a full size refrigerator, a kitchen, a living room (salon), heat and air conditioning, and all the latest electronic entertainment toys. On the bridge we have radar, GPS, auto pilot, and a multitude of radios. It's just the right boat to have in our retirement years for traveling, and enjoying the sun at home and in faraway places. A photo of *Mikara* with Admiral Barbara at the bow and me at the helm follows:

We have kept our boats at Stirling Harbor Marina, on the North Fork of Long Island in the seaport Village of Greenport for over 30 years, and consider it our home away from home in the summer months. We chose the location after spending time in the Hamptons, on the South Fork, because it was much lower keyed than its southern sister. The water in the area is deep compared to the South Shore, which makes boating a lot safer and more relaxing. It's also one of the best jumping-off points for boating on the East Coast, putting Connecticut, Rhode Island, Massachusetts, and Maine within reasonable boating distances. Cruising to Connecticut, Block Island, or Sag Harbor for lunch are some of our favorite short trips from our convenient homeport.

What attracted us to the quaint town of Greenport was the laidback attitude of its townspeople, and the farmers that could be seen around town wearing their blue, shoulder strap coveralls. It also didn't have the crowded restaurants and traffic jams that the popular South Fork is noted for. In addition, the inland boating waterways were less crowded and its islands, from a distance, reminded us of the friendly islands of the Mediterranean. We were always amazed that on some days the only boats to be seen were at a distance, which is very unusual for a popular seafaring area. The town itself has a rather checkered history, ranging from whaling, shipbuilding, rum running, and illegal whiskey trading to fishing and oyster harvesting. It was also home of the America's Cup winners, *Enterprise* in 1930, *Rainbow* in 1934, and *Ranger* in 1937. Its history has made the village the quaint but sophisticated place it is today. Needless to say, it no longer participates in any of the above illegal activities. The focal point of the village today is Mitchell Park, which became fully operational in 2007. Its main attraction is an Antique Carousel that was built in 1920 by the Herschell-Spillman Company and donated to the town by the Northrop/Grumman Corporation in 1995. It is fully enclosed in a glass pavilion and boasts of having one of the few brass ring dispensers in use today. Its hours during the season are from 10:00 A.M. to 9:00 P.M. These same hours apply on weekends and holidays during the off season, weather permitting. The park's amphitheater is connected to a harbor walk and is the site for band concerts, theatrical shows, and special local events. Its harbor walk connects the park to the Long Island Railroad Station, which travels to New York City, and also connects with the North Ferry, which carries cars and passengers across the narrow body of water in Greenport Harbor to Shelter Island. The park also has an ice-skating rink for outdoor winter sports, which is used as a mist walk in the summer months to cool the area. Its *Camera Obscura* is a medieval optical device that projects a live image from outside to a round projection table in its dark room, and is one of the only projections in the world that is open to the public free of charge. The park also has a harbormaster's building, observation deck, public toilets, and over 80 transient town boat slips.

Of special interest to us are the musical events that take place at the amphitheater during summer months. Once a week the residents bring their chairs and sit on the expansive lawn outside the theater to enjoy the Greenport Band, which is made up of approximately twenty local musicians, playing popular and marching music. Dancing bands are also scheduled throughout the season playing Dixieland, Jazz, Smooth, and hot Latin music. Our last dance session was to the music of the Mambo Loco Quartet of Brentwood, Long Island, which is considered one of the hottest bands on the Twin Forks.

Our dream of spending a month on *Mikara* cruising at our leisure had finally become a reality. We had our nautical charts out and began plotting courses to the far-away places we've dreamt of visiting with no restrictions as to how long to remain in each place. We were retired and the world was our oyster! The best time to travel along the eastern seaboard is in the middle of July when the seas are calm and rain and fog are less prevalent. But, there are no guarantees that traveling that time of year won't get a sailor in trouble with inclement weather. So it becomes difficult making reservations at planned ports-of-call, without saying a prayer or two. Reservations are required at popular marinas months in advance to secure docking space, which makes cruising totally reliant on weather conditions during planned vacations. There are many foolish sailors who will travel under any conditions and, somehow, live to tell of their ordeals as if they were gallant adventures. It's possible to plan a stay at a marina for two days and remain for a week, due to unexpected inclement weather conditions. But, if a person loves boating, as we do, they will throw caution to the wind, so to speak, and make early reservations in anticipation that the weather gods will cooperate. For our first extended vacation we made reservations at Montauk Yacht Club, in Montauk, Long Island; then on to Champlin's Marina in Block Island, Rhode Island; then to the town dock at Menemsha, on Martha's Vineyard, Massachusetts, with our next stops in the same state to Nantucket Boat Basin, in Nantucket and then to Hyannis, in Cape Cod. Leaving the "Bean State" we planned on cruising to Newport, Rhode Island for an extended period of time or until we tired of the place, if that's possible, considering the incredible amount of places to explore and its wonderful beaches.

We like casting off at around 10:00 A.M., which hopefully gives any fog in the area time to burn off. That was our plan as we began the first leg of our trip and it worked out well for us. As we entered Gardiner's Bay, the sun was burning through the fog as we settled in for a pleasant journey to the entrance of Montauk Harbor. It's always exciting and comforting when an inlet comes into view and we slow down to enter between the breakwaters. Upon entering this inlet, it's important not to make any wakes (waves) as there are people bathing on the left of the entrance and boaters are responsible for any damage caused by their carelessness. On the right are some pretty threatening rocks, some visible and others underwater, so it pays to be cautious and alert when entering this or any other inlet because it seems they all share the same characteristics: rocks above and below the water, and shallow water on either side of the entrance buoys.

We waited in line behind a couple of boats for the dock master of the Montauk Yacht Club to give us permission to enter the bulk-headed marina. Native Americans called Montauk "The land of many winds." Fortunately, there weren't any strong winds yet as they usually pick up around early afternoon, and we were able to dock our boat in our assigned slip without incident. I always breathe a sigh of relief when *Mikara* is tied up safely and the fresh water and dockside electricity are connected, which gives me an opportunity to wash the salt water off of her body while I calm down from the anxiety that accompanies me on all of my trips. The marina can accommodate over 200 boats, and boasts at being one of the top ten marina destinations in North America. It welcomes boats up to 225 feet and it's not uncommon to see several boats that size docked there, some with mini-helicopters on their decks. A great feature available to boaters staying at the marina is their use of the resort's land facilities, which include an indoor heated pool, two outdoor pools, a spa, a gym, a small beach, an outside restaurant overlooking the pool and Lake Montauk, and a first-class indoor restaurant with an extensive wine list that serves local fish specialties in addition to other delicious cuisine. In the evening, their indoor circular bar has a combo band for listening and dancing.

The resort was built by the famous Miami master builder Carl Fisher in 1928, as a playground for the rich and famous. He had successfully developed Miami Beach for winter fun and thought Montauk would be a great alternative for his "in crowd" to spend their summer months when it became too hot to play in Miami. To accommodate his friends' yachts, he dug a deep channel from freshwater Lake Montauk into saltwater Gardiner's Bay, making it the world's largest private harbor at that time. The members of his club included such dignitaries as Vincent Astor, J.P. Morgan, Nelson Doubleday, Edsel Ford, Harry Whitney, Thomas Eastman, John Wanamaker, and Harold S. Vanderbilt. According to legend, the "Island Club" became the most popular speakeasy and gambling casino on the East Coast. Unfortunately, the big stock market crash of 1929 put the *kibosh* on his plans, and the marina and resort soon fell into disrepair. It took many years to redevelop the "Montauk Yacht Club Luxury Resort Marina," and today it stands out as the "gem" of the East Coast, with its modern marine facilities and world-class hotel resort amenities.

Montauk is considered one of the sports fishing capitals of the world, hosting more than 40 charter and fishing boats, many reeling in world-record and prize-winning catches of tuna, shark, striped bass, and fluke, just to name a few. It also boasts some of the best Atlantic Ocean beaches on the East Coast, and draws over a million visitors a year to its shores. Walking through the pristine resort always gave me the feeling that the place was befitting my idea of where I belonged in the scheme of things; just the right place for me and mine—ha ha.

We took our traditional walk to Gosman's Dock, which is approximately one mile from the resort; we walked through other smaller marinas and past some local restaurants to arrive at Montauk's most famous eatery, known only as "Gosman's." The restaurant is made up of three different eating establishments, all on the same wharf. The largest is an indoor/outdoor sit-down restaurant facing the entrance to Montauk Point. The smallest is a counter "order and take out" eatery that provides outside seating for its patrons, also facing the entrance to the harbor. This eatery has many unwanted guests: "fat seagulls" or "baygulls" as many people call them as they are always hanging around the bay looking for free handouts. If diners aren't alert, these flying pirates will swipe the meal right off their plates. Our favorite place to eat is the two-story restaurant with indoor/outdoor seating facing the busy harbor entrance. We usually get a table on the spacious terrace facing Gardiner's Bay and the entrance to Lake Montauk and watch the comings and goings of every imaginable sized and shaped boat in existence entering and exiting the narrow inlet. It's always a memorable lunch spending a couple of hours eating sushi, mussels, and lobster salads, washed down with white wine for Barbara and a cold Budweiser for me. The food, coupled with one of the most beautiful boating scenes to be found in New York, makes for a perfect, relaxing afternoon far away from the stress and strain of our busy lives. Gosman's Dock also features a number of charming shops and boutiques selling nautical gifts, clothing, jewelry, fashionable women's wear (Barbara's favorite), home furnishings, a toy store, and my favorite, an ice cream take-out window.

The resort we were staying at had a complimentary jitney that traveled around the popular circuit for the convenience of its guests. After a long walk, large lunch, and some serious shopping by Barbara, it was a nice respite to return to our docking area in an air-conditioned jitney instead of walking back in the heat of the day. We spent our first evening having a light dinner at the open-air restaurant by the pool, watching the bright flickering lights of the boats moving about, wandering in and out of our view as if they were horizontal traveling stars. The dance music from the bar area attracted us so we immediately joined fellow boaters and hotel guests on the dance floor. We were quite exhausted from our busy day, but managed to do some Cha-Chas, Rumbas, and Mambos before retiring for the evening.

Like Greenport, Montauk also has a checkered history that went from whaling to illegal liquor trading during the days of Prohibition, with other diverse questionable activities in between. The first English settlers were from Massachusetts and found the island inhabited by Native Americans of the Algonquian group, who were loosely divided into bands, grouped together into a confederation under the leadership of the Montauk, Sachem, who was considered to be the ruler from Montauk to the western end of Long Island. The friendly natives taught their new friends how to hunt wild game, such as deer and wild birds, how to fish, grow corn, squash, and beans, and how to gather wild berries, herbs, and roots. They taught the Europeans how to hunt whales from canoes and how to make use of all the animals' body parts. Specifically, how to successfully extract oil from their carcasses by burning them in large clam shells and on rock piles. Over the years, the Indians sold off or had their land stolen by manipulative land grabbers. The most notorious case was in 1910, when the railroad heiress Jane Benson won her lawsuit against the Montauk Indians stating that they were not a tribe and had no rights under various treaties signed between the United States and tribal natives. The New York State Supreme Court ruled in her favor and the Montauk tribe was abolished, depriving them of any land rights. Eventually, the Benson family purchased Montauk for $151,000 from the state and opened the door to the evolution from a pasture culture into a resort area. Oddly, today the Montauk Tribe has a class action pending before the Supreme Court challenging the earlier court's decision.

One of the most important events at the eastern end of Montauk was when President George Washington commissioned the Montauk Lighthouse in 1797. It has been a Coast Guard station for many years and its light and foghorn have warned ships to stay clear of the treacherous rocky shoals that extend outward from its point. Today, the lighthouse is a museum and is visited by over one million tourists annually. Another interesting piece of history or legend has to do with the pirate Captain Kidd, who purportedly buried treasure chests of pirate booty in what is now called "Money Pond." No one has ever discovered his buried treasure and, as a matter of fact, the only booty found on the beaches of Montauk have been bottles of liquor, from the 13-year Prohibition period, that were buried on the beaches by bootleggers to be retrieved by their cohorts, when the coast was clear, to transport to New York City for the pleasure of their thirsty customers.

We took the resort's jitney for a 15-minute ride into the fishing and boating town of Montauk, where we had a delightful breakfast and then headed for its beautiful sandy beach, which was within walking distance from the town. We spread out on our blankets, books in hands, determined to spend the better part of the day just relaxing and enjoying the tranquility that the sounds of the ocean's surf and saltwater air seem to bring to most people. We rented a large umbrella to protect my delicate light skin from the sun's rays and I applied plenty of suntan lotion on my body for added protection. Barbara relishes sitting in the sun, perfecting her beautiful dark skin, which makes me envious of her relative immunity to the sun's rays. But when I think about having dark skin and sporting my reddish hair, my envy soon disappears as it doesn't seem like an attractive combination. When we returned to *Mikara*, we immediately showered to get rid of the sand that seemed to have invaded every part of our bodies, dressed, and headed to one of our favorite restaurants, the Sea Grill, which is located at Gurney's Inn and features freshly caught fish, Italian specialty dishes, and lots of dance music.

We've been visiting Gurney's for many years and always make it a point to have dinner at their oceanfront restaurant. But, dinner is only one part of the pleasure we experience when visiting this seaside resort. Having a cocktail before our meal while walking their ocean-view terrace, absorbing the Atlantic Ocean's dark blue water and salt air, and then moseying down to their 1,000-foot-long beach and spreading out on a chaise lounge, is something we both cherish. Being retired and not having to worry about schedules made the experience all the more enjoyable. The surf picks up in the early afternoon from the "Many Winds" that visit Montauk due to its location at the tip of the South Fork of Long Island. It's surrounded by water on three sides; from the south and east, the Atlantic Ocean pounds its beaches with long, large swells that relentlessly crash onto its shores. On the bay side, although it can get pretty rough at times, it's usually a calming relief from the ocean's intimidating activities.

By the time we sat down for dinner, the surf was pounding the beach with six- to eight-foot waves, which certainly is not a sailor's ideal boating conditions, but it does make for a panoramic and exciting view of the sea's activity from the safety of the restaurant, which has large viewing windows for their customers' pleasure. After enjoying the Italian cuisine, as is customary in Italy, we retired to the coffee and dessert bar for espresso and Italian cheesecake, while we danced the night away to the combo band that played soft romantic music and some hot Mambos. The fun on our first leg of our "dream retirement vacation" was that we were not in any rush; we were retired and could stay out as late as we pleased, or all night if we so desired; the alarm clocks in our heads were turned off and would remain so for the remainder of our journey.

We rose early the next morning so we could leave on the outgoing tide to our next destination, Block Island, Rhode Island, which is about 20 miles east of Montauk. We can always expect fog and unpleasant waves on the short trip, so we battened down the hatches and headed east. Before traveling we always check the weather report from NOAA to make sure that there are no small craft warnings (23 to 38 mph winds) in the area we're traveling to. If there are small craft warnings, we make it a practice not to leave our location until the inclement weather passes. The report for the day was for clear sailing, except for some fog and a reminder that there are many fishermen's lobster traps in the water that should be avoided at all costs when approaching Block Island. The traps are a major cruising problem as many of the bright-colored markers (usually orange) are either faded or underwater. Hitting one can disable a boat when its line wraps around one or both of a boat's propellers. While cruising around this body of water there is also lots of sea traffic, including large ferries coming to and from the north and west, and large cruise ships coming from or sailing out to sea. There is also commercial traffic zigzagging around the busy sea lanes, but the most hazardous vessels to be on the lookout for are naval submarines that practice in the deep waters and guard our shores. We have been hailed on many occasions by submarines while traveling in fog and told to steer clear of them. We started out very slowly, about 10 mph hoping to avoid lobster traps and praying that the heavy fog would burn off shortly. Well, as is common in this area, the fog stayed with us for the whole trip. It took over two hours to reach the entrance of Block Island. Sighting the red #2 entrance buoy was a relief from the stress of traveling under such uncomfortable weather conditions. The two main buoys when cruising are colored green and red. When returning from sea, the red buoy should be kept on the right (starboard) side of the boat and the green on the left (port) side. Straying out of their invisible safety lines can cause a boat to go aground and trigger the beginning of a boating nightmare, which could result in a boat sinking and having the Coast Guard come to the rescue. We entered the inlet doing about five miles per hour, which doesn't create a wake and prolongs the life of the protective rocks that are on both sides of the entrance. There are beaches on the port and starboard sides, which make it imperative not to send any dangerous waves at the bathers. Our destination after passing through the inlet and the Coast Guard Station's beach, which is on the right side, was Champlin's Marina and Resort. The mooring area outside of the marina is one of the most popular on the East Coast because it's considered a safe harbor for boats, has great clam beds for digging delicious soft (piss) clams, and is renowned for its pristine beaches. An added bonus is the 1,000-plus year-round residents who welcome sailors with their friendly and charming New England manners.

Champlin's Marina is a full-service facility, located in New Harbor on Great Salt Pond. It has fuel docks, showers, laundry service, a marine chandlery, an outdoor swimming pool with a restaurant, and a Tiki Bar. The renowned Trader's Tiki Bar is famous for its mudslide drinks, music, and aggressive dancing. The marina also boasts a picnic area, private beach, an ice cream parlor, its own movie theater, and all the water toys imaginable. The island has always been a place that we looked forward to visiting on our annual boating excursions, as it is, without a doubt, a well-thought-out vacation spot and a boater-friendly resort. When our kids traveled with us, this was their favorite play land, as there is a never-ending amount of activities to keep children busy, especially its large pool and children's playground. After tucking *Mikara into h*er slip and washing her down to show off her shiny hull, we embarked on our annual ritual of walking to the island's only town,

New Shoreham, which is approximately one mile from the marina. Walking to town along the surf of the gorgeous Baby Beach, which is a favorite place for parents to bring their children, brings to mind how few unspoiled places remain in the world. Block Island is certainly one of them, which is why it was named by The Nature Conservancy as one of the twelve natural "Last Great Places" remaining in the Western Hemisphere. Exiting the beach at the Surf Hotel put us in the center of the bustling town.

The busy little three-block-long town is lined with boutique shops, a supermarket, a couple of ice cream parlors, several Victorian-style hotels, and, at the end of the strip, Ballard's Restaurant, which is next to the ferry dock in Old Harbor, which has a small, 30 slip boat marina for transients. It was this area that the Italian explorer Giovanni de Verrazzano, who was in the service of France, sighted land in 1524. He named the island Luisa after Louise of Savoy, the Queen Mother of France. At that time, it seemed all the first explorers to this hemisphere were Italians, but weren't in the employ of Italy. Columbus sailed for Spain, John Cabot (Giovanni Capoto) sailed for England, and Amerigo Vespucci sailed for Portugal and Spain. Although Verrazano was the first to sight the island, it was named after the Dutch explorer, Adriaen Block, who explored the area almost 100 years later in 1614. The Europeans found the Manissean tribe of the Narragansett's Indians living in peace on the island and quickly, through barter or manipulation, conquered the island and raised flags of conquest as proof of their sovereignty. The natives called the island Manisses, which meant, "Island of Little God"; they lived there for centuries in peace and within the unspoiled splendor of nature's bounty. Fortunately, we can still find a major portion of the island in the same condition that the Native Americans enjoyed. On the southeast part of the island is Mohegan Bluff, still pretty much the same natural beauty as in pre-European days, except for a stairway from the cliff down to "Bluffs Beach." There are 141 wooden steps from the top of the stairs to the rocky bottom, and then onto a beautiful pristine beach, where nude bathers, although against the law on the island, are scattered throughout the isolated area. Mohegan Bluffs got its name from the unfortunate fate of invading Mohegan Indians, who were defeated in battle by the Narragansett Indians on the cliff and were thrown down to their final resting places on the rocks surrounding the site (these were not the last of the Mohegans). Sharing the area is the Atlantic seacoast's brightest lighthouse, perched over 200 feet above sea level that warns seamen of the perils of the many treacherous rocks surrounding the region. On a clear day from that high vantage point, you can see Montauk Point with the naked eye, just peeking out above the blue waters of the Atlantic Ocean, truly one of nature's visual delights. Many of the dunes surrounding the island are part of the Block Island National Wildlife Refuge, home to many wildlife species, including the Piping Plover and American Burying Beetle. Also, there is a 230-acre glacial outwash basin, Rodman's Hollow, near the southern shore of the island that has several nature walking trails. The northern section of the island is a great undeveloped natural area that is often visited by birds making a stop along the Atlantic Flyway. On and on and on, the beauty continues. Hopefully, Block Island will remain an unspoiled natural treasure to be enjoyed by never-ending visiting nature lovers.

We returned to *Mikara* for a well-deserved afternoon nap, and when we awoke the sun was setting and it was starting to get dark; what a great snooze we had. We put on some comfortable clothing and took a cab over to Ballard's Restaurant for dinner and dancing. Another delight of the island is its comfortable temperatures; in July, the average high is 77 degrees dropping to about 65degrees in the evenings. This makes Barbara very happy, as she can wear a nice outfit while dancing without becoming too uncomfortable.

How does one explain Ballard's Beach Club and Restaurant? It's truly a hybrid consisting of a hotel with a porch that welcomes visitors to sit and relax; it has a tempting ice cream window, a spacious beach with a lifeguard on duty and volley ball nets, and an outside Tiki Bar overlooking the Atlantic Ocean, where one can enjoy a sea breeze drink while enjoying the ocean's sea breeze. It employs a combo band that fills the air with music all day long, a large al fresco dining area, and an indoor circular bar that seems to accommodate up to 100 happy customers. It also has an inside dining area that services over 100 diners at once, boasts a piano bar, dance floor, and, in the evenings, a variety of dance bands. A unique feature of the building is the collection of boat name plaques that hang on the inside walls, such as "Smugglers Cove," "Our Dream," "SeaRest," "Our Home," "Trident," and "Mikara III" (our 35-foot Chris-Craft). Well, all of this went up in smoke many years ago, which totally depressed us at the time. It took a couple of years to rebuild the facility exactly as it was before the fire, minus the old boat plaques that decorated its ancient walls, which were replaced by shiny and beat-up new ones. So we visited the new Ballard's and were pleasantly surprised to see an exact replica of one of our favorite entertainment places totally restored and swinging.

Ballard's is renowned for its family-style lobsters that are cracked in pieces and served at the dinner table in a hot pot, ready to be devoured. It boasts of serving more lobster plates than any other restaurant in the world. Looking around and watching the many diners enjoying their meals validates their claim. Customers were eating inside and also enjoying al fresco dining to the sound of music from the band that was harmonizing with the Atlantic Ocean's pounding surf. Some of the diners seemed to be in somewhat of a trance, eyeballs rolling and making pleasant sounds while savoring their ambrosia. Although I'm not a lobster lover, I joined Barbara in ordering a pot full of the red pieces of crustaceans that seem to be universally loved by everyone, except me. She loves when I join her in this feast, as she can have all the pieces that I find visually difficult to eat. We strategically chose our seats so that after dinner we could be near the piano bar and our favorite robust piano man, Jim Kelly. Jim was known as Ballard's Balladeer due to the many songs that he sang that have folk tales, such as, "Michael Row the Boat Ashore," "Good Night Irene," and "You are my Sunshine." That night everyone enjoyed singing along with him till his tour of duty ended. His famous Chicken Dance is a favorite of many customers. The dancers imitate chickens, including their clucks, while bending and raising their arms and squatting and walking around in that position like chickens. It has to be the most embarrassing display that anyone can perform, but we all did it, and totally enjoyed the fun, especially after a couple of drinks.

We woke up the next morning to the call of *"Andiamo, Andiamo"* (*Listen, Listen*). It was Aldo from the island's popular Aldo's Bakery selling morning treats, such as blueberry and cranberry muffins,

Danishes, and finger cakes, all freshly baked and being sold from his 18-foot Boston Whaler run-about. It's amazing how many boaters wait for his *"Andiamo"* so they can begin their breakfasts, especially those sailors that are anchored out in the bay or on moorings that do not have easy access to the restaurants on shore. We ordered our favorite blueberry muffins and quickly demolished them while drinking our morning hazelnut-flavored coffee; what a great way to start a morning in the picture-perfect marina at Block Island. After a leisurely breakfast we decided to take an alternate path into town by walking along the streets through Block Island Boat Basin Marina and Payne's docks. Both docks accommodate ferries from the West and North mainland. Passing Smugglers Cover brought to mind our old friend Captain Kidd, who tried to negotiate his freedom when visiting this Island, but was soon captured and returned to "Dear Old England" for his final appearance at the end of a hangman's noose. He is purported to have buried some of his treasure on this island, but none has ever been discovered, or if it was located, no one advertised the event.

Walking along the ocean side of Water Street into town, we stopped at the Victorian-style Surf Hotel, built in 1873, to enjoy a cup of their delicious fresh coffee and sit down for a spell on their rocking chairs, which were located on their expansive porch facing the center of the town. This was a great spot to rock away while watching the promenade of people passing by, while we played a game of checkers. After drinking our coffee and congratulating Barbara for beating me at checkers without any mercy or sympathy, we proceeded to visit some trinket shops, trendy boutiques, the book store, and a couple of local craft shops. By the time Barbara satisfied her "daily shopping fix," it was time for lunch. There were many al fresco bistros to choose from, but one of our favorites is the Victorian-style Harbor Inn, which has an extensive lunch and dinner menu and turn-of-the-20th-century dated furniture throughout its lobby and dining area. It has a great vantage point to view the comings and goings of the ferry and boat traffic traversing Old Harbor. The Inn has an exemplary salad bar that we took advantage of to complement their New England clam chowder, which was served in a bread bowl and was delicious beyond words, especially when drinking their house specialty beer; a concoction called

"Black and Tan," which is dark Guinness beer mixed with regular ale. When stirred briskly, it turns into delicious beer malt. Umm!

It is from the porch at the Harborside Inn, facing due east, that the location of the sinking of the submarine *Unterseeboot 853* can be seen. It was sunk by the U.S. Navy near the end of WWII. It had just been in the successful Battle of Point Judith, in Rhode Island, and sunk a collier (a ship for carrying coal), *Black Point,* when American warships located her and sent her to the bottom of the ocean, just seven miles from where we were sitting. The same submarine attacked the *Queen Mary* in the Atlantic Ocean when she was carrying American soldiers and equipment to Europe, but the sub was warded off by planes from nearby aircraft carriers, but not without damaging three planes before making her escape. So it must have been a celebrated day when the *Unterseeboot 853* was sent down to the bottom of the sea to fulfill its destiny as an artificial fishing reef along with two other German U-Boats that were sunk in the general vicinity earlier in the war. While having lunch, we heard that John F. Kennedy, Jr.'s plane had crashed on its way to Martha's Vineyard, which was the next stop on our itinerary. It happened on July 16, 1999; he was going to drop off his sister-in-law, Lauren Bessette, on the island, while he and his wife Carolyn were on their way to the Kennedy Compound in Hyannis Port, Massachusetts, to attend the wedding of his cousin, Rory Kennedy. His flight plan indicated that he was piloting a Piper Saratoga II Hp Single-engine aircraft from Essex, New Jersey, to the island, and then on to his final destination in Hyannis. The Coast Guard and other naval crafts were desperately searching for the wreckage. Radio transmissions warned everyone to avoid the area around Martha's Vineyard as rescue crafts were zigzagging the area trying to locate the wreckage. It was determined that he didn't have much experience flying at night or in fog. The dense fog probably was responsible for his crashing somewhere in the vicinity of the Vineyard. We were scheduled to arrive at Menemsha, Martha's Vineyard, the next day, and immediately called the marina we had reservations with to determine if the port was open; it was not, and the whole area was off-limits until further notice. Everyone on Block Island seemed to be in a state of shock at the news of our country's fair-haired JFK Jr. having met such a tragic demise at the young age of 38. It was inconceivable that another Kennedy could meet such a horrible fate so early in life. We spent the rest of the day in a vigil with everyone else on the island, waiting and praying for some good news.

We joined some friends for dinner and prayer at the Spring House Hotel, which is considered one of the island's most elegant historic landmarks. It is one of the oldest Victorian-style buildings on the island. Built in 1852, it has withstood over 150 years of nature's challenges. Its wrap-around veranda, mansard roof, and distinctive cupola, rises from a 15-acre promontory overlooking the Atlantic Ocean and Block Island's foothills. The view from the veranda is considered one of the most magnificent seascapes on the East Coast. Coincidentally, this picturesque location has provided the formal setting for many of the Kennedys' weddings. The atmosphere in the restaurant was solemn as religious services were being conducted for the recovery of the passengers of the ill-fated plane. Their survival was no longer a possibility based on information from the authorities at the search site; the best that could be hoped for was the recovery of their bodies. Everyone at our dinner table ordered modestly, as if semi-fasting in some way would change the events to a more palatable conclusion.

We left Block Island for Martha's Vineyard the next day, and were told by the Harbor Master of the island that the area was still under surveillance by naval vessels and helicopters and that we would have to bypass it. We headed for our next destination, the island of Nantucket in Massachusetts, which was approximately 80 miles from Block Island. If we were lucky and had good weather with no unforeseen mishaps, it would take about five to six hours to reach the "The Grey Lady," which got its name due to the dense fog that visits the island so frequently. The NOAA weather forecast was pretty good for the day, so we were off on the next leg of our trip by 10:00 A.M. The body of water that we were traveling can be very tricky as currents from several different directions meet along the route to Vineyard and Nantucket Sounds. The strong currents from Buzzards Bay can cause some large broadside waves on the port (left) side of the boat, or the Atlantic Ocean's currents can cause some pretty big swells on the starboard (right) side of the vessel. While approaching Menemsha Bight, our original destination, we spotted some debris in the water that looked strange and could possibly have been from the plane crash. We immediately called the Coast Guard and gave them our latitude and longitude positions so they could locate and investigate the scene; they thanked us and before the conversation was over a search vessel was at the site. Unfortunately, it was debris from the aircraft, which sent us into a depressed state, causing Barbara to cry uncontrollably. We moved from the area slowly and had to do some tricky maneuvering to get past all the naval vessels in the water around the island. We called Nantucket Boat Basin and spoke to the dock master, George, who we have known for many years, and explained our circumstances hoping he would have an empty slip for us. He said, "Come on in, very few people have been able to move their boats because of the restricted area around the accident." We were delighted and relieved that he had a slip available for us. It prevented our having to make an unexpected stop in Cape Cod, which meant we would then have to cross over to Nantucket and back to the Cape again, passing some pretty nasty shallow water, especially dangerous when pea soup (fog) is present. The currents were very strong as we approached Nantucket Sound; luckily for us, they were coming from behind us and pushed *Mikara* to a cruising speed of 22 mph, which we had never achieved at 3,400 rpms; it usually takes the engines about 4,000 rpms for her to move that fast. We got to Nantucket much sooner than anticipated, just in time to avoid the strong winds that are so prevalent in the early afternoons from the Atlantic Ocean, which were just starting to pick up. There is a very narrow inlet at the entrance to Nantucket, so it's imperative that boats entering stay on the right side of the channel, especially if ferries or large commercial vessels are exiting. Once past the channel, Nantucket Boat Basin's bulk-headed marina is immediately apparent on the right side of the harbor.

Waiting for permission to enter the marina from the dock master George is always tricky, especially when the wind starts to kick up, as it did. *Mikara* has a tendency to be pushed away from the entrance of the protected area when it gets windy, so getting behind the bulk-headed sea walls took some nifty maneuvering. George gave us our docking assignment on our VHF radio. I throttled up to get to the marina's entrance, but had to immediately throttle down upon entering as the steering area is very narrow and winding, with boats docked on all sides. After zigzagging past the boats that were securely tied to their docks, I finally reached my slip and backed in with the help of the prevailing strong winds. It was a long and tedious trip, and we were glad to be secure at such a pristine and boater-friendly facility. We have been going to this marina for over 15 years and were always thrilled when tying *Mikara* up at our temporary home. This year was special because we had no deadline as to when we had to leave; we were retired and decided that we would leave whenever the weather and "call-to-the-next-port" beckoned us. The marina is located at the end of the town, which makes for a picturesque view when looking from the town at the marina or from the marina at the beautifully landscaped town. *The Waterway Guide*, Northern edition, describes the marina perfectly: "Nantucket Boat Basin sets an industry standard for service at its transient marina. You will find 243 slips to accommodate boats from 30 to 280 feet in length, as well as dockside electricity, water, fuel, ice, public phones and waste disposal, with individualized pump-out stations designed to reach virtually every slip. Ashore are restrooms and showers, a large 24/7 coin-operated laundry, rental cottages, rustic artists' studios along the wharves, and even a park for pets' needs. The Boat Basin concierge, whose headquarters is located at the fuel dock, can arrange restaurant reservations, sightseeing trips, car rentals, medical appointments, and babysitting services." Well, I guess that just about says it all for this pristine marina whose staff is professional and boasts of having the world's most polite, experienced dock boys and girls to accommodate their guests' every wish.

Nantucket Island is one of the most natural and beautiful islands that I have ever had the pleasure of visiting. It has its own idyllic persona derived from its beaches and the abundance of beautifully landscaped designed and natural wild flowers. The island is only three and a half miles from north to south and is 14miles long, with miles of clean, well-maintained beaches. It's rich with fields of Scotch broom, bayberries, beach plum, grapes, bearberries, and hundreds of varieties of wildflowers. Its Milestone Road cranberry bog is one of the largest on the East Coast and its aromatic flavor seems to capture the air that flows throughout the island. We have seen deer, pheasants, cottontail rabbits, and all kinds of birds on our walks around the island. As a bonus from nature, Harbor Seals are seen year round sun bathing and playing off the beaches. Whale watching is still viable by sightseeing boats that guarantee sighting them on every excursion. One of the island's biggest tourist attractions is biking; people travel from all over the country with their bikes, crossing over on one of the many ferries from the mainland, and spend days biking and camping on the many excellent paths throughout one of nature's few remnants of paradise. Some years ago, our son Steve and his wife Donna joined us on the island after crossing over on one of the ferries with their bikes ready to explore the unique island. We thought we would spend some quality time with them, but we lost them for most of their visit to the "Call of the Wild," beautiful Nantucket. On each of their excursions, Donna would gather wild flowers and return to *Mikara* with them. By the time they left the island, our boat looked like a florist's shop with flowers decorating our bridge, deck, salon, and bedrooms. Biking is one of the most popular methods of transportation on the island; cars are discouraged and must pay exorbitant fees to cross over on the ferries, but there are many auto rentals on the island at relatively reasonable rates. Taxis are an alternative if other transportation is not available, but the shuttle bus system is the most efficient and affordable method of getting around if biking isn't feasible. The Nantucket Regional Transit Authority (NRTA) provides an island-wide seasonal fixed-rate shuttle service and a year-round "Your Island Ride" van service. In season, the shuttle buses run every 15 minutes from the center of the town and circle the island. The fares are reasonable, from $1.00 to $2.00 each way with discounts for senior citizens and no charge for children under six. Our favorite method of transportation is by foot, as walking around the island can be a pleasant way to spend the day, if the temperature is in the low 80s. When it gets near 90 degrees, we prefer the convenient shuttle buses.

We kept tuned to the radio to get up-to-date information on the rescue ships; the bodies still were not found, but some wreckage had been located. I'm sure the debris that we alerted the Coast Guard to was a part of that recovery, but nothing significant had been uncovered about the passengers of the ill-fated plane. We decided to take advantage of the cool weather, about 80 degrees, and walk around the island ending our journey at the Nantucket Memorial Airport, which was the fictitious setting for the sit-com *Wings*. But as the great Scottish poet, Robert Burns, wrote: "The best laid plans of mice and men gang aft agley." Truer words were never spoken, for we were in for some surprises on our journey. We mapped our walkathon carefully, beginning at the cobblestone streets outside our marina. The streets are inhabited by surprising colonial, Georgian, and Greek revival houses of ship captains and whaling merchants, dating back to the 18th century that still remain intact. Many of the houses have engraved plates that identify the dates they were built and the original occupant's names. We stopped at the Nantucket Whaling and Life-Saving Museums, which gave us some insight and a better understanding of the dangers that the mariners faced at a time when they had to go to sea to survive, but didn't always return home due to the hazardous nature of the elements and their dangerous encounters with the giant whales. To appreciate the importance of whaling on the lives of these brave seamen, some history of Nantucket is necessary. It wasn't until 1602 that Captain Bartholomew Gosnold of Falmouth, England, sailed his bark *Concord* past the bluff of Siasconset and mapped out the territory for dear old England. The 2,500 native Americans living in peace on the island were the Wampanoag Indians; they called their home *Nantican, Natocke,* or *Naytucan,* which is thought to mean "Far away island" or "In the midst of waters." The island was deeded to Thomas Mayhew by the English Crown in 1641. Up until that time, Indians from Cape Cod and Martha's Vineyard sought refuge on Nantucket from the European interlopers and consolidated their energy and skills with the local natives to fish and harvest the whales that washed up on the shore. The Europeans didn't settle on the island until 1659, when Mayhew sold his interest to the "Nine original purchasers," for 30 English pounds and two beaver hats, one for himself and the other for his wife. English ingenuity brought whaling offshore and, with the help and skill of the Native Americans, Nantucket became the world's leading whaling port from the mid-17th to the early 18th centuries. Prior to the colonials' invasion, the natives harvested Drift and Right whales that were near the shore or were washed up on the beaches. The whales were 30 to 60 feet in length and weighed upwards of 60 tons. The English readily saw that a profit could be made by commercializing whale hunting. Whale oil for lamps, whalebone and ivory for ladies' corsets, buggy whips, parasol ribs and scrimshaw, proved to be a rainmaker and the main industry of the island.

Walking along the bustling cobblestone, three-block town, we stopped and browsed antique galleries specializing in scrimshaw, China trade porcelain, old hooked rugs, country furniture, weather vanes, English antiques, and maritime artifacts. The most fascinating items sold in many of the up-scale stores were whale ivory lightship pocketbook-baskets, which are decorated with nautical scrimshaw created by sailors of bygone days and lightship attendants. The starting prices of these begin at around $800 and can cost into the tens of thousands of dollars if they are very old and designed by famous artists. Today it is illegal to use whalebones or ivory for artistic purposes, so these original baskets keep increasing in value. It's amusing to see many ladies walking around town with these baskets hanging from their arms, as if they were showing off trophies or badges of honor. I bought a miniature one decorated with a plastic design of a whale for my Xmas tree that cost 50 bucks and proudly hang it on my seven-foot artificial tree annually, with a smile and chuckle, as I picture the expensive baskets dangling from the Nantucket ladies' arms.

During the summer season, the population of the island reaches 50,000-plus people from its year-round residency of 10,000. The influx of tourists and summer residents keeps the island's commercial establishment busy and the town's streets crowded, so it was a relief to head out of town away from the crowds to our final location for the day, the Nantucket Memorial Airport, which is located a little over three miles from the center of the town. I was wearing comfortable sneakers, but my feet were killing me from walking on the town's cobblestone pavement. It was also close to noon, and the sun was starting to throw off more heat than we expected. But we were retired and had all the time in the world to walk and explore the roads leading up to the airport. So we headed south on Orange Street toward Gardener Court and walked a mile to the traffic circle. That is where we got into trouble. We stopped and asked a woman in a coffee shop how far it was to the airport. She said "Just a few minutes up the road." So we purchased some large cold soft drinks, which we desperately needed as we were both getting weary from walking on the uneven roads and from the temperature that was rising to the upper 80s. We began our "Few minutes' walk" and couldn't fathom why we weren't reaching our destination in that period of time. Well, evidently the lady we asked for directions thought we were traveling by car and her "Few minutes" was in motorized time, not walking time. The two-mile walk took forever; we were sweating out of control and our feet were literally on fire. There was absolutely no place along the road to take shelter and when we finally reached the airport, I was tempted to run to it for shelter, but lacked the energy to do so.

We were facing the entrance to a three-runway airport, expecting to see some resemblance to the fictional Tom Never Field in the popular television sit-com *Wings* that ran from 1990 to 1997, but there was none. The show was one of our favorites; it was about the Hackett brothers, Joe and Brian, played by Timothy Daly and Steven Weber, who were pilots and operated Sandpiper Airline from Nantucket's only airport. Mr. Daly played a highly responsible but mildly neurotic and compulsively neat pilot who owned the one-plane Sandpiper Airline. He originally planned to launch the airline with Carol, his finance, who worked behind the ticket counter, but his brother Brian ran off with her, causing a falling out between the brothers that lasted throughout the comedy's long TV run. Other cast members were Tony Shalhoub, of TV's *Monk* fame, as an oddball cab driver, and Crystal Bernard as the on-again, off-again girlfriend. We rushed into the air-conditioned waiting room and almost collapsed with delight from the refreshing cold air caressing our overheated sweaty bodies. The inside of the airport was a facsimile of the one in the sit-com, so we were immediately at home with sitting on the small cafeteria counter seats and ordering extra large glasses of water to cool us off and large ice cream sodas to make sure our bodies would pleasantly recover from our uncomfortable walkathon. We decided then and there that in the future, we would either ride bikes, take the shuttle bus, or a taxicab for any walking distance of over one mile. Accordingly, we called a cab to take us back to *Mikara,* which took all of 15 air-conditioned refreshing minutes.

As soon as we got back to our boat, we showered, donned our bathing suits, and went directly to the White Elephant Hotel, which was a short walk from our marina, and jumped into their deliciously cool swimming pool. I could feel my body sizzling as I swam underwater for the full length of the pool, coming up for air, and then re-submerging for the return underwater trip. The pool is one of our mandatory stops on our visits to the island. Fortunately, it's owned by the same organization that operates the marina that we were staying at, which gave us unlimited use of the hotel and its facilities at no additional cost. We had made previous arrangements to meet our dear friends Elaine and Austin Lyon (both retired), who are the owners of a 48-foot Gulf Star, *Sea Lyon.* They docked their boat at the Nantucket marina for the summer and returned to our marina in Greenport for winter storage. The couple is so well liked that they are considered honorary citizens of Nantucket by the locals. We also enjoy their company in Florida where we have homes only a few miles from each other. After lots of hugs and kisses, we spread out on our shaded chaise lounges and ordered refreshing drinks to sip while we caught up on the latest gossip. After a couple of hours of pure relaxation, befitting retired folks, we decided to meet for dinner that evening. We said our goodbyes and headed back for well-deserved naps. There was still no news about locating the bodies of the shocking JFK, Jr. crash.

We met Elaine and Austin at the "Brotherhood of Thieves" restaurant, which was a short walk from our marina. The name of the eatery was taken from the title of an 1844 pamphlet written on Nantucket by Stephen S. Foster, in which he vigorously attacked those who continued to support slavery. The island has always been known for its religious and racial tolerance. Even during the Revolutionary War, Patriots, Tories, and Quaker pacifists coexisted on the island. The Quakers were the first Europeans to develop the island, and believed that all their children, male and female, should have the same education and nurtured independence and freedom as a way of life. That spirit provided fertile ground for abolishing slavery and encouraging women's rights on the island. The island boasts of such distinguished women as Abiah Folger, mother of Benjamin Franklin, who was born on the island in 1667, and Maria Mitchell, a groundbreaker for women in American science, who was also born on the island in the year 1818.

With that bit of history, we entered the bistro and found what I had hoped for: rustic brick, wooden beams, darkly stained furniture, and a roaring fireplace. It immediately gave me the feeling of what it must have been like during those historic days of yesteryear. We were in a Revolutionary War atmosphere and I was ready to order some "dark ale and pork loins." Everyone had different ideas of what food to order, but they all went for fish dishes, except for me. Broiled Seasonal Scallops for Barbara, Fisherman's Stew for Austin, and baked Seafood Casserole for Elaine. I ordered the dark ale and crispy pork loin, which was unbelievably delicious. I pictured myself as a young sailor enjoying a late supper at the "Brotherhood of Thieves" restaurant, being kept warm by the blazing fireplace, after a long chilling day at sea whale hunting.

The first thing the next morning we turned on our TV for an update of the naval search. Additional ships with sophisticated sensors had arrived and gathered offshore to continue probing for any wreckage of the fallen aircraft. Investigators released new data that portrayed the final half minute of JFK Jr.'s doomed flight as an "**UNCONTROLLED PLUNGE INTO THE SEA.**" Although we expected that news, we were greatly saddened by the event and decided to do some sightseeing as a distraction.

A particular piece of American history that we learned at the "Brotherhood of Thieves" restaurant tweaked our curiosity, especially Barbara's, as she is an avid amateur stargazer. Maria (pronounced Ma-RYE-ah) Mitchell, astronomer, librarian, and 19th century intellectual, first cousin to Benjamin Franklin, four times removed, was born on the island in 1818. She earned international fame and was awarded a gold medal from the King of Denmark for discovering a telescopic comet. The discovery resulted in her being the first woman elected to a fellowship in the American Academy of Arts and Science, and the first woman Professor of Astronomy in the United States. She also promoted women's suffrage and higher education and, as President of the American Association for the Advancement of Women, she was able to forward her beliefs with authority. We headed straight for the Maria

Mitchell Observatory and Museum to learn more about this incredible lady who also discovered that sunspots are whirling vertical cavities and not clouds, as previously thought.

We were surprised to see about 50 children, ranging from 10 to 15 years of age, attending celestial demonstrations at the observatory. We joined in one of the classes and learned how to observe the sun by making a hole in a piece of paper and allowing the sun to shine through and reflect onto a table. We joined another tour and explored a scale model of the solar system, a planar sundial, and even observed sunspots. Barbara couldn't wait to climb the ladder to an old telescope and sample some of the daylight sights in the distant sky. She was determined to return in the evening, time permitting, to further explore the solar system. We spent the remaining week on the island playing golf, swimming at several of the beaches, eating lunch and dinner at rustic restaurants, and socializing with our friends and the friendly people of Nantucket.

We were excited that our last evening in Nantucket would include enjoying the music of the Boston Pops Orchestra's "Great Social" that was to be performed at Jetties Beach, which was adjacent to our marina. We left a half hour before the scheduled performance with our beach chairs and walked the short distance so we could find good seating locations; the beach was already crowded, so we had to settle for a spot that was quite a distance from the bandstand. We got comfortable and then applied anti-mosquito lotion to all the exposed parts of our bodies to avoid becoming the flying cannibals' evening BBQs. The program indicated that, during and after the concert, there would be fireworks by the world-renowned firm of Grucci (officially called Pyrotechnique by Grucci, Inc.). The theme for the evening was "A Dedication to the Music of John Williams," conducted by the man himself. He is considered the most prolific writer in the history of movie music and probably one of the most widely heard composers of the 20th and 21st centuries. His awards for music compositions are endless; he is the recipient of five Academy Awards, four Golden Globes, seven BAFTA Awards (British Academy of Film and Television Arts), and ten Grammy Awards. He was inducted into the Hollywood Bowl Hall of Fame in the year 2000 and was the recipient of the Kennedy Center's

Honors in 2004. Some of his movie compositions were in *Schindler's List*, the six *Star Wars* films of George Lucas, Steven Spielberg's *Raiders of the Lost Ark*, the *Indiana Jones* movies, *Jaws*, *Jurassic Park*, *Superman*, and numerous other movies and TV scores. The native Long Islander (born in Floral Park) was the conductor of the Boston Pops Orchestra from 1980 until 1993, and also has been a guest conductor at venues throughout the world during his illustrious career.

The orchestra played many of his compositions from famous movies and TV shows while the Grucci team displayed their expertise in producing state-of-the-art, spectacular fireworks. The evening ended with the orchestra playing "God Bless America" as the crowd of thousands joined in singing the beautiful lyrics. This was complemented by an incredible display of firework replicas of the American flag and atomic bomb-like explosions. Multi-colored flares decorated and illuminated the sky, and their sonic sounds and vibrations shook the surrounding beach front, which made the hair on the back of my neck stand straight up from the noise and the feeling of pride in singing one of our nation's sacred patriotic songs.

On our way back to *Mikara,* we stopped for a nightcap at one of the restaurants that had a panoramic view of the harbor and shared its docks with our marina. We were still concerned about the JFK, Jr. crash and were sort of spooked about crossing from Nantucket to Hyannis because of the ever-present fog that seems to engulf the preferred traveling route across the Sound. We returned to our resting place and reviewed our charts, carefully highlighting any possible dangerous areas that might have rocks or shallow water. We decided that we should leave a little later than usual to give any morning fog a chance to burn off from the sun's rays.

In the morning, we received news that JFK, Jr.'s plane and its occupants had been recovered. This upset us to no end, considering we were about to travel the same general route of the crash. I said a silent prayer for JFK, Jr. and his companions, and then remembered that in the area we were traveling there had also been a major ship collision between Italy's pride and joy cruise ship, *SS Andrea Doria* and the *MS Stockholm,* a smaller passenger liner of the Swedish American Line. On the *Andrea Doria's* 100th Atlantic crossing, it collided with, or to be more precise, was rammed on its right side by, the *Stockholm*. On that fateful day, July 25, 1956, the *Andrea Doria* was heading west passing the shores of Nantucket on its voyage to New York, while the *Stockholm* was heading from New York, eastward toward the Nantucket Lighthouse, and then continuing across the North Atlantic Ocean to Sweden. The Italian liner had about 1,200 passengers and 500 crew members; the *Stockholm* had over 600 passengers including crew members. Deaths due to the infamous maritime collision were 46 on the Italian liner and 5 on the Swedish-American ship. What happened? What caused the horrific collision that sank *Andrea Doria* the next day? It all boiled down to **"POOR VISIBILITY AND CARELESS SEAMANSHIP."** The Italian liner was traveling at about 25 mph while the *Stockholm* was cruising at about 20 mph in dense fog. Both ships saw each other on their respective radar screens, but neither attempted radio communication with the other. The *Stockholm* followed the "International Rules of the Road" and steered to the right to avoid collision; the *Andrea Doria* mistakenly steered to the left, bringing the right side of the ship directly in front of the *Stockholm*. Neither reduced their speed, which is customary when cruising in fog, and only slowed down after impact. In addition to the fatalities, hundreds were injured during the impact and the subsequent evacuation rescue, but fortunately, due to improved communication methods, and the fact that they were on a busy sea lane, which allowed nearby ships to respond to their distress calls quickly, most of the passengers avoided the horrific destiny of the 1,512 passengers on the *Titanic* in 1912 when it hit an iceberg while traveling **at night at high speeds;** even though they were forewarned that icebergs were in the vicinity of their route **(poor seamanship).**

How similar was the JFK, Jr. incident to the above collisions? He was traveling at night with poor visibility, and, although his GPS was on, his autopilot was off. If it were on, it would have kept his plane on course and upright, giving him an opportunity to safely follow an electronic heading. Again, **"POOR VISIBILITY AND CARELESS SEAMANSHIP" caused an avoidable misfortune to become an unfortunate reality.** The air tower at Nantucket's airport stated that seconds before the crash, his plane veered to the right and then suddenly went nose first into the sea. The technical information that was gathered after retrieving the wreckage of the plane, unfortunately, resulted in a lawsuit for negligence between the Bessette family and the estate of JFK, Jr. The case was settled out of court for the benefit of the plaintiff without prolonged publicity, but it didn't discount the fact that he was not an experienced pilot when it came to flying under adverse weather conditions.

We were concerned, but prepared, about traveling into some pretty unstable water and weather conditions for our short and possibly nasty 25 mile trip. Barbara suggested that we follow the twelve o'clock ferry from Nantucket to Hyannis and play it safe; great idea from my competent first mate (she calls herself the Admiral). After her suggestion, I was inclined to agree with her and pay more attention to her nautical advice. We reviewed our pre-cruise checklist, filled our tanks with fuel, and followed the ferry out of the inlet. The weather conditions and forecast were for clear weather, soft winds, and the usual possible patches of fog, which is so common in that area. We followed the ferry at a safe distance, as the large vessel created an undercurrent from its huge propellers that we had to avoid or we would end up zigzagging across the Sound. The first half of the trip went according to our plans, but dense fog soon encompassed our vessel, resulting in zero visibility. I immediately reduced our speed and put on the automatic fog horn and our running lights. From that point on, we were on our own, as the ferry continued full speed ahead to its destination. Our LORAN and GPS got us to the entrance buoy of Hyannis Harbor and our radar guided us in. We traveled buoy to buoy until we reached the Hyannis Marina, where we had reservations for the next few days, but could extend if our fancy dictated, as we were retired and could travel at our leisure. It's so important to trust *Mikara's* instruments, which are necessary aids to navigation, and not to rely on one's own instincts when traveling in blind conditions. Only experience and patience can build the confidence that is required to trust inanimate pieces of electronic equipment. Anyone traveling without proper experience and confidence, which are developed over time, invariably gets into trouble, whether piloting a boat or an airplane.

As we traveled from Hyannis Harbor into Lewis Bay our visibility improved considerably, and we were able to appreciate seeing yachts under sail, charter fishing boats on their way to a bountiful day's catch, wind surfboarders, small sailfish boats, and the large ferries going to Nantucket and Martha's Vineyard. We could also see the Kennedy Compound with its flag flying at half mast, which quickly brought us back to the reality and sweet comfort of arriving safely at a planned destination. Hyannis Marina has been our preferred dockage when traveling to the Cape, as it has all of the comforts of home, plus some, including clean private showers and toilet facilities, dockside water and electricity, cable television hook-ups, a marine supply store, and the Harborside swimming pool with Trader Ed's Cabana Bar at the poolside. It also boasts a full-menu restaurant named Tugboat's, floating docks, and one of the best marine repair shops on the Cape. The resort-type location is an ideal place to spend a few days sightseeing, walking around Hyannis, relaxing at the pool, or spending time on the abundance of sandy beaches that are open to the public free of charge. I gave *Mikara* her desalting fresh water bath while Barbara cleaned the stainless steel railings that were caked with salt from the moist salty air that accumulated from our crossing from Nantucket to Hyannis.

After thoroughly cleaning our baby, we strolled for about 15 minutes to the town of Hyannis, stopping at one of our favorite used bookstores to indulge in one of our pet pastimes, browsing for out-of-print books; mysteries for Barbara and books on the Age of Discovery (14th and 15th centuries) for me. Many of the stores in town were closed due to the death of another young favorite son of the Kennedy clan. Store windows were draped with American flags and all flag poles were flying their colors at half mast. The details of the discovery of the wreck were posted at the Kennedy Museum: "Navy divers recovered the bodies of JFK, Jr., his wife, and sister-in-law in 116 feet of murky waters off of the island of Martha's Vineyard, seven and one half miles from shore." The atmosphere in the museum and town was solemn as most of the people seemed to be in a trance and state of denial that there was yet another Kennedy's death under tragic circumstances.

We returned to *Mikara,* sharing the sorrow of the people we met in town, and decided that a refreshing dip in the pool would perk us up.

We changed and walked over to the swimming area and ordered two margaritas, stretched out on chaise lounges, and sipped the edge off of our depressed states of mind. After enjoying the pool's cool refreshing water, we returned to our boat for well-needed naps. While trying to nap, I read some history about Cape Cod and the surrounding area. It's a peninsula that opens to the waters of Massachusetts Bay on the north side, Nantucket Sound on its south shore, the Atlantic Ocean on its east side, and Buzzards Bay on the west side. Its history parallels that of Nantucket, except for one big exception: Native Americans fled from the Cape Cod Peninsula to Nantucket for a short-lived respite from the cruelty of the European interlopers. The English also manipulated Hyannis and the surrounding area away from the natives as they did in Nantucket, but for a lot less: 20 English pounds and two small pairs of pants purchased the rights to all of the Native American's valuable land. Both islands share the same pirate myths. On the Cape, Captain Kidd is purported to have buried his gold at "Money Head on Hog Island in Pleasant Bay," off of the town of Orleans, just northeast of Hyannis. Once a year, it's whispered by the town's people, there is a chance of finding Captain Kidd's treasure, especially if the treasure seekers purchase maps to guide them, which, of course, are available for sale at the local shops.

The Hyannis Marina has a courtesy car at the disposal of its boating guests, which we were able to secure for our trip to the Regatta Restaurant in the town of Cotuit, which was a short distance from our temporary home. The restaurant was recommended by friends who said, "It's beyond an eating experience, it's an event." How right they were! Two cranberry red colonial-style buildings, the smaller one dating back to 1790, immediately transported my mind back to a time when our nation was struggling to become a democracy well over 200 years ago. Its brochure "invites guests to enter through its large Federal period front door and to hear the laughter of patrons of a bygone era." The entrance hall is inviting with the "Good Morning Stairway" leading to a second floor dining area with an entrance to the Adams Room on the left, which was previously used as Cotuit's first public library in 1872. On the right is the entrance to the Washington Room, which was originally a sitting area and down the hallway to the right is the

Jefferson Room, which was the original kitchen. Behind what was once the summer kitchen is the cozy Crocker Room with its low, beautifully carved, wood-beamed ceiling. To the left at the end of the hall is the Tap Room with a striking oak bar, where one can enjoy a before and after drink in a cozy, smoke-free atmosphere. The Tap Room, as well as the Adams, Washington, and Jefferson rooms, each employs one of the eight fireplaces found in this Federal twin-chimney Colonial national treasure. All construction is of hand-pegged posts and beams, which are most visible in the bar area where hurricane braces are also exposed, as are the 18 x 24-inch pine planking of the overhead beamed ceiling. We decided to have dinner in the Tap Room with a window view of the outside road and the passing traffic.

The menu was extensive; it took our enjoying a good part of an outstanding bottle of French chardonnay wine before we could choose our dinners. Barbara ordered "Fire & Ice Oysters" for an appetizer and "Crispy Georgia Bank Scallops" for her main course. I skipped the appetizer and ordered an extra plate so I could join Barbara with her choice of oysters. I ordered the evening's special, which we had never seen or heard of, "Shoulder of Swordfish." It was a daring choice, but I figured that swordfish has always been one of my favorite meals, so why not try a different part of the fish and hope for the best. We both made excellent choices. The oysters were beyond delicious. Barbara savored every morsel of the scallops, with small hesitations and deep breaths between each bite. The swordfish presentation, aroma, and taste were out of a culinary fairytale. It was above and beyond any fish I have ever tasted; thick, succulent, and exotically flavored with a charcoal and honey aftertaste. We decided it would be worth a return trip to Cape Cod just to dine at the "one-of-a-kind" bistro. We both finished our meals with espresso and a shared glass of Black Sambuca, which complemented and added to our unforgettable dining experience.

We headed back to our floating vacation home and turned on the TV for an update on the memorial and burial status of JFK, Jr., and his party; the services and burials were planned for the following morning. At 9:00 A.M. the ashes of John F. Kennedy, Jr., Carolyn Bessette Kennedy, and Lauren Bessette, were scattered at sea from the US Navy destroyer, USS Briscoe. JFK, Jr., son of the 35th president of the

United States, was returned to the waters off the Massachusetts coast where he enjoyed sailing, sea kayaking, and searching for sunken pirate ships. His uncle, Massachusetts Democratic Senator, Ted Kennedy, stated at the memorial services: "We dared to think that this John Kennedy would live to comb gray hair with his beloved Carolyn by his side. But like his father, he had every gift but length of years." And of his nephew's marriage he said, "Both his father's presidency and his marriage lasted 1,000 days." The incomprehensible death and final burial brought down the curtain on the life of one of America's beloved sons. Goodbye young John!

Doing anything but mourning on that day seemed to be sacrilegious, but it was one of those situations that required keeping busy to distract one's attention from the deep sorrow that was being felt. So we decided to rent a car and leisurely drive to Provincetown, also known as "P-Town," which is located at the furthest northern part of Cape Cod. Checking the local maps, we determined that the scenic Route 6A, originally called Old Kings Highway, would take us through many local towns and shops along the way, and would also give us intermittent views of the Atlantic Ocean on our right. The trip would be a "no rush event" to help us shake off the depressed feelings we both were carrying around with us due to the inconceivable events of the past few days.

We began our journey on Route 6A, which runs the full length of Cape Cod, beginning at the foot of Sagamore Bridge on the west and traveling down through the horseshoe-shaped peninsula to Yarmouth at the shoe's bottom, and extending upward to Provincetown. Hyannis is somewhere left of the halfway point, so we had a long ride ahead of us on a very slow-moving scenic road. We passed many antique, gift, and local craft shops, which we visited, stopping to stretch our legs while enjoying some refreshment, especially delicious ice cream in sugared cones, vanilla for me and chocolate for my beloved. Our first sightseeing stop was in Wellfleet, located just before our main destination. Of the many beautiful attractions of the town, such as pristine beaches, gorgeous sandy dunes, and an abundance of boutiques, the main reason we chose to stop there was to visit the Marconi Wireless sight and to explore the area where the infamous pirate, Black Same Bellamy's ship, *Whydah*, was discovered in 1984.

The Marconi Station today is a far cry from the original four 210-foot transmitting and receiving towers that sparked the birth of global two-way wireless communication on January 18, 1903. On that day, Marconi's dream to send signals across the Atlantic became a reality. He chose the location because of its elevation and the writings of the great American author Thoreau's description of the Cape as "A place where a man may stand and put all of America behind him." The location at Wellfleet was conducive to his plans for a quiet, secluded site to build his towers without interruption from the local residents. Marconi somehow convinced President Teddy Roosevelt to take part in a wireless experiment where a message would be sent from the Cape to the King of England. On that eventful day, the president's message was tapped out in Morse code from South Wellfleet, Massachusetts, to King Edward VII in Cornwall England. It was the first two-way transatlantic communication and the first wireless telegram between America and Europe. The message read, "His Majesty, Edward VII, London, Eng. In taking advantage of the wonderful triumph of scientific research and ingenuity, which has been achieved in perfecting a system of wireless telegraphy, I extend on behalf of the American people a most cordial greeting and good wishes to you and to all the people of the British Empire. Signed: Theodore Roosevelt, Wellfleet, Mass., Jan. 18, 1903."

Expecting a confirmation from that station in England, Marconi instead received a direct response from the king's private estate in Sandringham, England on January 19, 1903, that read: "To the President, White House, Washington, America. I thank you most sincerely for the kind message which I have received from you, through Marconi's trans-Atlantic wireless telegraphy. I sincerely reciprocate in the name of the British Empire the cordial greeting and friendly sentiment expressed by you on behalf of the American Nation; I heartily wish you and your country every possible prosperity, Signed: King Edward." And so the windows of Europe and the World were opened to communicating instantly with people around the globe, hopefully for the betterment of mankind.

The station was short lived, as it lasted only 16 years. Beach erosion, inclement weather, and new radio technology resulted in the closure of the site in 1920. Sand and trees now cover both sides of the road and there are few traces of life remaining in the once-important Marconi Station. There is an observation platform that looks out across the Atlantic Ocean toward England and a rather rundown exhibit shelter, built to house a model of the station and various related displays. This area has become part of the National Seashore and a habitat for many fragile beach species. Inside the shelter is a model of the station as it was at the time of the momentous transmission, a schematic of the original spark gap transmitter, a map showing the original relay towers, a bust of Marconi, and some history about the important inventor.

In addition to Guglielmo Marconi's many inventions and improvements in wireless communication, one of his most significant contributions was the foundation he created for developments in radio, radar, microwaves, and cellular communication. Upon his death in 1937, this Nobel Prize winner for physics was honored when all wireless radios around the world were temporarily silenced to pay homage to the man whose wireless invention was instrumental in rescuing over 700 passengers from the doomed ocean liner, *Titanic* in 1912. This honor has not been repeated for any other person to date.

Down the coast from the shelter is Marconi Beach, where the ship of pirate Samuel Bellamy, aka "Black Sam Bellamy," the *Whydah,* was shipwrecked in a violent storm on April 27, 1717, killing the notorious pirate and over 100 of his shipmates. He was one of the more successful pirates of his time, associating with such infamous buccaneers as Captain Benjamin Hornigold, aka "Horn of Gold," Captain Edward "Blackbeard" Teach, and our old friend, Captain William Kidd. He got his name "Black Sam" because he wore his black hair wild and in a ponytail instead of wearing the popular white wigs that gentlemen and sea captains wore in those days. He is known to have captured and looted over 50 ships before he drowned with his shipmates at the early age of 28. He was leading a pirate flotilla of five ships from the Caribbean to Maine, where they intended to divide their booty and decide on their futures, when they were caught in a violent nor'easter storm with heavy rain and fog. He went aground and sunk, killing all but two of his 143 crew members and losing what is estimated today to be around 400 million dollars worth of loot. His companion ship, the *Mary Anne,* also went aground and sunk, killing all but seven sailors. His intention was to pick up his sweetheart Maria Hallet and their child in Cape Cod and to continue on their journey with their fortune and establish a place where they could live in peace and luxury. Unfortunately, his young life ended when his ship "deep sixed," joining over 3,000 other ships that went to the bottom of the sea in that area. Due to the dangerous waters and the great number of sunken ships, the Cape Cod Canal was eventually built to avoid the ocean side, turning Cape Cod from a peninsula into a man-made island. His most formidable conquest was the *Whydah Gally,* a new 300-ton slave ship that had just finished the second leg of the Atlantic slave trade and was loaded with a fortune in gold and precious trade goods. The ship carried 600 slaves, which made it a prize catch for the pirate. He was affectionately known as "The Prince of Pirates," as his men took pride in calling themselves "Robin Hood's Band," because of his mercy and generosity toward captains of the ships he plundered. He would usually let them retain possession of their vessels and their lives after asking them if they wanted to join his group. When he captured the *Whydah Galley,* he offered the captain and crew of that ship a chance to join his league; when they refused, he reprimanded them and then gave them his smaller ship, the *Sultana,* with adequate provisions and sent them on their way, keeping the larger vessel as his new floating fortress.

From time to time after his death, his name would be resurrected, most recently in the movie, *Pirates of the Caribbean: The Curse of the Black Pearl.* The piece of land on which Jack Sparrow was twice marooned by Hector Barbossa was "Black Sam's Spit," which was named after Captain Black Sam Bellamy. Over 20 years ago, his name was in the headlines again when the wreckage of his ship was finally discovered in 1984 by underwater treasure hunter Barry Clifford. He spent over 20 years trying to locate the wreck, but to no avail. With the help of John F. Kennedy, Jr.'s drawings of the underwater site, which he located and charted in 1982, Clifford was able to finally locate the ship. JFK, Jr. was a passionate treasure hunter and spent a considerable amount of time exploring the area with his friends. He is credited with making Clifford's dream a reality that uncovered over 200,000 artifacts including coins, jewelry, pistols, and swords. Many of the artifacts are stored at the "Expedition Whydah Sea-Lab and Learning Center" in Provincetown, which is dedicated to Captain Black Sam Bellamy. Clifford wholeheartedly gave Kennedy and his friends, who were specifically looking for that ship, credit for his success in uncovering the remains of the ship and expressed his deepest gratitude for their many dives and their meticulous charting that resulted in his success.

On to Provincetown, aka P-Town. It is considered one of the most eclectic towns in the United States. How did it become such a glamorous place with a worldwide reputation for its progressive life-styles? Well, the Nauset Indians originally settled the area and established a settlement known as *Meeshawn*. Other Indian tribes shared their waters in the summers and took advantage of the abundance of fish and the hospitality of the Nauset Indians. Unfortunately for the natives, the English explorer Gosnold landed on the tip of P-Town in 1602, naming the area Cape Cod due the great quantity of cod fish in the surrounding waters. The tip of the Cape was also the first landing place of the *Mayflower* and its pioneer Pilgrims, in 1620. They didn't consider the region safe due to its exposure to rough waters on both sides of the tip and, therefore, sailed on to Plymouth where they established their famous colony. For the very reason that the Pilgrims didn't settle there, other unsavory types were attracted to the area, as it presented a great escape route to the sea and was a safe distance from the mainland. The area attracted smugglers and privateers, including Captain Kidd, Captain Blackbeard, and Captain Black Sam. As law-abiding English settlers migrated to the region, the more colorful shady characters moved on to friendlier shores.

A relatively safe harbor near P-Town is where the Pilgrims signed the "Mayflower Compact"; this document would become part of the foundation of American democracy and nurture the town's growing reputation as a place of tolerance. Portuguese fishermen were eventually attracted to the area due to the abundance of fish and easy access to the ocean and whales. It was a pleasure to see the Portuguese fishermen still plying their centuries-old trade and traditions in an area that seems to be engrossed with tourism.

An interesting part of the town developed at the turn of the 20th century. Charles Hawthorne established an art school that attracted artists and writers from all over the world. Soon poets, novelists, journalists, radicals, and dilettantes formed a colony and opened the "Provincetown Players' Theater" in a converted fish house on an abandoned wharf. They turned the town into a Mecca for the arts, which is currently the oldest art colony in the United States. Over the years, such famous artists and writers as Eugene O'Neil, Tennessee Williams, Susan Glaspell, Charles Hawthorne, Hans Hoffman, Norman Mailer, Michael Cunningham, John Waters, and a long list of others called P-Town their temporary home away from home. Known for its unique brand of tolerance dating back to the original Indian settlers and the marauding pirates, the unconventional population soon became a haven for gays and lesbians, and today is probably one of the most popular gay and lesbian resort towns in the world. The town's population is about 4,000 and grows to approximately 60,000 during its beautiful summer months, when people flock from around the globe to enjoy its agreeable climate, fishing, whale watching, artists' colony, theater, miles of bike trails, and pristine beaches.

The most striking structure in town is the Pilgrim Monument, rising over 250 feet above the 100-foot hill that it was built on. Its cornerstone was laid in 1907 as President Teddy Roosevelt looked on. The granite tower looms over the town and acts as a compass and focal point, reassuring travelers of their location at all times. At the bottom of the tower is a museum featuring memorabilia and the history of the town from the Native Indian period to the present. There are exhibits showing Indian arrowheads, tools and head gear; images of a Native American Wampanoag tribe's living conditions; artifacts of a polar bear, musk ox, and Inuit Indian relics brought back by the town's native son, Donald B. MacMillan, who explored the Arctic with Commodore Perry.

We were anxious to discover what artifacts were housed at the "Expedition Whydah Sea Lab and Learning Center," which opened in 1997 and was still developing as the foremost pirate museum in existence, with the first verified pirate shipwreck and its artifacts on display. It has a choice location on MacMillan Wharf right next to the ferry dock, with a great view of the ocean. In addition to the relics rescued from the wreck, information about pirates heretofore unknown or questionable was being accumulated and verified. Pirates have always been depicted as "blood thirsty, murdering criminals," but the information gathered from the wreck and the history of that era seemed to prove that there was a more humane side to the buccaneers. At a time when seamen were shanghaied into the service of naval and merchant vessels and treated no better than slaves for years or "until death do we part," pirates had a whole different code of conduct for their members. The pirates, including ex-slaves, were, in comparison, free men living in a modified democracy, sharing equally in plundered booty and actually voting on important matters, such as who the captain should be or if a captured ship should be sunk or released. Many were convinced that they were fighting the corruption of autocratic governments and business institutions. Recovered artifacts confirmed many points made about pirates by contemporary observers, including important features of their society, such as their egalitarianism, internationalism, racial tolerance (there were more than 30 Africans serving as equal crew members on the *Whydah*), and their unique brand of democracy. An interesting observation can be made from some of the new data taken from the wreck: Captain Black Sam, Prince of Pirates, was leading a flotilla of five ships; if he was commanding those ships, then it must be assumed that many of the captains had the same beliefs as he did, which was: "Only plunder for profit and don't sink captured ships or kill unnecessarily." I'm sure that pirate aficionados and admirers will have many heated debates over this issue for many years to come. It certainly would be interesting if it were determined that **pirates were the good guys.**

The most striking artifact at the museum is the 2-foot wide by 2 ½-foot high ship's bell with the inscription "The *Whydah Gally* 1716." That discovery confirmed that the ship was truly Captain Black Sam's, thereby making it the first verified pirate ship to be discovered. Since its discovery, over 200,000 and still counting, artifacts have been recovered. Some were suspended in tanks to show what they looked like in the sea where they were found. There were also gold coins from various parts of the world, and fascinating Akan gold jewelry from Africa. There is a wonderful children's hands-on section where kids can touch gold coins, utensils, and pistols, and ask questions of the on-site archeologist.

We decided to have a light dinner and then go to the Atlantic House for some dancing. Several of the town folks that we spoke to recommended it as the "in place" for music, dancing, and lots of fun. The oldest section of the complex was built in 1798 and is one of the oldest establishments in P-Town; it also boasts of being the oldest disco in the country. The "A-House," as it is called, turned out to be a lot more than a dance venue. It is more of a compound consisting of the Little Bar, with a jukebox; the Macho Bar, aka the "Leather and Levi Bar"; the Big Room, P-Town's #1 Disco Club; and the Patio Bar. The overall texture of the place was nautical, and had a blazing fireplace and cozy sitting areas. When we arrived, the only bar open was the Little Bar. It was somewhat of a shock to see photographs hanging over the bar of Tennessee Williams strolling on one of the town's beaches in his birthday suit with some of his companions. We nestled in next to the roaring fireplace and watched gays, lesbian, and male and female couples dancing. We didn't know whether to stay seated or run for our lives. But after some refreshing drinks and sing-a-along songs from the jukebox, we got up and did some nice Swing and Disco dancing; we even did a couple of Cha-Chas and a Hustle. We struck up conversations with some of the patrons who were quite friendly and impressed with our dancing. At about 10:00 P.M., the other bars opened and people started to gradually fill the rooms. Within a half an hour, the rooms were jammed packed with every combination of couples: male-male, female-female, and male-female. Many of the men were dancing without shirts and seemed to be enjoying themselves while flexing and showing off their overly developed biceps. It was getting late so we bid our new friends goodnight and returned to our car for the long ride back to the marina. We had a local map that indicated we should take the four-lane highway, Route 6, back to Hyannis. It was a good choice, as it was well lit and got us to our homeport in a lot less time than the scenic Route 6A.

It was comforting to see *Mikara* again after our busy day. We didn't waste any time in preparing for bed and a delightful night's sleep to the familiar soft sways and the rhythmic movements of our vessel's body as she obeyed the current of the water beneath her hull and rocked us to sleep. When we woke in the late morning, we were undecided as to what we should do for the day. Should we just hang around and enjoy the swimming pool and the bright sun that warmed the area? Should we take a sightseeing train ride around Hyannis or a trolley car around town? Or should we maybe take the Duck Mobile for an amphibious ride that included a tour of the town on land and then a plunge into the harbor for a sightseeing tour of the beautiful homes, including the Kennedy Compound, that dress the beautiful waters surrounding Hyannis? Another choice could be traveling westerly in the opposite direction from the day before on Route 6A to see what we would discover traveling to the other end of the Cape. Whatever we chose to do, we had to leave plenty of time for evening entertainment at the Melody Tent in Hyannis that boasts of such entertainers as Kenny Rogers, Dolly Parton, and the Beach Boys. Another evening option was a visit to the Cape Playhouse in the Town of Dennis, which is the oldest professional theater in the United States, and boasts of such illustrious past performers as Betty Davis, Gregory Peck, Lana Turner, Humphrey Bogart, and Tallulah Bankhead, just to name a few. Well, in our week in Hyannis we did all of the above while still finding time to enjoy the magnificent beaches and the many friendly towns as well.

Being that we were retired and in no rush to arrive at our scheduled ports, we chose a day to head for Newport, Rhode Island, which had a good weather forecast for the area we were going to cruise. Before changing our planned time schedule, we would always call the marina that was our next destination in advance to make sure that modifying our reservations was okay. Rarely did we have a problem with any of the establishments as reservations in the boating world are not always written in stone, as there are many reasons for not arriving as scheduled, such as inclement weather, unexpected boat repairs, or in our case, we just decided to stay in a location that we were enjoying longer than originally planned. So we started our voyage to Newport early in the morning after fueling and checking our pre-cruise safety list. The trip is about 60 miles and usually takes between four to seven hours, depending on sea conditions and the mechanical efficiency of our boat.

We headed out of Hyannis Harbor and into Nantucket Sound, which is usually rough riding; that day was no exception. I set my GPS and LORAN to take me past Falmouth and Woods Hole and into Vineyard Sound. The ride was bouncy, but with the aid of our autopilot, we held the course and were able to travel an average of 15 mph. Boating between the Elizabeth Islands on our right and Martha's Vineyard on the left calmed the water and wind considerably, which allowed *Mikara* to perform at her best, holding her course and riding the waves smoothly. Passing the protection of the beautiful tip of Cuttyhunk on our right and Gay Head in Martha's Vineyard on our left, brought us into the cross currents of Rhode Island Sound, Buzzard Bay, and the Atlantic Ocean. This is not a happy location for traveling. The rough and quick currents from Buzzards Bay and the waves and winds from the Atlantic Ocean gave us a plowing and bumpy ride for over an hour. Buzzards Bay got its name from the Pilgrims in the early 17th century, when they mistook osprey birds for turkey buzzards; the name has stuck ever since. Considering the hazardous water conditions of the bay, due to its strong tides, undercurrents, shallow water, and winds, many an unsuspecting ship has gone down to "Davey Jones' Locker," which is a more appropriate explanation of its name. It's also one of the few recorded places in Massachusetts where a shark attack resulted in the death of the victim. So, when traversing this area, we are always cognizant of the impending dangers and keep our radio weather and alert stations on at all times, while both of us keep a very sharp eye out for any possible problems, like lobster traps, floating logs, general debris, and submarine telescopes. To balance the frightening name of Buzzards Bay to the north, there is an island just past Martha's Vineyard on the Atlantic Ocean's side named "Nomans Land." The island has a checkered history. It was discovered by Captain Gosnold in 1602 and named Martha's Vineyard after his oldest daughter. The name was subsequently transferred to the larger island to the northeast while it took on the name "Nomans Land." Its current name probably comes from the Wampanoag Sachem Indian, "Teque**noman**." The U.S. Navy built an airfield there in 1942, which was used as a practice area for 53 years for its bombers. The field was abandoned, although its use as a target bombing range continued until 1996. It's now a Fish and

Wildlife Sanctuary and is closed to the public due to the unexploded ordnance still remaining there.

The fun story of the island concerns the "Leif Eriksson Runestone" that was photographed there in 1927 by the controversial author Edward F. Gray. He was researching the *Norse Voyages to North America* for his book, which was published in 1930 by Oxford University Press. Two lines of letters on a large black stone, which were only exposed at low tides, were translated to read "Leif Eriksson, 1001," and "Vineland." Some scholars have disproved the possibility that Leif ever landed on the island or that there was ever such a stone inscribed by him in runic (the written Norse language). There is no record of the stone being removed from the island, but because of restrictions imposed by the authorities that closed the area to the public, further in-depth research has not been possible. It's also possible that the bombing drills may have destroyed the black stone. Hopefully further exploration of the island will be conducted in the future to get to the bottom of Leif Eriksson's mysterious "Runestone."

Our destination was the coordinates of the old Brenton Reef Light, which was once a steel 87-foot-high tower at the entrance to Narragansett Bay that leads to Newport and ends north at the State's Capital, Providence, Rhode Island. Seeing the tower when it was operational on our radar screen was always reassuring, especially when we would get a visual sighting that told us our port of call was close by. The 87-foot structure has been replaced by a small red and white "NB" lighted horn buoy that flashes every four seconds, so navigating to the marker must be exact with little room for error. We found the buoy with no trouble, thanks to the clear weather, our GPS, and trustworthy LORAN. We have found that when we traveled this area, it was always a good practice to use both direction finders as the U.S. Navy makes a habit of jamming the airways for security purposes. If both electronic aids fail, *Mikara's* magnetic compass is always the final backup to lead us to our destination by using "dead reckoning."

Narragansett Bay is New England's largest estuary, which functions as an expansive natural harbor that includes a small archipelago. The bay has over 30 islands of which Goat Island is one of our favorites and lies across from our preferred boating destination, Newport. Our usual morning walks to Goat Island from Newport would take us over a suspension bridge that has an eclectic panoramic view of the bay and the exciting colorful quilt-like nautical activity, including lighthouses, sailboats, powerboats, gorgeous waterfront homes, and people bathing at local pristine beaches.

It's about a fifteen-minute ride from the wide opening of the bay to Newport, which is on Aquidneck Island. Passing two locations on the high cliffs at the right are sites that have made their place in history. The first is Hammersmith Farms, where Jacqueline Bouvier Kennedy Onassis grew up and had her wedding reception when she married the young senator from Massachusetts, John F. Kennedy. The 28-room Victorian mansion on 48-acres was built in 1887 by John W. Auchincloss. The place was often used by the Kennedy family and was referred to as the Summer White House during President JFK's time in office. We were fortunate to have toured the working farm when it was open to the public and were astonished at the size of the many small rooms and toilets in the mansion; not what one would expect of a mansion of that size. One of our most memorable sights was the view of Newport Harbor and the surrounding waterways from atop the wide cliffs of the farm. It's certainly one of the most beautiful nautical sights in America, incorporating large bridges in the distance, an abundance of large and small sailboats, power boats of every size, Naval vessels of every description, and the ocean on the left with the expansive bay on the right showing off its beautiful scattered islands, including our destination, Newport. Also appearing on the right at a strategic vantage point is the largest coastal fortification in the United States, Fort Adams. It was active from 1824 to 1950 and spreads out on a six-acre parade field with breathtaking views of the harbor and surrounding areas. The fort is now a State Park and has tours of its massive (and somewhat scary) underground tunnel system, casements, and barracks. Today it hosts many spectacular events, such as the Summer Music Festival, the Annual Kite Flying Competitions, military reenactments, and antique car shows, which are just some of the many exciting open-air events.

It's understandable why Newport is considered one of the boating capitals of the world. It's also considered the center of yachting in the

Northeast, as just about every boat traveling the coast makes it a port-of-call. Large sail and power boats stop over for repairs in the many world-class yards or for provisioning and refurbishing. The harbor is well protected, has a wide mouth, and water depths of up to 100 feet, which is probably one of the main reasons that it's the home of the United States Naval War College, the Naval Undersea Warfare Center, and a United States Navy training Center. Newport boasts that its Naval War College was the Summer White House of President Dwight D. Eisenhower, who spent many a hot summer enjoying the coolness of the constant breezes that visit the area.

Newport has come a long way since its discovery by Giovanni da Verrazano in 1524 on his ship *La Dauphine,* after he successfully visited New York Bay. It took over 100 years before a European settlement was established by Pilgrim Roger Williams in the 1630s. Following the Pilgrims were the infamous pirates of the 17th and 18th centuries. Newport was considered one of the most notorious pirate havens during the Golden Age of Piracy. They thrived under the protection of the government and the people; they were actually treated as celebrities. One of the most famous pirates was Captain Thomas Tew, who was so beloved by the people that they would celebrate his conquests with merriment and partying. Captains Blackbeard and Kidd were also frequently welcomed guests of the locals. In the early 18th century, colonial leaders, acting under pressure from the British government, arrested many of the pirates and sent them to their final resting places on Goat Island. Out of that checkered history, Newport has grown into one of the world's busiest and most beautiful waterways with some interesting nicknames, such as "City of the Sea," "Sailing Capital of the World," "Queen of Summer Resorts," and "America's Society Capital."

Approaching the Newport Harbor marina, our final destination, required some patience and tricky maneuvering as the area is busy with boats in motion or on moorings, and many at anchor. It required moving through some pretty tight places for at least 15 minutes until the dock master and his aides could coordinate where and how we were to dock and secure *Mikara*. We have been docking at this marina for many years and are always relieved to be tied up to the safety of their floating docks, with our ropes, electricity, and water connected. I cheerfully gave *Mikara* her post-cruise celebratory bath for a job well done, which always makes her shine with pride and produces an imaginary smile on her bow, which only I am privileged to see. The marina is considered one of the best on the island and, fortunately, is attached to the Newport Harbor Hotel, which has a convenient indoor pool and sauna with excellent showers and a gym. Marina guests have hotel privileges, which we've used frequently, at no additional charge. The marina is located in the heart of Newport and a short walk to shops, restaurants, parks, and supermarkets. We usually spend our first hours in the busy city at the Visitors' Information Center, which is only a couple of blocks away. It's a pleasure going there, as it is very modern and spacious. It has half a dozen people working behind its circular information kiosk ready to help with maps, hotel reservations, sightseeing tours, restaurant accommodations, and helpful hints about current entertainment in the area.

We gathered the information we needed to occupy our stay and were excited that the Newport Classical Music Festival was having their annual extravaganza. The annual Japanese Black Ship Festival was also appearing throughout the town, and one of our favorite entertainment places, the Newport Playhouse & Cabaret, was open, featuring a buffet dinner, a stage show, and cabaret entertainment. While walking back to our marina, we passed every imaginable type of retail store in existence, lined up one after the other on each side of the street and around every corner, beginning at Brick Alley and continuing on to America's Cup Avenue. The alley was one of the largest slave markets on the East Coast of the United States in the 17th and 18th centuries as well as a notorious pirates' hangout. Today it has evolved into a major section of the city, and is filled with trendy boutiques, an overabundance of T-shirt and miniature lighthouse stores, a fudge factory, several ice cream parlors, candy stores, a Xmas shop, children's clothing stores, and quality restaurants of every ethnicity. Just walking around the main street, America's Cup Avenue, is a treat, especially while devouring a giant ice cream sugar cone with chocolate sprinkles, or a freshly made candy apple or hot fudge. There are many marinas lined along the waterway just one block from the main avenue, each with its own personality, depending on the type and size of the vessels occupying their docks. Newport shipyards can accommodate sail and power boats up to 315 feet, while the marina we stayed at handles boats from 20 to 180 feet. There is a place for every type of vessel in Newport, but it does favor sailboats. It proudly boasts of being a sailors' haven that provides a resting place and a small restaurant for weary underprivileged seaman at moderate or no cost, depending on the sailor's circumstances.

The America's Cup races were one of the mainstays of Newport from 1852 till 1983. The New York Yacht Club's schooner *America* raced 15 yachts in 1851 that represented the Royal Yacht Squadron of England around their Isle of Wight and won by 20 minutes, forever changing the name of the trophy from the Queen's Cup to the America's Cup. The American Club won 25 consecutive races over the next 130 years, making it the longest-held championship in sports history. The Cup is the most prestigious regatta and match race in the sport of sailing, and the oldest active trophy in international sports. The sport attracts top sailors and yacht designers from all over the world who put their seamanship and boats' designs through the tests and trials of the rigorous race. This competition made Newport the undisputed sailboat capital of the world for over 100 years. As all good things must come to an end, we lost the Cup in 1983 to Australia when *Australia II* took the prize from us, forever surrendering Newport as the Cup's homeport. The loss of pride and business due to the relocating of the Cup's home brought hard financial times to the city. It took over ten years for it to begin the slow process of reinventing itself as a tourist attraction with world-class music festivals (jazz and classical), and entertainment at the opulent mansions (summer cottages) of the rich and famous American industrialists of the 19th century.

We decided to spend the first night onboard enjoying a lobster feast that Barbara anxiously put together. A short distance from our berth is the Aquidneck Lobster Co. on Bowen's Wharf. It's a unique lobster market in the heart of the bustling city that sells its products to commercial businesses as well as the ultimate consumer. We ordered a five-pound steamed lobster, cracked and ready for consumption earlier in the day, and picked it up at about 6:00 P.M., ready for our dinner table. Our lobster, combined with Barbara's delicious Greek salad and a bottle of Pinot Grigio, transported us to an ambrosial paradise. We enjoyed the feast on our outside deck with soft music provided by *Mikara's* CD player. Passersby complimented us on the wonderful aroma coming from the beautiful scene of our picturesque setting. Some even asked if they could join us; my reply was "Maybe next time." After some espresso, we walked the marina's docks striking up conversations with some of the other mariners who were also enjoying the cool evening breeze and the coolness of the fog that was overcoming the area. A wonderful day came to an end with our retiring to our place of rest on *Mikara*.

The next morning we had our breakfast on our outdoor dining table, which always seems to attract mariners who are walking along the docks enjoying the invigorating smell of the morning's fresh salt air. Quite a few stopped to inhale the coffee aroma coming from our table and spent some time chatting about how beautiful *Mikara* looked. This is a common boating ritual; walking the docks and meeting new fellow sailors and sometimes old friends, and passing the time asking, "Where are you from? Where are you going? How long is your trip?" And so on. Just pleasant conversation with people that have a common love— boating. After breakfast we decided to visit one of the mansions and sit in on a concert sponsored by the International Newport Classical Music Festival. The nonprofit organization has sponsored the festival for over 30 years and attracts some of the best musicians from around the world who are proud to be a part of the spectacular event. An abundance of classical music lovers travel from far and wide to enjoy the talents of the musicians and their interpretations of some of the most beautiful music ever written. The event usually covers 17 days with up to five concerts daily at the mansions, parks, and on evening boat cruises. Over 60 musicians perform as many as 600 pieces of music to the delight of their audiences, and can be found playing at morning, afternoon, evening, and even midnight concerts. Some concerts have box lunches included in the price of admission, which can be enjoyed on the luscious lawns of the palatial mansions. The dress code is rather casual because most of the venues are not air conditioned, and wearing shorts is quite common and most certainly comfortable. Many patrons dress well for the crowded evening performances; each attracts from 100 to 300 hundred classical music lovers. The nearby Salve Regina University has been gracious enough to extend their welcome and facilities to the multitude of musicians and staff, which makes coordinating such a complicated endeavor manageable.

We would join the many classical music lovers at the Breakers and Elms Mansions every day for our week's stay in Newport. We also visited the International Tennis Hall of Fame courts and enjoyed a Japanese Taiko Drum Exhibition that was part of the Japanese Black Ship Festival commemorating the signing of the peace treaty between the United States and Japan in 1854. The treaty was signed by Newport's favorite son Mathew C. Perry, USN, who was the commander of the American Exhibition. There were several Sumo wrestling shows around town that we visited, enjoying the history of the sport, and watching matches between giant-sized men who carry an amazing amount of weight, which the wrestlers are required to have so they can participate in the ancient sport. Some weigh over 300 pounds and are very proud to be part of an ancient sport that seems to be slowly disappearing. We also made a point of seeing Andrew Lloyd Webber's *Joseph and the Amazing Technicolor Coat,* which was playing at the Newport Playhouse and Cabaret. This was a five-hour event that included an elaborate buffet dinner, a 150-seat theater presentation, and, after the theater, a cabaret show in their main club, which included dancing, singing, and lots of jokes.

Our week came to an abrupt end, when we realized that our one-month dream vacation was over; so we prepared *Mikara* for her voyage back to Greenport, New York, prayed for calm seas and clear skies, and completed our circular trip back to our home port. Our dream vacation on our boat had become a reality; what we didn't realized was that spending extended periods of time in our confined home was not as wonderful as we thought it would be, and that traveling to Florida and down to the Bahamas was something we decided we might leave for another lifetime.

What is interesting and so important when deciding what sports are right for you are the social aspects of the activities that are available within the sport. As can be determined from the above story, there are social gatherings with the United States Power Squadron; there is lots of traveling, usually with companion boats; entertainment becomes available that would otherwise be difficult to attain, such as the music festivals and beach fireworks. There is, without a doubt, an opportunity to meet new friends and develop lifetime relationships, which becomes so important in our golden years as they expand our interests and keep adding to our physical as well as our brain power.

Sports – Tennis

I first became interested in tennis when I was in the United States Air Force. I was stationed at Nagoya Air Base in Japan awaiting my next assignment, which would be for two years. While hanging around the base with not much to do, I met a young WAF (Women in the Air Force), Joan, who was wearing the cutest tennis outfit that complemented her picture-perfect gorgeous figure. We became friendly in a very short time; one of the benefits of our friendship was that she volunteered to teach me how to play tennis, which I thought at that time was a rich man's sport, based on the movies that I had seen where the rich and famous monopolized the game. So I made a V-line to the PX (Post Exchange) and bought all the necessary garments and equipment that made me look like a bona-fide tennis player. The look was okay, but the learning process was difficult and frustrating for a young twenty year old who thought that there was nothing in the world that he couldn't master. We played, at one thing or another, for the whole month that I was stationed at that base. Her advice to me, among many other words of wisdom, was "Make sure you get a professional to teach you the game before you hurt yourself or some innocent bystander." I played on and off for two years while stationed in Tokyo. It was a great place to learn and enjoy the game as almost every Japanese person I met was a devout tennis player and was willing to teach the young redhead the finer points of the game. There were many places to play; luckily for me, most venues were free to servicemen, which made the game all the more attractive, as a corporal's pay didn't go very far in those days. Unfortunately I didn't take Joan's advice about hiring an instructor, as my pay scale didn't provide for that luxury, so although I looked good on the courts, my game was far from perfect, which gave many of the Japanese girls that I played with great satisfaction, as beating an American at anything was thought to be very honorable.

After leaving the military when my four-year enlistment ended, I didn't have much opportunity to play again, as it was too expensive for a hard-working young underpaid person, and tennis courts were not readily available in my Brooklyn, N.Y. neighborhood. It wasn't until attending Long Island University, in Brooklyn, that the opportunity to play again became attractive. There were tennis courts on the campus and I was finally able to follow Joan's advice, as instructors were available at very nominal fees, especially for ex-servicemen. So during my years at the university, whenever time allowed, I took lessons and played as much of the sport as I could fit into my tight schedule. After college I played tennis very infrequently, as time, money, and opportunity rarely seemed to coincide with each other. When I had the time, money or opportunity was scarce. When I had the money, time or opportunity seemed to dictate that other priorities were more important. When I had the opportunity, time or money seemed to be lacking. So time went by with me playing very little tennis until I married and had two children, Stephen and Laurie. When they were about ten and eleven years of age, they insisted that we take tennis lessons together. My wife Barbara also thought that a family sport would be a worthwhile way to spend quality time with our children. So we went to the indoor tennis courts that were in our neighborhood and began a series of tennis lessons that lasted three months. The kids loved the game, but Barbara and I just couldn't develop a passion for the sport; maybe our aged bodies were too set in their ways to introduce a new muscle stretcher into their routines. So the kids continued with their game while Barbara decided that shopping would be a better alternative. In the mean time, golf, which is a less strenuous game, became my game of choice and would remain so into my retirement years.

Many of our friends are still playing tennis in their retirement years and couldn't imagine their lives without frequently sweating on the tennis courts. For my active friends, the passion of the game began with playing with friends and on teams, and then graduated to attending games locally and then the ultimate tennis experience of traveling around the world to watch many of the Grand Slam tournaments that are hosted in Australia, France, England, and the United States. There are an abundance of locations that can be easily accessed on the website WWW.tennismaps.com. The site not only gives the location of the courts but actually allows for zooming onto an actual court of interest and outlines the details and rules for playing at a particular venue.

The cost of playing can be from zero, except for the cost of tennis balls, to expensive membership in fancy clubs, such as the Polo Club in Boca Raton, Florida. Many municipal and town parks have courts that residents can use at minimal or no charge, that also may accommodate non residents. Another aspect of the sport is the wheelchair games. The sport began when Brad Parks in 1976 hit the first tennis ball from a wheelchair; the rest is history. The wheelchaired games today are an international sport with 11 international tournaments and over 170 events. The qualifications are as follows: "A player must have a medically diagnosed permanent mobility related physical disability which must result in a substantial loss of function in one or both lower extremities." An excellent place to obtain information on this activity that has opened new horizons to disabled people is to Google "NEC Wheelchair Tennis Tours."

The social aspects of this sport are endless, and range from playing on teams and traveling to tennis matches of professionals locally and around the world, to having tennis parties while watching matches in the comfort of your home. The physical and social events of the sport can certainly add to the enjoyment and health of active senior citizens, and if one is so inclined, new doors to friendships can be explored that will keep one quite busy during retirement.

Sports – Golf

Most people who decide that they would like to give golf a try make the same mistakes that I did. I bought a 3 Wood (it was really made from titanium) for hitting the golf ball from the tee, a 7 iron for fairway shots, and an inexpensive putter for tapping the balls into practice holes. For the first couple of years the only golf that I played was at various driving ranges in my neighborhood, except when I would carry the three pieces with me to vacation places around the country, always satisfied with hitting golf balls from tee areas on driving ranges and experimenting with my putter on practice greens. Well, what my method accomplished was that I picked up lots of bad habits from my experience at driving ranges that were exacerbated by the bad advice I received from other novice golfers. It wasn't till I began spending time in Florida where my company had an office that I decided getting a set of clubs would be the most logical next step in my learning experience. But, what brand of clubs should I buy? My golf buddies that had been playing the game for years all had their own preferences, such as Adams, Callaway, Cobra, Wilson, and a long list of other manufacturers. According to them, before buying an expensive set of clubs certain considerations had to be addressed. My height and the size of my hands were very important as clubs that are too long or too short or handles that were too small or too big would reduce my efficiency and could possibly cause back, neck, arm, and leg injuries. After purchasing the **right clubs,** using the **right balls** was the second most important part of the gear that was necessary in making me a champion golfer; the main choices seemed to be Top Flite, Titleist, or Maxifli. After selecting the right hardware, how I looked on the golf course seemed to be an important part of the game. So, wearing the right clothing became a hot topic of discussion between me and my friends. According to the "unwritten rules" of the game, shorts should be no more than two inches above the knees with no bulging pockets. Short-sleeved shirts with no pockets and knitted collars, which make them lie flat and even, should also be part of the golf ensemble. Socks could be either short or long sweats, but must be white. Golf shoes should be white, or a combination of white and a limited number of other colors, preferably black or brown, and at all times should be spotlessly clean. Last but not least, the proper gloves should be worn so that when swinging at the golf ball the club remains in the holder's hands and not on the fairway. All of the above attire should be neutral in color so as not to distract other players; "No loud colors allowed."

Needless to say, speaking to my casual golf friends about their preferences became a dizzying experience as each had their own sure-fire method of playing the game. The best advice that I received was to hire a professional instructor and let him guide me through the fundamentals of the game, especially the rules, vocabulary, and the proper equipment that would suit my body and experience.

I purchased a book by Jack Nicklaus for beginners that discussed the vocabulary of the sport and many of its complex rules. An understanding of the vocabulary that is unique to the sport took quite a bit of time for me to learn, but eventually I got "into the swing of it." Some common words that should be memorized and understood before playing the game are:

- **Ace**......................A hole in one is when the ball is hit from the tee and goes, one way or another, into a small targeted hole.
- **Birdie**....................One stroke under par, which is the pre-designated standard score for the hole.
- **Bogey**....................One stroke over par.
- **Bunker**...................A sand trap or hazard.
- **Cart or Buggy**........Small vehicle for transporting two players and their golf bags.
- **Chip**......................A low short shot to the green where the targeted hole resides.
- **Course**...................A large area of land designed for playing golf.
- **Dog Leg**.................A fairway that turns left or right.
- **Drive**.....................The first shot on every hole.
- **Driver**....................The number 1 wood (which isn't made of wood but a variety of metals).
- **Driving Range**........Practice area with mats or grass. Many ranges are designated for the use of irons or woods.
- **Eagle**.....................Two strokes under par.
- **Fairway**.................Part of the course between the tee and the green, which is kept free of rough grass.
- **Flag Stick**..............Pin supporting a flag on the green.
- **Fore!**....................A warning call when a ball is heading towards another player.
- **Green**....................Part of the golf course with grass cut very short, surrounding a hole. The hole contains a cup into which players try to "putt" their balls.

- **Handicap**.................A numerical system of a golfer's playing ability, measured as under par or over par.
- **Hazard**....................A difficulty or obstruction on golf courses such as lakes, ponds, fences, or bunkers.
- **Irons**.......................Metal golf clubs numbered from 1 to 9.
- **Lie**..........................Position in which the ball lies on the course.
- **Links**.......................A golf course besides the sea.
- **Mulligan**.................A second drive, which players grant each others in a friendly game on the tee only. Mulligans are not officially permitted in professional play.
- **O.B.** ....An abbreviation for "out of bounds" or beyond the limits of stakes or fences.
- **Par**...........................The pre-designated standard score or number of strokes given to each hole on the golf course.
- **Rough**.....................Area on the golf course where the grass is longer and thicker than on the fairway.
- **Scratch**...................A scratch player is one who has a "0" handicap and plays a par game.
- **Stroke or Shot**.......Movement of the club aimed at hitting the ball.

While learning the unique vocabulary of the sport I read every book I could get my hands on about the rules of the game. There are basically two forms of play, one which is decided by the holes won and lost (match play), and the more popular form, which is decided by the total number of strokes taken to complete the round (stroke play). The primary rule is that the game is a gentlemen's sport and at all times the players must conduct themselves accordingly. The etiquette of the game covers both **Courtesy and Priority on the Course as well as the Care of the Course**. Some of the rules of the game are:

1-Don't move, talk, or stand close to the player making a stroke.

2-Don't play until the group in front is safely out of the way.

3-Always play without delay and leave the putting green as soon as all the players in your group have holed out.

4-Invite faster groups to play ahead of you (play through).

5-Repair divots (holes) on fairway, and smooth footprints and disruptions in sand bunkers.

6-Don't step on the line of another player's putt.

7-Don't drop clubs on the putting green.

8-Replace the flag stick carefully.

I was fortunate that my company maintained an office in Boca Raton, Florida. It gave me an opportunity to spend the months of January and February in the sun. We rented a townhouse at Pelican Harbor in Delray Beach, which was only a 10-minute ride to my office. We searched for a private place to play golf and settled for the Boca Country Club where golf and tennis are the primary sports; they also allowed players that were not residents to become members. I was determined to take the advice of some of my friends to take the sport seriously and find a good golf instructor to undo many of the bad habits that I accumulated over the years, and hopefully learn the right way to play the game to the best of my ability.

I asked some of the better players in the club who they would recommend as a good coach; the name Steve seemed to be the favorite instructor for most of them. So I asked Steve if he would consider taking me on as a student, he said he would like to see me hit some balls from the driving range to determine if I had the physical capacity for him to be interested in coaching me. On a clear windless day, we headed for the driving range, where he laid out six balls in a row for me. I had no trouble hitting them with my driver, but not one was straight; they were all over the place. I thought I was doomed, but he laid out another set of six and told me to step back and do some stretching; arms first then hamstrings, then 20 soft practice swings. With that out of the way, he gave me my first lesson: "Always warm up before starting to swing." Then he corrected my grip, and I hit most of the balls dead center to the fairway. He told me that I had lots of bad habits that needed to be undone, but in time he thought that I would do just fine as a golfer. He told me to throw my clubs away and immediately go to the Golf Center to purchase a set of measured clubs. It was determined that Cobra offset clubs would do the trick. I was measured for arm length and club grip and told to return in a week to practice with the club pro to see if the clubs were okay. The clubs were made from titanium, which made them light and easy to swing, which made my practice session fun and informative. My big question was, "When do I use the different clubs?" The answer was, "That depends on you and your experience, so practice and play often, then you'll know what each club will do in your hands."

At that point in time I had all the proper attire, and with my new set of clubs I was ready to start playing the game in earnest. But as I learned when I began taking dancing seriously, "A new pair of dancing shoes doesn't mean that you know how to dance." I told Steve I would like to play in a game; he strongly suggested that I wait until at least six lessons and *mucho* practice before attempting to play, as playing badly at the beginning of a golf experience is one of the top reasons that many golfers give up the sport. So I took my six lessons and practiced every day after work and several hours on weekends. Soon, I knew which clubs to use and thought I was ready to play the game with some degree of success. My first game was a nightmare; I played the game with my brains instead of my body, which resulted in my hitting the ball in every wrong direction possible. Steve was right; I played so badly that I almost gave up the sport. Steve suggested that we play a game together so he could see what was wrong. His first suggestion was to relax and not think of anything but the ball and where it should be headed. Relaxing seemed to be the key ingredient in my game; with him alongside me, my game improved considerably and helped me develop some confidence, which is another main ingredient to successfully play golf.

The club had a Senior Men's League, which Steve suggested I join. I was surprised to learn that I was the **kid on the block.** Most of the members were in their seventies and eighties; I was just in my sixties.

The advantage that the older players had over me was that they knew the course very well and they were in no rush to finish their play. I got many pointers from my fellow golfers, which in time would allow me to play a game to my satisfaction. At that time I was still a working person so I had to find time to play between my other responsibilities, but it laid the groundwork for my being comfortable with the sport when I retired several years later; it gave me something to look forward to with what developed into a passion for the game. The most important thing I learned was that there is no age limit in the sport. I played with members that were in their nineties—much to my embarrassment, as they beat me in my first year of play, every time. Our club also had a 9 hole league for players who were not able to complete an 18 hole game or didn't have the time or inclination required to play a longer game. One of the side advantages of playing golf for me is that our long yearly drives from New York to Florida are always planned around stops that have places for me to play my favorite game.

For those with computers, finding a place to play golf is as easy as typing in www.golfdigest.com or www.golflink.com. Each website displays information about locations, course profiles, course rules, and the cost to play. I use these sites when we travel down south in the winter to locate the courses that I would like to try. I usually call the facility and tell them when I'll be arriving so that they can set me up with a partner. While I'm playing, Barbara manages to locate places to shop, enjoying the quality time away from me while she indulges in her favorite pastime.

Golf, like tennis, is another sport that is intertwined with social activity. Making friends on the golf course is easy, especially if using a golf cart as it accommodates two people. When competing, there are usually two carts per team with prizes for the ball closest to the hole from an initial drive, lowest overall score, best play on the difficult holes, and a number of other competitive prizes. The camaraderie and competiveness results in making numerous friends, all with a love for the sport. In addition, there are many social events that include dinners, dancing, and traveling with fellow golfers to vacations spots to play the game.

Writing

Many of the activities that keep retirees busy in their golden years are planned based on lifetime dreams as previously mentioned, such as traveling, dancing, boating, fishing, tennis, and golf. In Barbara's case it was her love of dancing that introduced her to writing. She was asked to write a column by the publisher of Long Island's New York Ballroom Dance Newsletter: "Around the Floor." Her column covered our travels around the world and the many dancing experiences we've enjoyed. The newsletter evolved from a local paper into an international website with links around the world including China, England, Australia, South Africa, Korea, and many Latin American countries. Other links connected to Bridge to World Championships, colleges and universities, Swing dance sites, and, my favorite, Tango dance sites. I soon had a column on the same website under the name, "Tangohombre," covering ballroom dancing on Long Island, with emphasis on the Argentine Tango. We were fortunate that an opportunity presented itself where Barbara and I could indulge in a pastime that would carry into our retirement years and would keep both of us occupied doing something that we didn't realize we had a passion for until we tried writing. The stories that appeared on the website were quite condensed from the original ones submitted to the publisher. At that time I thought it would be fun to present the articles as they appeared in the newsletter and website, and then tell the full stories as originally experienced. In addition to the published articles, many of our dancing experiences were not presented for publication, so I thought, why not include those stories too? It took several years of serious writing on my part, and intense editing by Barbara to get our 600-plus page book *Dancing Around the World with Mike and Barbara Bivona* published at the beginning of 2010. Two of the condensed stories as they appeared in the newsletters follow:

Traveling Around: "Chicken Soup and Chocolate Pudding," by Barbara Bivona

As a child growing up during World War II in Brooklyn, New York, the popular sound of that era was big band music. We listened to Swing and Jive, ballads alluding to loved ones who were far from home during the war, and patriotic music. The Rumba was making a good showing on the dance floor, and the Andrew Sisters sang "Rum and Coca Cola" to a Rumba beat. I was young and innocent of the ways of the world; my memories of that time were not so much of the devastation and horrors of war, but of growing up in Brownsville, my neighborhood in Brooklyn, my close circle of friends, going fishing with my dad and brother, and my mother's wonderful chicken soup and chocolate pudding. Mom collected records, the old 78 and 33 rpm discs, and was always buying the latest hits. We listened to Helen O'Connell, Buddy Clark, and The Dorsey Brothers; I was amazed when Mom came home with the first LP (long playing) recording that I had ever seen: "Sing, Sing, Sing." Mom would take my hand and dance with me in our tiny living room. If she knew the words, she would sing along with the recording, and my brother George and I would soon join in. That's why when I saw an ad many, many years later for Joe Battaglia and his New York Band at the Huntington Town House, in Huntington, Long Island; I didn't waste any time making reservations for an evening of dinner and big band dancing.

I was fascinated with Joe's background. Until he retired, he worked in the garment industry in New York City. He started as a young man and after many years of hard work, owned his own business. After retiring, he decided to pursue a life-long dream of taking trumpet lessons. After just six years of lessons, Joe was ready to take on the big band sounds. He played trumpet with several bands and soon decided to form his own, fulfilling another life-long dream. His success was rapid, and soon he and his band were being booked to repeat engagements in New York's theater district and supper clubs. The icing on the cake was a Grammy in the year 2000 for best instrumental recording titled "Close Your Eyes," a tribute to Harry James and Ray Anthony. The band performs music from this album in clubs and is enjoyable either for listening or dancing. That night we danced to "Embraceable You," "It Had to Be You," "Ain't That a Kick in the Head," as well as more contemporary music, such as "On a Clear Day," and "Misty."

All of these and more are on his album. Joe has been compared to Harry James; however, he told me, "I feel that I have my own sound." And, while he may be using some of Harry James' arrangements, this is definitely not what I would call a cover band. Joe's sounds are his own. True, they are inspired by the master, but they emanate from his own soul. They take me back in time to those wonderful days when my main concerns were homework and what Saturday matinee my friends and I would be seeing. They take me back to the days of Mom's **Chicken Soup and Chocolate Pudding.**

Barbara occupied many pleasant retirement years visiting different dance venues locally and globally and relating her experiences in her "Traveling Around" articles. Of her many stories, I chose to include the one above because it had an exciting retirement story within a story, of Joe Battaglia retiring and fulfilling two of his dreams while in his golden years, which included learning how to play the trumpet and eventually having his own big band. It is living proof that it is never too late to begin exploring new experiences, especially those that stimulate the brain and eventually become a passion and something to look forward to every retirement day. Joe's story also clearly shows that in many cases, when someone tries something new, it leads beyond the new experience and can open doors to a new lifestyle. Joe's experimenting and passion for playing the trumpet led him to become a big band leader and forever changed his life from a retired garment person to a very active senior citizen. What an incredible change of direction at a time of life when most people are looking to curtail their activities and slow down.

When the publisher of "Around the Floor" asked me to develop a column about Tango dancing and its popularity with today's dancers, I asked him, "Why me?" He said, being that my e-mail address is "Tangohombre," that I probably had some insight into the feel of the Tango and its popularity in today's dance scene. Of course flattery can go a long way and I decided to give it a try. One of my first articles follows:

"Tangohombre," by Michael Bivona

When discussing Tango dancing, you might wonder if we are talking about American Tango, International Tango, or the original, Argentine Tango. It just so happens that we are referring to all three styles of dancing. Discussing the technical differences of these incredible dances is beyond my ability, but I can discuss the differences from my point of view as a social dancer.

About 15-years ago, my wife Barbara and I decided to take dance lessons. We both loved Tango music and decided it would be a good starting dance for us. At the time, the most popular, and probably the only readily available lessons in our area, were in American Tango. The choice of that dance went from a whim to an infatuation and then love in a short time. We became so passionate with the feeling of the dance and the music that we encouraged many of our friends to take Tango lessons.

The image of the actor Anthony Dexter* portraying the great Latin lover Rudolph Valentino in the movie *Valentino* (1951) and dancing a passionate Tango was in my mind often as we progressed with our infatuation with the dance. I recall seeing him portray the great Valentino on screen and remembered how many times my teenage friends and I saw the same picture over and over again, totally absorbed with the music and the passion of the dance.

Over the years, we observed the development of International Tango, enjoying the complexity of the steps, body and head movements, and its strict syllabus. We tried to get into the dance, but for us it lacked the passion and freedom of movement that dancing the other Tangos gave us. Last year we were invited to participate in an exhibition where the three tangos were performed to show their differences. We danced the Argentine Tango and were followed by a professional-amateur couple dancing the International Tango. The professional, who was from Australia, picked up the mic and said, "Well, you just saw how the Tango came to my country, full of passion and softness of movement, now we will show you how we and the English took the sex out of the dance." Their performance was exemplary, their movements and precision were remarkable; certainly the right dance for competition dancing, but, as social dancers, we still preferred the Argentine Tango. Well, how did we go from the American Tango to the Argentine Tango?

We fell in love with the Argentine style when we saw the show "Tango Argentino" that appeared off-Broadway in Manhattan. Our dance instructor, Electra, of Swing Street Studios in Farmingdale, New York, thought it would be a good idea to expose her students to this type of dancing, so we made group reservations to see the show, and began our journey into the world of Argentine Tango. Little did we know that this style would take many of us to a new level of passion for dancing. We immediately took lessons from Electra, who was waiting for the opportunity to teach this original Tango dance that her father taught her as a child so many years ago. She had a deep love for the dance as it brought back memories of when she was a young girl and of her parents and their friends, who danced only that style of Tango. Thanks to the "Tango Argentino" show, she was able to purchase a great Tango teaching tape and made copies for her students so we could get a true feel for the dance by listening to the sweet, warm, exotic music.

Our lessons were difficult, as we had to learn new patterns that were not familiar to us from other dances that we knew: swaying *cortes*, body balancing, leg rubs, *ochos* (figure eights), kicks, and the most unusual, stopping to allow your partner to improvise and, in turn, to do the same.

About ten years after our introduction to this exotic Tango style, I was reading a travel brochure, "Puente al Tango" (Bridge to the Tango), published by Dan Trenner with a website at www.BridgetotheTango.com. He was organizing a tour to Buenos Aires, Argentina, limited to 40 lucky students. It was an eleven-day tour and included daily lessons, dancing at different *milonga*s (clubs) every evening, lectures and demonstrations by the world's great male and female Tango dancers, and most important of all, one instructor for every two students. I booked the tour and gave it to Barbara as a birthday gift; luckily she was as excited as I was about our new adventure.

On our trip we learned new *cortes*, turns, kicks, and fine-tuned improvising. But the most exciting and difficult thing to be learned was emphasized by one of our renowned instructors, Mingo Pugliese—"**ATTITUDE.**" He said, "There is no dance if you do not have the right **ATTITUDE.**"

That was the end of my article. I wrote about our adventure to Buenos Aires in more detail in my book *Dancing Around the World with Mike and Barbara Bivona.*

*There is an incredible website, "The Anthony Dexter Homepage," established for his memorial, 1913-2001. It includes the theme song for the movie *Valentino*, "Valentino Tango," and the history of this most fascinating and versatile man who played Valentino in the 1951 film. The sophistication of the site is something to behold... **Pure Enjoyment.** Page two of the site is presented below with the permission of Gilda Tabarez:

View Pictures and Facts about *Valentino* (1951)

Anthony Dexter Photo Gallery
Click on each image to view a larger version.

Collecting Books and Reading

Who of us hasn't dreamt of sitting down in a comfortable chair, in a quiet place, without interruption and reading all the books that we never had a chance to read when we were in our productive time of life with limited time for such a luxury? Well, Barbara and I are among those who just didn't have time between our busy schedules to read all the books we accumulated over the years but had never read. We tried during our preretirement years to join book clubs, but could never put the time aside to participate and enjoy the camaraderie and exchange of ideas that is the essence of these clubs. So we did the next best thing, we started collecting books from used book stores in our travels, with the intention that when we had the time in our retirement, we would catch up on all the reading that we missed during our productive years. Not to say that we didn't get some book reading in, but there were so many books we wanted to delve into, but just couldn't due to the time constraints in our busy lives. Barbara collected as many books as she could get her hands on from her favorite authors, including Stephen King, Dean Koontz, Mary Higgins Clark, Anne Rice, John Saul, and many of the classics. I was always fascinated with information on Christopher Columbus and the Age of Discovery. So I in turn started collecting books from the 14th through the 18th centuries, especially those that pertained to Italian explorers such as Marco Polo, who sailed for Italy and traveled to China overland; Christopher Columbus, who sailed for Spain and added the better part of the "new world" to the holdings of that country; Amerigo Vespucci, who sailed for Spain and supposedly was the first European to realize that the land mass was a new continent; Giovanni da Verrazzano, who sailed for France and explored the East Coast of the new lands, and finally, James Cabot (Giovanni Capoto), who sailed for England and was responsible for adding the northern part of the American continent to the English map of conquests. Captain Caputo had to change his name during his employment with the English Crown as they didn't want the world to think that they had to go outside of their homeland to find someone to head their exploration into the new world.

So when we retired, we had hundreds of books that we had collected and finally had time to read in the comfort of our home, while sunning ourselves on the beach, and in our travels. It's interesting how one's passion can open doors to other unrelated happenings. Due to my obsession with collecting books and material on Columbus and the Age of Discovery, I became a charter member of the congressionally designated "Christopher Columbus-500 Quincentenary Jubilee Commission" and the New York "Countdown 1992" organization that promoted the Expo '92 event. From our association with these organizations, Barbara and I went to Seville, Spain to take part in the Universal World's Fair-Expo '92, "Columbus and the age of Discovery," as spectators for the New York organization "Countdown 1992." The Expo was from April 29 to October 12, 1992, on La Isla de La Cartuja, in Seville. Over 100-countries were spread out over 500-acres displaying their pride and ethnic joy in every type of exhibition imaginable. We were there for several days, including the finale on October 12, and became part of the history of that event, which recorded over 41 million visitors. A poster of the 1992 Seville-Expo '92 follows:

GRAN
REGATA
COLON
92 QUINTO CENTENARIO

GRAND
REGATTA
COLUMBUS
92 QUINCENTENARY

GRANDE
REGATA
COLOMBO
92 QUINTO CENTENÁRIO

GRAN
REGATA
COLOMBO
92 CINQUECENTESIMO

PROGRAMA
OFICIAL

OFFICIAL
PROGRAMME

PROGRAMA
OFICIAL

PROGRAMMA
UFFICIALE

Well into my retirement I realized that I had collected in excess of 400 books, maps, and documents on the Age of Discovery. I realized after a friend's demise that many of the possessions that he had accumulated over his lifetime and were so dear to him, were of no interest to his heirs or friends and were disposed of like pieces of junk. So I began looking for a home for my collection. Providence was instrumental in my having the opportunity to place my collection at the Columbus Foundation, the organization that is the sponsor of the annual Columbus Day Parade in New York City. We were at Dan Maloney's Empress Ballroom in Delray Beach, Florida enjoying our usual Friday night social dance party, when I was introduced to Lou Mangone, who was a member of the foundation and in charge of their library. I mentioned that I was in negotiations with Brown University, in Providence, Rhode Island, about donating some of my collection to their extensive, world-renowned Americana Collection of books on that period. I was a long-standing member of the Brown University Library and was excited that they were considering adding some of my books to their collection. Lou said his organization would be very interested in my books and could probably keep them as a collection in a separate area of their extensive library as they only had a sprinkling of books about their namesake. The prospect of having the collection stay intact under my name was very compelling; Brown University would have scattered the books in their respective categories throughout their humongous library, which meant that I would lose the recognition of the collection. So to make a long story short, I indexed my collection and shipped them off to the foundation, where they reside today for the pleasure of their members and researchers. My fear of having my beloved collection scattered or discarded was no longer a concern; I found a home for them and was very pleased when I visited the foundation and saw a place set aside for my collection. A copy of the foundation's newsletter mentioning my donation follows as well as a picture of the library that was set aside for the collection:

Michael Bivona Collection:
Columbus, the Age of Discovery and Related Books
Donated, March 2006

Bivona Collection Donated

The Foundation has received an enormously generous and essential donation, the Michael Bivona Collection: Columbus, The Age of Discovery and Related Books. The collection, which Mr. Bivona acquired over the course of 30 years, contains approximately 300 books and immediately gives us an extensive group of works about the Foundation's namesake. It will reside in the Ambassador Charles A. Gargano Library.

"This remarkable donation, by Michael Bivona, vastly increases and improves the quality of our library's holdings," said President Louis Tallarini. " We are deeply grateful to Mr. Bivona for his donation, and we are proud that our Member Louis Mangone made the introduction that has brought the Michael Bivona Collection to the Foundation."

"The age of discovery was roughly 1400 to 1700, and of course Columbus was central to the period," said Mr. Bivona. "He had the audacity and the courage to venture out into unknown areas. At that time, very few people would venture out on the water beyond the sight of land. He had few navigational instruments to guide him when he became the first European to discover and record this unknown continent. He found his way back to Spain using his knowledge of celestial navigation, ocean currents and prevailing winds. The route he took is still being used today because of the favorable winds and currents. What he did was just amazing."

Mr. Bivona, 72, and his wife Barbara live in Dix Hills, Long Island and have two grown children and two grandchildren. Now retired, he was a CPA and co-owner and CFO of Manchester Technologies. His main hobbies are boating and ballroom dancing. He owns a 42-foot Cris-Craft boat, which they've taken to Block Island, Cape Cod, Nantucket and Plymouth, among other places, but, unlike Columbus, he said, "with very sophisticated electronic navigational devices."

Foundation News

Mr. Bivona and Foundation Member Louis Mangone belong to a dancing group that meets regularly. Several months ago, Mr. Bivona was in discussions with Brown University, in Providence, Rhode Island, about donating the collection to the school. "I mentioned to Lou Mangone that I was talking to Brown, and he told me that the Foundation would be interested in the collection," Mr. Mangone pursued the collection, which is now coming to the Foundation.

Book collector, philanthropist and ballroom dance aficionado Michael Bivona with wife Barbara in a tango

The Michael Bivona Collection has great depth in its holdings of books about Columbus, from his own letters and journals and con temporary accounts of his voyages to the works of later historians who interpret and comment on the lasting changes brought about by his explorations. Mr. Bivona acquired the books from every type of source imaginable, from specialized booksellers to bookstores and flea markets, and the books range in age from recent to over 100 years old.

"It is wonderful to know that my collection will have a meaningful place at the Foundation to honor a great explorer," Mr. Bivona said. ❖

In addition to the wonderful experience of visiting Spain for the 500th anniversary of Columbus' discoveries, earlier in the year we helped New Orleans celebrate the discovery by spending one week on the *Mississippi Queen* Paddlewheel exploring the Mississippi River and a week at the Mardi Gras; the theme again was "Columbus and the Age of discovery." So my love of reading and my hobby of collecting books of that period resulted in our visiting Spain and New Orleans chasing one of our dreams, which resulted in two unforgettable lifetime experiences.

I can't express how much pleasure Barbara and I have had over the years collecting and then reading the many books we've accumulated. Collecting and reading books is certainly a pastime that can be enjoyed by everyone regardless of their financial or physical health. Some books that we purchased cost as little as two dollars. What better way is there to spend some quality time when one's body is aching from advancing age, than by picking up a book, stretching out on a comfortable chair, opening to the first page, and taking part in a new adventure.

Today the younger generation doesn't seem to enjoy reading from printed pages. Their heads tend to be glued to computer screens of every size. So for those who are not inclined to open a book and explore its contents, there is an alternative that has become very popular with many of the "**electronic folks,**" and that's eBooks. It is an **electronic book,** (also known as e-book, eBook or digital book), and seems to be the wave of the future for reading books and magazines. E-books are usually read on dedicated hardware devices known as e-Readers or e-books. The most popular readers are the Amazon Kindle and Barnes & Noble NOOK. For a fraction of the cost of a printed paged book, the book's contents can be read using the aforementioned devices for under ten dollars and in many cases at no charge. Many seniors can be seen on air flights to and from Florida enjoying the benefit of the lightweight eBooks; some are so small that they can be put into a pocketbook or inside jacket pocket, which makes it a lot more convenient than carrying a clumsy printed book. Other advantages of the small lightweight devices are the applications that are available for accessing magazines, games, and the Internet. Seniors that do not have eyesight limitations should certainly try using the electronic devices as they are easy to carry around and have an abundance of applications and information that can stimulate a person's brain cells.

Exercising

Wouldn't it be nice to start an exercise regimen when we are young and our bodies are flexible and our muscles toned, and continue with a healthy routine into our senior years? We certainly know that our bodies were meant to move and the expression "Use it or lose it" certainly applies to body motion and its relationship to exercising. We were taught early on that if our muscles become too flabby and weak that our heart and lungs won't function efficiently, and that our joints will become stiff and easily injured. Not only are our bodies meant to move, they actually crave exercise on a regular basis for physical fitness and good health. A good exercise and stretching schedule can reduce the risk of heart disease, cancer, high blood pressure, diabetes, and other maladies; plus it will no doubt improve our appearance and delay the aging process.

Knowing all the positive results that can be obtained from a good exercise program, why aren't we more conscientious about keeping active with a regular exercise routine? Well, the obvious reasons are that when we were young, we felt good and probably looked good. We were busy working and raising a family, and doing any activity on a regular basis that required time and energy wasn't easy. The two things that most of us didn't have in our early lives was spare time, and exercising unfortunately was on the bottom of the list of "things to do that I like." Unfortunately, most of us begin an exercise program out of necessity rather than on a voluntary basis, at least that's the way Barbara and I began our journey into a healthier lifestyle that continues well into our senior years.

In 1988 when Barbara was 52-years of age, we drove our oldest child Stephen to the State University at Albany to begin his life as a college student. After helping him move into the 17-story dormitory, which took a better part of the day, we checked into the Ramada Inn in town and had a leisurely dinner and a well-deserved night's sleep. In the morning we decided that Barbara would take the first leg of our 200-mile trip back to Long Island, and that I would finish driving the last part of the journey. Well, as "the best laid plans of mice and men" don't always go according to plans, that day was the beginning of a horrific nightmare. A few minutes after awakening and discussing our plans for the day, Barbara had a seizure and passed out. I couldn't revive her and quickly called the hotel manager, who appeared as soon as I hung up the phone. He called for an ambulance and within minutes Barbara was on her way to the Albany Medical Center, which, thank God, was a short five-minute ride from the hotel. After a cat scan, it was determined that she had an aneurysm that had burst in the left side of her head and the prognosis was not very good. I was told to make funeral arrangements as the chances of her surviving the night were very slim. Needless to say, I was in a state of shock; she was very rarely sick during our 20-plus years of marriage, and being told that we were going to lose her seemed to be an impossibility that my mind would not accept. I wasn't too sure about the quality of the hospital, so I called my doctor back home and inquired about the credentials of the facility. I was told by him and others that I called that the Albany Medical Center was one of the best facilities in the country for taking care of the serious medical problem that she had.

I was also told by my regular doctor to make sure that the Chief of Staff of Neurosurgery was assigned to her case. I insisted that Doctor Pop handle her, which he did to perfection. He told me that he would have to wait until her brain settled from the blood burst, and when she was strong enough, he would perform an operation and remove the blood from her agitated brain and hopefully insert a metal clip on the weak part of the vessel that had caused the aneurysm. It took a week before she had enough strength for him to perform the critical operation, and two additional weeks for her to recover. After three weeks at the center, we were able to take her home for her long three-month recovery. During my three-week stay in Albany, my 18-year-old son had to plough his way through the beginning of his first semester at the university, and my 16-year-old daughter Laurie, who was starting a new term in high school, had to fend for herself back in Long Island. Fortunately, my brother Vic and sisters Anne and Mae and their spouses Rose and Sal made sure that someone was with me every day during that trying time. The only bright side to the experience was that Barbara didn't have the seizure while driving the first part of our trip back to our home on Long Island or we both would probably have perished in a car crash taking God only knows how many other people with us.

Well, what does all this have to do with exercising? As any good doctor will tell someone that is recuperating from surgery, exercising is paramount to recovery and a healthy life. Barbara followed the good doctor's advice and began a walking regimen that eventually included some of the girls in our neighborhood. She and her friends walked for three days a week, and in inclement weather, they happily would walk through the local mall, rewarding themselves with serious shopping when their routine was done. So there we have it, out of necessity due to a horrific experience, my wife began her exercise program that would last into retirement. But, her experience didn't encourage me to start an exercise program, as I felt great and looked pretty good in my friendly mirror. It took a big "Kick in the ass" for me to wake up and begin my exercise routine.

In 1993, when I was 59, I went for a stress test and failed dismally. My story began when my good friend and fellow worker, Charles Kaufman, age 42, had a heart attack and died on the spot. He was the youngest of the executives in our company and the shock of his passing made the remaining 12 officers think hard about their sedentary lives. We decided that we should all have thorough medical exams including stress tests to see if we were possibly candidates for joining Chuck in the hereafter. Well, to make a long story short, everyone passed with flying colors, except for me. I was taken off the treadmill before the test was over and told to rest; it seemed my heart was jumping all over the place. Although I was the oldest in the group, I thought that my body was in better shape than most, as I was only slightly overweight and stayed pretty active with boating and dancing whenever I had the time. The only discomfort I experienced at that time was occasional heartburn. The cardiologist told me that I had to undergo an angiogram to determine which arteries were clogged. He also told me not to drive or go to work until the test was done. I immediately went into denial and walked out of his office in a state of confusion; my wife, who was waiting for me, seemed to be in an even greater state of confusion when I told her of my unhappy experience. A couple of days later I went to St. John's Hospital in Smithtown and had the procedure done. While under valium—thank God for the pacifying drug—I was told that a heart attack was imminent and that I should be transported immediately to St. Luke's Hospital in Manhattan for open heart surgery. As I was still in a happy mood from the drug, I agreed and within a short period of time I was strapped onto a gurney, with an intravenous stent in my arm, and was on my way by ambulance from Smithtown to New York City, which took over two hours.

It was determined that I needed double bypass open heart surgery. My two main arteries were 90 and 70 percent closed and had to be bypassed using both mammary arteries from my chest, which were supposed to be the preferred arteries to use in that type of procedure. Still under the influence of the peaceful drug, I agreed to everything the doctors said, and the next day the operation was done successfully, although I didn't remember a thing and awoke two days later with all the usual tubes sticking into my body and my brother Vic leaning over my bed. His first words that I remember so clearly were, "Are you sure you needed this operation?" That was his sense of humor and it caused me to laugh and disrupt some of the tubes that made me look like a Borg from the series "Star Trek." Because of some blood complications, I spent 11 days in the hospital instead of the usual week, and when I finally got home and looked in the mirror, I didn't recognize the emaciated person starring back at me. In that short period of time my muscles had atrophied and I looked ten years older.

In a little over a month I was driving my car and was able to return to work. The doctors insisted that I begin a physical therapy program, preferably at the St. John's Hospital gym. I agreed, knowing that if I was left unsupervised, in time I would lose interest in working out and would return to my old bad habits that were probably responsible for my medical emergency. The program consisted of working out at their gym for two days a week for one hour each day with other recuperating heart patients. I continued for almost two years, using treadmills, bicycles, Stairmasters, and minor weights. The therapy began slowly and in time my muscles and speed surpassed the levels prior to the surgery. When exercising became a permanent part of my lifestyle, I began working out at Bally's gym and eventually bought equipment that I was accustomed to for my finished basement. It took a medical emergency for me to start living a healthier life, which included exercising, the Mediterranean diet, and stress avoidance, when possible.

One of the most bewildering things about retiring is that there doesn't seem to be enough time to do the things that are planned; we always seem to be running out of time and in a rush to get things done. So out of desperation I developed a **priority list** to remove the stress that accompanies the feeling of not getting things accomplished in a timely manner. The list follows:

1-Excercising three times a week.
2-Dancing, at least twice a week.
3-Writing as much as possible (I'm now on my fourth book).
4-Boating and fishing, whenever the opportunity arises.
5-Golf in good weather only.
6-Charitable work, whenever the need arises.

If there is ever a conflict in any of the above, I always try to use my **priority list** as a guide; for instance, if there is a dance on a particular night and a golf game scheduled for the same day, the golf game is skipped as it is number 5 and dancing number 2 on my list.

One of the advantages of an exercise schedule during retirement, if planned properly, is that we have all the time necessary to firm up. We always seemed to have had excuses, when we were in our productive working years and raising families, for not having enough time to take care of our bodies through proper exercise. In our golden years, what better way to spend a few hours a week than at a gym or in our homes using equipment of our choice? Many people use the excuse that they play baseball, golf, tennis, or many of the other physical sports, so they don't have to enter an exercise program. I found that to enjoy the full potential of any sport, one must be in good physical condition, and it's not the sport that gets you there, it's the condition that is developed by working out on a consistent basis that makes you excel at any sport. In our case, we certainly couldn't do ballroom dancing at an aerobic level if we weren't in good physical condition. Therefore my advice to retired folks is to stretch for at least 15-minutes every morning before getting out of bed, and exercise three times a week from 45-minutes to one hour. For those not inclined to working out indoors, aggressive walking or cycling is a good alternative, but should be done consistently and scheduled for at least three days a week. As previously mentioned, ballroom dancing done in earnest is certainly an aerobic activity and so are many of the popular line exercises such as Zumba and Dancercise, which are done to music and are favorites of the ladies. None of these activities should be tried unless the participants are in relatively good physical shape before the activity, and at the beginning should be supervised by a professional, as unconditioned bodies can be damaged if not properly prepared for the task. Always remember, before participating in any physical activity, stretch for at least 10 to 15 minutes; it prepares your muscles for the forthcoming strenuous events.

Volunteering – "Paying it Forward"

I personally think that our "golden years" are the perfect time to share our good fortune with others. The fact that we reached retirement "without too many kinks in our armor" should give us an opportunity to "pay it forward." Paying back a little can be accomplished on a financial or a personal basis. I'm sure that during our lifetimes we in some way donated funds to religious and secular organizations, such as churches, synagogues, hospitals, and the many other worthy causes that are always in need of support. In retirement, when we have time available, the many organizations that provide charitable and other essential services to the public could use our hands to help them in achieving their goals. What better way for senior citizens to contribute their time than to donate their precious talents for the betterment of the worthy goals of these useful organizations.

The essence of this book is to show by example rather than by lecturing, how "old folks" can spend their time in a constructive and gratifying manner, and one of the ways is by volunteering time to worthwhile causes, preferably one that is dear to our hearts. In my case, working with the Salvation Army in their Homeless Veterans Program caught my attention and eventually my time. I didn't seek out the program, as a matter of fact, I wasn't even aware that homeless veterans were an issue in the United States. My story starts with visiting the Northport Veterans Medical Facility in Northport, Long Island for post-bypass surgery examinations and medication, which I was entitled to as a Korean War vet. I heard that the Salvation Army was considering setting up a homeless shelter and rehabilitation program and that our government was donating one of their vacant buildings at the huge complex to them for that purpose. I can't express how outraged I was in learning that we had veterans living on the streets of our neighborhood and that many were actually living in the woods on the facility's grounds in make-shift wooden shacks. I managed to get a meeting with the Salvation Army's leader of the program and asked what I could do to be of help. He explained that the program was to get vets off the streets for 90 days and provide them with food, shelter, and encouragement, and if possible, getting them back into the workforce with meaningful jobs.

He gave me a tour of the huge vacant building, which was in dire need of repair. He explained his optimistic program in detail and his dream of having the government put the building in a condition so he could begin hiring, furnishing, and, hopefully within a short period of time, getting veterans into the rest and rehabilitation program. He told me how important my volunteering would be to him as he was having a meeting with the neighborhood leaders to explain to them what the Salvation Army's plans were, and that my presence as a professional accountant and veteran would help him convince them that the homeless program would not be detrimental to them or their neighborhood.

One of the few experiences I had had with the Salvation Army was during Christmas time when their soldiers, in full blue dress uniforms, invaded the streets of Manhattan and the entrances of major department stores with their donation kettles and bell ringing. A very vivid encounter with their soldiers was when I was in the United States Air Force. At each embarkation point that I shipped out of, they were there serving coffee, cake, and good cheer to the airmen going overseas. Other than during the holidays and my military experience, the only other experience I had with them was when the musical film *Guys and*

Dolls came out in 1959, which I saw several times, starring Marlon Brando as Sky Masterson, a high-ranking gambler, and Frank Sinatra as Nathan Detroit, a low-ranking gambler. What they both had in common was making a fast buck, and their way of getting some quick and safe dough was by conning the Salvation Army's Sergeant Sarah Brown, played by the beautiful actress Jean Simmons, into allowing them to use her facility as a cover for their gambling operations. Up until my agreeing to join the Army's homeless shelter program, all of my memories of the organization were pleasant ones, so I went head over heels into the project of assisting in getting the homeless shelter up and running.

I think a little history about the organization is in order:

The Salvation Army began in 1865 when William Booth, a London minister, gave up the comfort of his pulpit and decided to take his message into the street where it would reach the poor and homeless, the hungry and the destitute. His original plan was to send the street converts to established churches, but he soon realized that the poor did not feel comfortable or welcome in the pews of most of the churches and chapels of Victorian England. Regular churchgoers were appalled when these shabbily dressed, unwashed people came to join them in worship. So he decided to found a church especially for them—the East London Christian Mission. Although the mission grew slowly his faith in God remained undiminished.

By the early 1900s the Army spread around the world. It soon had officers and soldiers in 36 countries, including the United States. This well-organized flexible structured organization inspired a great many much-needed services such as: women's social work, the first food depot for the poor, the first day nursery and the first Salvation Army hospital. During World War II, they operated over 3,000 service units for the armed forces, which led to the formation of the USO. Today the organization is stronger and more powerful than ever. Now, in over 106 nations around the world, they continue to work where the need is greatest, guided by faith in God and love for all people. In 2010 over 3 million volunteers gave of their time, talents, and resources to assist the organization's goal of "Doing the most good for everyone in need."

So I became a volunteer of the astonishing Army as a civilian representative on the Neighborhood Committee, which had periodic meetings to keep the people in the surrounding area abreast of what the Army was accomplishing and to act as a sounding board for any complaints from either side. I was also a representative of the Suffolk County Veteran's Committee, whose main purpose was overseeing the welfare and care of the homeless veterans. We met once a month to discuss the progress of the Army's programs and contributed our advice to them based on our experiences in the military. We helped resolve many of the issues that they were having with the unfortunate veterans, especially the Viet Nam Vets, who seemed to think that the world was against them, and that they were the bad guys. Two of our primary goals were to raise funds to build a kitchen and laundry room that would make the shelter self-sufficient and would introduce the patients to working in these environments as cooks, waiters, machine maintenance men, etc. By accomplishing our objectives the patients would again join others in productive endeavors and hopefully be helped to regain their self-confidence and composure as civilized human beings. Our group of volunteers accomplished our goals and much more. We not only raised enough funds for the kitchen and laundry room, but we also supplied the furniture for their small dining area, TV lounge, exercise room, and library.

The facility had the capacity to house 80-men and women. The essence of the program was to get homeless vets off the streets and rehabilitate them by providing a clean place to sleep, eat, learn, socialize, and work. The program was usually for 90-days and if they were ready, willing, and able, many of them were provided with jobs through the Salvation Army's employment service. The satisfaction that I received while working with fellow veterans, and in some small way contributing to their reentry into useful lives, remains one of the highlights of my life.

While I was busy with my various charitable endeavors, my wife Barbara donated her time and knowledge as a Council Member Overseer at the Tilles Center for the Performing Arts, which is located on the C.W. Post Campus of Long Island University in Brookville, Long Island, N.Y. The Center's Concert Hall seats over 2,500 theatergoers and features orchestral performances, fully staged operas, ballets, and modern dance, along with Broadway shows, and all forms of music, dance, and theater from around the world. Chamber music, cabaret, solo recitals, and theater productions for children and adults are presented in their more intimate 500-seat Hillwood Recital Hall. They host more than 100 performances a year by world-renowned artists in music, theater, and dance. Among the artists and ensembles that have been presented by the Center are the Boston Symphony Orchestra conducted by Seiji Ozawa, cellist Yo-Yo-Ma, violinist Itzhak Perlman, the Big Apple Circus, Bill Cosby, James Taylor, Liza Minnelli, and the Met Orchestra with James Levine. In addition, Tilles Center is home to important regional arts organizations including the Long Island Philharmonic and Eglevsky Ballet.

What got Barbara interested in the Council was her love of music, especially classical. In her formative years she studied piano and classical guitar for ten years, and continued with her passion well into retirement. As a Council Overseer she attends meetings that review the programs and progress of Tilles Center. The President of Long Island University, David Steinberg, heads the early morning meetings and lends his energy and talent to all the discussions. Fund raising for the Center is usually one of the main topics. It seems that performing arts can only exist today by the donations of generous sponsors and the many volunteers who donate their time as ushers, guides, or whatever jobs are necessary to keep the venue performing at its peak.

A major endeavor of the Council is to introduce classical music to children with the hope that they will become the music lovers of the future. Its popular "Swing for Kids" program is funded by an annual golf and tennis tournament that takes place at "Meadow Brook Club" in Jericho, and the "Creek Golf Course" in Locust Valley. The annual tournament benefits Arts Education, which includes the "Swing for Kids" program. The effort is primarily run by senior volunteers who are devoted music lovers and enjoy being a part of programs that they are passionate about.

Peter Tilles, one of the leaders of the program, made the following statement:

With funds provided by "Swing for Kids" over the years, Tilles Center for the Performing Arts has been able to strengthen its commitment to the artists and audiences of tomorrow. As part of the arts education program, thousands of school children participate in master classes, in-school workshops, and performances at Tilles Center by world-class artists renowned for their multicultural work in classical music, jazz, dance, theater, and opera. Additionally, through Tilles Center's residency program with the New York Philharmonic, young musicians have an opportunity to work with Philharmonic soloists in rehearsals, master classes, and panel discussions. The Center's "Arts Start Here" program introduces youngsters to live performance by highly acclaimed artists from the world of dance, music, and theater. The ambitious Arts Education Program, modeled on the prestigious Lincoln Center Institute for Arts in Education Program, provides Long Island school districts with high-caliber weekday performances which support and expands schools' curricula through the use of study guides, in-school workshops, and extensive teacher training. Tilles Center strives to nurture the audiences and the visual and performing artists of tomorrow through such outreach activities as "Performance for Schools," "Tilles Scholars," an annual residence program with the New York Philharmonic and regular student art exhibitions.

These programs are successful thanks to the many volunteers who devote their time and energy to enhancing and sustaining the Performing Arts.

Two popular volunteer organizations that many retirees are active in are the Smithsonian Institute and its extensive museum network and the Memorial Sloan-Kettering Hospital organization. A little history on both may interest readers as they are representative of other associations that have volunteer opportunities available on a local and national level. Volunteers have provided a primary means of support for the Smithsonian since its establishment in the mid 19th century. "Strong volunteer partnerships are essential for the Institution to successfully carry out its work." Some of the opportunities are:

- **Docent Programs** – Docents are volunteer teachers who provide group learning experiences in the form of museum tours, demonstrations, or instructions in special activity areas.

- **Museum Information Desk Program** – Volunteers in this program work at a museum information desk where they are on the front lines interacting with visitors of all ages on a daily basis.

- **Telephone Information Program** – These volunteers handle public inquiries from around the world on all aspects of the Smithsonian activities, administrative functions, and services.

- **Special Support Programs** – Offers volunteers an opportunity to enhance the museum experience for visitors in various ways, from assisting with hands-on activities to providing the staff with administrative support.

- **Citizen Science** – Offers special opportunities to assist in the various research programs.

- **Behind-the-Scenes Volunteer Program** – Offers challenging alternatives to public-oriented volunteer activities. Opportunities are generally available in: archives; libraries; administrative offices; conservation laboratories; and curatorial divisions related to art, history, and science collections.

- **Seasonal Programs** – Includes summer opportunities including the Smithsonian Folklife Festival, which is presented for a two-week period during the summer. This endeavor relies upon the services of hundreds of volunteers who assist with every aspect of the annual celebration including folk crafts, music, food, and culture. For more information e-mail info@si.edu. The opportunities at the Smithsonian are endless for volunteers. The same e-mail address will get information on volunteer activities at the Smithsonian Zoo and the Institute's locations around the country.

I was introduced to the Memorial Sloan-Kettering organization under very unhappy circumstances. In my younger days when my hair was noticeably red, I was guilty of spending too much time at Coney Island Beach lying in the sun with no hat and only the hair on my arms and legs protecting my very light skin. The expression "Play today, pay tomorrow" is certainly the case with skin cancer. My many visits to their Hauppauge, Long Island, facility to get rid of the unwelcomed visitors on my body made me realize their importance in body cancer preventive maintenance, and the organization's "cutting edge" research and technology. The institute has a unique volunteer program, which is outlined on their website www.MSKCC.org as follows:

> Since its establishment more than 60 years ago, Memorial Sloan-Kettering's Department of Volunteer Resources has grown to include many participants who donate a combined 75,000 hours of service per year.
> The volunteer department is an integral part of the culture of the organization. Our volunteers provide services that enhance the quality of life in the hospital through activities ranging from transporting patients to staffing the Thrift Shop.
> We also offer several specialized volunteer opportunities. Cancer survivors treated at Memorial Sloan-Kettering and their caregivers may participate in the "Patient-to-Patient Support Program." Volunteers with writing backgrounds can share their expertise with patients through the "Visible Ink Program." In addition those who have certified therapy dogs can interact with patients through the "Caring Canine Program."
> Alongside outstanding medical care, volunteers' humanity and spirit are at the core of the organization. Our volunteers vary in age and background, from

high school students fulfilling service requirement to employed and retired adults wishing to give back to the community. Each member of our dynamic group is committed to providing a welcoming and compassionate environment for patients, families, and visitors.

Volunteers serve at least three hours per week, and must maintain a good attendance record. Though we accept volunteers for all shifts, our greatest need is for those who can work Monday through Friday between the hours of 9:00 AM to 5:00 PM. Our adult volunteers generally commit to at least one year of service, while the average tenure of a volunteer is more than two years; some continue to serve for decades.

It is estimated that over 63 million Americans will donate their time this year for an average of 34.2 hours a year, providing $163 billion worth of services annually, free of charge. So if any readers are feeling bashful or uneasy about volunteering, they shouldn't; just ask your neighbors, I'm sure you'll find many of them are already donating their time at churches, hospitals, museums, and art centers. Two good website to explore for volunteer placement are: www.mygooddeed.org and www.serve.gov.

Chapter Five – Part-Time Jobs for Retirees

Whether your needs are financial or you simply enjoy having a place to go to every day to mingle with coworkers, being employed on a part time basis after retirement can be a smart decision. But continuing to work doesn't necessarily condemn you to a 9 to 5-grind.

Many of my friends have combined part-time jobs with pleasure. Cruise ships have offered them an opportunity to earn pocket money while traveling around the world. The ships provide room and board and the use of the facilities when the workers are not plying their trade. In many cases the retirees escort tour guides on sightseeing trips, which gives them an opportunity to travel in style at no charge. Some of the job openings, descriptions, and requirements that cruise lines use for hiring aboard their ships are listed below:

- **Golf Instructors**—The job entails operating golf simulators, playing golf with passengers, and other cruise staff duties; the instructors must be fluent in English. These positions call for very independent individuals who have the capacity and patience to teach at all levels of the game and must have the ability to interact in social situations with the cruise line's guests and staff personnel. They must also possess the motivation and business acumen to operate an on-board operation in its entirety, including self-promotion and instruction, and must also assist with shore excursions.

- **Scuba Diving/Water Sports Instructors**—They conduct daily diving and snorkeling programs and meticulously maintain equipment. Diving instructor's certificate and Cardiopulmonary Resuscitation (CPR) and First Aid certificates are required.

- **Bridge Instructors**—Must be experienced bridge teachers and ACBL-certified directors who have achieved Life Masters standing. The directors must be proficient at both Standard American and ACOL and must be excellent socializers with outgoing, dynamic personalities. The directors will be responsible for teaching bridge for intermediate and advanced players followed by afternoons of duplicate and social bridge play on each day the ship is at sea and on select port days. Depending on the ship, the instructors may also be asked to offer lessons to absolute beginners. The bridge instructors will also be responsible for submitting any master points earned by passengers who are members of the ACBL.

- **Texas 42 Instructors**—Often referred to as "the National Game of Texas." It's a popular domino game similar in strategy to the card game of bridge, but not as complicated. Experts of the game will teach passengers how to play and improve their games and will host game plays on each sea day. The instructors must be friendly, flexible, and excellent socializers with outgoing, dynamic personalities. The instructors will be responsible for teaching lessons to absolute beginners and intermediate and advanced players. Lessons are followed by game plays on each of the days that the ship is at sea and on select port days. The instructors will also be responsible for consumable supplies, such as dominos, pads of paper, and pens.

- **Arts and Craft Instructors**—Must be friendly, patient, and creative and enjoy teaching craft projects to the guests. The instructors will be responsible for providing the supplies needed to make the crafts and must prepare an original project for each class. Examples of craft lessons may include "The Joy of Scrapbooking," "Easy-to-Make Christmas ornaments," or "The Art of Watercolor."

- **Caricature Artists**—They serve as part of the ship's enrichment staff. Everyone loves to bring home a fun, visual memory of their cruise vacation, which is why the artists are so popular aboard ships. During a cruise assignment, a Caricaturist's responsibilities include quick and fun drawings, which are offered at no charge to passengers. Usually the Caricaturist is located in a popular high traffic area of the ship sketching individuals, as well as groups of family and friends traveling together. As a general rule of thumb, less than five minutes should be spent on each drawing. The artists must be friendly, creative, and have excellent social skills.

- **Dance Instructors**—Should apply as a couple and must be proficient in all dance styles—from the classics to the current fads—and offer lessons to passengers of all ages and abilities. One day might feature lessons on traditional ballroom dance techniques, including Waltz and the Foxtrot, while the next might be spent teaching line dancing or the Macarena. Dance instructors must be outgoing, friendly, and prepared for any unusual situations on the dance floors, such as students falling. They may also be asked to assist with shore excursions. Some ships allow instructors to give private lessons and pocket the money. Certainly a great way to earn money while enjoying one's self.

The opportunities for part-time work on cruise ships are endless. Where else can retirees spend time teaching what they enjoy, while traveling around the world and eating wonderful food and also, where the opportunity is available, earn extra pocket money? I have a friend that has been a dance host on ships for the last six years, and plans on continuing for as long as his legs hold out. The amazing thing about him is that he has managed to maintain his weight, considering the availability of the tempting food on large cruise ships. If anyone is interested it's easy to find job openings by accessing cruise lines' websites.

Of the many part-time opportunities, some of the more popular that combine flexible working hours with pleasure for retirees are the following:

- **Librarians**—The duties include answering customers' questions, shelving books, helping patrons check out books, tracking overdue material, and sending notices, as well as cataloging and keeping an eye out for lost and damaged items.

- **Bookkeepers**—Usually the opportunities are with small businesses and entails a full sweep of financial recordkeeping. Some of the duties may include establishing and maintaining inventory database systems, tracing accounts receivable and accounts payable, maintaining checking and savings accounts, producing financial reports, following up on delinquent accounts, and assisting in audits and reviews. Needless to say, this type of work requires previous experience in bookkeeping and computer applications. The old method of handwritten information data entry is rapidly disappearing, so it's essential to be familiar with computer bookkeeping to secure this type of position.

- **Personal and Home Care Aides**—This type of work typically includes caring for the elderly, ill, or disabled with everyday activities ranging from bathing and getting dressed to running errands. Other duties might include light housekeeping, companionship, grocery shopping, meal preparation, and medication monitoring.

For those who prefer working at home there are many opportunities available. Of course some of the advantages are working in a familiar surrounding, no longer having to commute or dealing with annoying co-workers. Working at home certainly has a nice ring to it— sometimes too nice. **Work-at-home scams** are something that must be kept in mind when considering allowing your home to be used for someone else's business. The Federal Trade Commission (FTC) states that the number of scams reported have doubled over the last year. Two glaring red flags to look for are jobs touted via e-mail that promise to pay more than you've ever dreamed of, and firms that charge a fee to obtain more information about a job or paying for supplies. "Payment for the privilege of working is rarely acceptable, in our view," says Christine Durst, an Internet fraud and safety expert and co-founder of "ratracerevebellion.com," a website on home-based work that screens job leads for at-home work.

That being said, there are certainly many legitimate at-home jobs waiting to be filled by seniors, but checking them out for scams is imperative. Some nice safe job opportunities are:

- **Customer Service Representatives**—It is surprising how many overseas jobs have returned to the United States from India, the Philippines, and other offshore locations in this field. Many companies such as Home Depot, Hilton Hotels, American Airlines, and 1-800-flowers hire representatives directly, but there is a growing market for **virtual call center operators**. One of the largest is Alpine Access at WWW.alpineaccess.com, which is headquartered in Denver and has over 4,500 part-time at-home employees in 1,700 cities across the United States. Those applying for the jobs must have an up-to-date computer, a high-speed Internet connection, a dedicated land line, a telephone headset, and a quiet place to work. In general they answer incoming calls, take orders, track existing orders, and in some cases troubleshoot and help out with technical support. Some of the advantages of this type of at-home work are flexible hours, lucrative hourly wages, and, in many cases, vacations and fringe benefits. In addition to Alpine, other virtual call center operators' websites include WWW.Liveops.com, WWW.WestatHome.com, and WWW.WorkingSolutions. com. It is estimated that there are over 50,000 people employed in the U.S. as operators; the number is growing as our citizens continue to complain about their difficulties with understanding the foreign accents of outsourced workers.

- **Virtual Assistants**—The main purpose of the position is to assist busy business executives who do not have in-house staff to attend to various administrative functions. The position has become available due to small companies trying to keep permanent overhead costs down. Training programs are available at community colleges, many of which offer online certifications. The duties of an assistant range from making traveling arrangements to sending out letters and other support services which are easily handled remotely via e-mail and telephone. Job openings can be explored at www.virtualassistanjobs.com and at www.teamdoubleclick.com.

- **Online Tutoring**—Private online tutoring sessions with students is a growing job market due to the super-competitive college admissions programs. The subjects in demand are the core topics: world history, physics, science, math, and English. Foreign languages especially are seeing an increase in demand for this kind of service. An online employer at www.Tutor.com offers one-on-one help to students and is set up so that when students need help with their homework, they enter their grade level and subject of interest into their computer log-on screen. Based on the information, an appropriate tutor (the firm has over two thousand on board) is assigned and a relationship is born. Some other tutoring firms with job openings are found at www.Kaplan.com and www.SmarThinking.com.

In the part-time job market some of the most exciting opportunities have become available for **snowbirds.** With more and more seniors flying to Florida and Arizona during the cold winter months, jobs in their winter states are plentiful and require only a little or no experience. For instance, Disney in Florida and California have job openings that run the gamut from dressing as a member of the mouse family to escorting tourists around the vast entertainment facilities. Some of the available jobs in both resorts are: loading and unloading passengers from rides, doling out costumes at wardrobe facilities across the parks, staffing gift shops and concessions, and being costumed cast members throughout the parks. For those who like being around airplanes, there are also openings for airport representatives who greet guests at arrival and usher them to waiting shuttles. Of course there are many opportunities for responsible seniors in the resorts transportation departments, as older and wiser is preferred to younger and somewhat carefree drivers. Checking the Walt Disney World website for job openings and qualifications is easily accomplished for anyone that "Believes in magic," and loves dealing with children from one to ninety.

Disney doesn't have a monopoly on seasonal employment opportunities at resorts. All kinds of jobs become available across the Sunbelt when snowbirds flock down South. Jobs as bartenders or gardeners to parking valets and room cleaners are in demand during the winter season, at very lucrative pay rates. If a senior loves golf or tennis there might be openings in pro shops or as a caddy or ball retriever. Gambling fans should investigate casinos as should boating enthusiasts who will find many job openings at marinas.

For those that have good eyesight, a valid driver's license, and enjoy the open road, delivering cars up and down the East Coast can pay very nicely, while picking up frequent flyer miles on the return trips. The busiest months are December and May, but departures and returns are ongoing, though at a reduced rate between those peak months. These jobs can net a driver up to $200-a-day, with all costs paid including service to airports and air flights on return trips.

To emphasis that dreams can come true in our golden years, I know someone who is a diehard baseball fan that was able to get a job at a spring training camp for a Major League Baseball team. This relatively quiet person has become the most gregarious person I know and can't stop talking about the fun and satisfaction that he gets from being around baseball stars and fans. Some job openings are: ushering fans to their seats, selling programs, fielding ticket inquiries, working concession booths, and driving players and staff to and from airports. There are many job opportunities for seniors with experience in sales as seasonal assistants, helping in marketing and special promotions. Former Information Technicians can usually find seasonal work making sure wireless networks and computers run smoothly for the press and players. While duties might be routine, the chance to rub shoulders with a World Series ring bearer is certainly a dream come true for any baseball fan. A good place to find job openings is the Major League Baseball's website; click on the link to your favorite baseball team, then click on "job opportunities," and if you are one of the lucky ones, you'll be on your way to having a **dream come true.**

Chapter Six – Intellectual Decisions Must Be Made

Much of my writing so far has been related to the fun things that concern retirees. It is appropriate now to delve into the not-so-happy topics, those that require changing how we think and our capacity to try to anticipate our futures in a financial and physical way. Where do we begin when discussing computer technology and how it impacts our everyday lives, whether through laptops, desktops, iPods, telephones, or the multitude of other applications that are computer software based? In the year 2000 I wrote a book, *Business Infrastructure in a Computer Environment*. At that time, personal computers were in an experimental stage, with initial users exploring their usefulness in the commercial and personal user markets. As a matter of fact, IBM gave away most of its rights to personal computer software development as it was convinced that the **small babies** would be a distraction from their profitable, large mainframe computer markets. They in effect restricted the sales of their personal computers to a handful of resellers, thereby limiting their market and allowing an opening for other manufacturers, such as Epson, Panasonic, H.P., and Dell to surpass them in the personal computer marketplace. Their thinking unfortunately has carried over into the minds of many people who still believe that personal computers have no place in their lives or who refuse to experiment with the amazing technology. A copy of the covers of my book *Business Infrastructure in a Computer Environment* follows:

Within the structure of today's increasingly complex corporate world, author Michael Bivona's *Business Infrastructure: In a Computer Environment* is a blueprint for success.

As technology and finance shape tomorrow's companies, organizational issues become more and more crucial. The author's analysis clearly shows how wise development can translate into increased profits and productivity. The complexities of infrastructure are examined with regard to internal operations, such as customer service departments.

This is a book that is certain to be welcomed by managers and supervisors in large and small firms; and a must for young people starting out in the business world.

Many seniors are reluctant to experiment with a computer mouse or keyboard, and seem to avoid contact with PCs at any cost, probably because they are intimidated by the keyboard and fear that they are not capable of mastering the equipment. What they don't seem to realize is that the **little babies** already have an impact on almost every facet of their lives even though they don't own one. There are different kinds of computers other than the personal ones that help us in more ways than we realize. There are basically four kinds that impact our lives in different ways, in different places and for different purposes. So, what are they, and how do they affect our lives?

- **Personal Computers**—These are used by one person at a time and are probably found on desktops in a majority of homes in the United States and other first-world countries. Many have additional microprocessors so that they can perform special tasks like graphics, math, sounds, etc. They are also used in businesses, and have many features that help with simple to complicated tasks. These tasks may include word-processing, storing information in a file, researching subjects, etc. They can also be used for educational purposes, leisure (games), and listening to music, watching movies, Skype, e-mail, accessing the Internet, and much more. Under this type there are desktops, laptops, notebook computers, and PDAs.

- **Mainframes**—This type of computer is the fastest of them all. These are significantly larger than their little sisters with some having almost infinite storage capacities. Some mainframes may have hundreds or more people at the same time accessing their intelligence and sharing information. Supercomputers, the fastest of the mainframes, are used to do even more complex projects like the design of aircraft or building skyscrapers. These computers are primarily used for commercial and government purposes and can cost into the millions of dollars.

- **Dedicated Computers**—These are special-purpose machines. Some examples are word processors and video-game units. The smallest of the video-game units are battery-operated ones such as Gameboy. Larger ones are plug-ins into televisions like Xbox and PlayStation. The largest of these are found in game arcades and gambling casinos.

- **Embedded Computers**—These are control units built into the devices they control. Examples are telephones, digital watches, and VCRs. Aircraft and robots also have embedded computers, while guided missiles use them to find their targets.

So as we can see, many of us, although we do not own or use personal computers, do use computer technology in our everyday lives. As a matter of fact, who of us hasn't watched the weather reports on television and enjoyed the information that was derived from mainframes connected throughout the world? Who of us hasn't played with video games, if not our own then with those of our grandchildren? Who of us hasn't taken their grandchildren to an arcade and joined them in playing with the amazing games that light up the environment and increase the noise level beyond our tolerance?

Considering that we are dependent on computers in our everyday lives without owning or actually using them, I think the next logical step for those who do not possess the magical machines should be to go out and buy one. Well, what does all this have to do with making life a little more intellectual and interesting during retirement? Remember the article by Professor Richard Powers, "Use it or Lose it," that I wrote about previously? According to Professor Powers, the more new things we learn the more building blocks get added to our brain; the more building blocks added to our brain the longer our intellectual awareness will prevail. When it comes to learning new things, I can't think of a better place than in your home maneuvering through a personal computer and exploring the infinite possibilities for intellectual growth. Again, you may ask, what does this have to do with senior citizens? The answer is obvious: at that time of life when our brains begin to play tricks on us, what better way to forestall the inevitable then to force new brain cells to develop in our minds? An example of increasing our prowess with the use of PCs and having fun at the same time is using Skype. This is accomplished by having cameras attached to personal computers that allow people to see and converse with each other free of charge. In our case, we had a new grandson Michael born on October 1, 2010 in Atlanta, Ga. We live in Long Island N.Y. and communicate with our daughter and her son almost every day, watching our baby make sounds and take baths without being with him, but certainly enjoying his experience as if we were there. Facebook is another fun computer application through which people can keep in touch with family and friends at no charge. It seems that today the only way to keep in touch with the young people in our lives on an ongoing basis is to participate with them in their love affair with Facebook.

Again, what does owning a computer have to do with retirement plans? The reality is that it makes life a lot easier, as I found in my case. I'm not as patient as I was in days gone-by and find it a lot easier to use the Internet to get information, buy products, and deal with companies than I did by calling on the telephone or shopping at stores. In addition, traveling information, movie schedules and reviews, and restaurants and their menus are at your fingertips as well as most other information that we might need. The bottom line is it makes us more **self-reliant** at a time in life when we're expected to be more dependent on others for many of our necessities. As previously mentioned, the many job opportunities that are available to seniors can easily be accessed if a computer is at hand. The advantages are endless, especially when trying to decide where to spend our retirement years without having to travel to faraway places to investigate for ourselves. Today one can use virtual reality applications to actually see houses and their contents, get pricing information, travel through neighborhoods, and, finally, visit only those that look like possible places to live during retirement. What an amazing time saver at that point in our lives when time is so precious and running out at what seems to be an accelerated pace.

We shouldn't discount the importance of computer use in the financial activities that seem to become more burdensome in our senior years. Especially useful is the reduction in record keeping, more so for those of us who are snowbirds. When we became members of the winged family about ten years ago, I was overwhelmed with writing duplicate monthly checks for our telephone, electricity, insurance, heat, air conditioning, mortgage payments, and my other miscellaneous bills. Living at two locations compounded the dreaded task of paying additional monthly bills that included snow removal, which I used to do myself when I spent the white months in New York, and house-sitting bills for winter and summer house sitters. Keeping track of bills, paying them manually with hand-written checks, inserting the bills and payments into envelops after addressing them, and finally after stamping the envelopes, posting them at the most convenient mail box, became an overwhelming task. Making sure that all of my bills were paid promptly became a "pain-in-the-butt" due to the multitude and the different times that bills had to be paid. A nightmare was when there were disputes with creditors; especially aggravating was proving that bills were paid and trying to explain to them why they didn't receive the payment or received it late, which resulted in late payment charges.

What to do? Considering that I was retired from the computer industry, one would assume that I paid my bills with the help of a computer over the Internet long before retiring. Well, I guess I'm as guilty as the next person when it comes to using a PC to break old habits. Out of desperation, I went to my bank and told them that they must come up with a better method for me to satisfy my obligations before I went crazy trying to keep up with the ever-growing stack of paperwork. Their answer was quite clear; they had a better method, at no charge, and began indoctrinating me in all the reasons why I should be paying my bills from my PC keyboard instead of handwriting them from my checkbook. It didn't take too long for me to appreciate the advantages of not having to write checks manually, of not having to insert bills into envelopes, of not having to address envelopes, of not having to buy and place stamps on envelopes, and then finally posting the mail. Just saving on postage stamps, which seemed to be increasing in price every year, was worth changing my life-long habit of doing things by hand and in a familiar way.

I know that many retirees already use computers to pay their bills. Some even have telephone payments set up with their banks or even have direct payment withdrawals from their checking accounts. If a person doesn't have too many bills to pay, telephone payments can be an option to using a computer, but is not as efficient and requires accumulating bills and calling several times a month to have timely payments made. For those who have direct withdrawals, I give them credit for being very trusting; I'm never comfortable with having money withdrawn from my bank accounts by vendors automatically without my first reviewing bills, and it certainly becomes very frustrating resolving bill disputes with creditors over the phone after a bill is paid, that is, if you can find a person on the other end that understands English.

For those who don't use the telephone or direct withdrawals methods, or who wish to change, I'm going to go through the steps that led me to being a less stressed person in my senior years by eliminating a task that I detested. My first step was to set up a creditor list for my monthly payments for telephone bills, electric bills, garbage collection, etc., by name, address, and my customer numbers. **How sweet it was** when I paid my first series of bills without having to touch my checkbook. I selected the creditors that I wanted to pay, they appeared one by one on my computer screen, I inserted the dollar amounts and the dates that I wanted the bank to make payments, and *voila*, electronic instructions to the bank were written in "computer stone." One major advantage that I noticed right away was that if the payee had what is known as "Electronic Transfers," I was able to set up a payment for two days prior to the due date and not worry about the payment ever being late, as I had proof at my fingertips as to when my bank transferred the funds directly into the payee's account. Next, I set up automatic recurring payments for automobiles, mortgages, insurance, and association fees; being that the payments are for the same amounts each time, it was easy to schedule them for monthly, quarterly, or whatever timeframe was necessary to satisfy the obligation. **Bingo!** After setting up the scheduled payments, the bank honors your payment requests without missing a beat and at every time period issues a check to the payee without my getting involved. After my computerized payment method became routine, I felt the stress of my monthly bill-paying nightmare disappear. A major bonus was that if I wanted to know if a bill had been paid and the date it cleared the creditor's bank, by the touch of the proper keys on my PC, I could access the information and have the ability to send a copy of the check or receipt to anyone that claimed a payment wasn't received. Another bonus is that there are no more checks to store as the bank keeps all of your records in their electronic files. A really sweet feature is that if you miss a payment, whether it's because you didn't receive a bill or just plain forgot to make it, the system could be set up to remind you that a payment was missed.

A real efficient time saver was when paying subsequent bills. If the payments were not on the "Recurring List," which means they are paid automatically without my help, when preparing to pay a current bill, the last payment date and amount appears on the screen next to the current information that is being input into the computer. This helps you determine if a previous payment was missed, or if the current bill is out of line with a previous one, or if the bill is a duplicate. Another great feature is that the amounts paid to individual vendors are accumulated and you know at any given moment how much was paid to each. This is especially useful when planning future spending budgets and in determining how much money is needed during retirement years to live comfortably.

Computerized banking almost forces people to check their bank accounts frequently to make sure that payments are made as scheduled and that deposits are recorded correctly. You go from being an active player to an overseer; your main purpose is to make sure that your instructions have been followed correctly. I check my account almost every day, which makes me aware of my financial obligations and status. It is imperative that seniors control their own finances as long as they are able, and keeping an eye on our bank accounts frequently is certainly one way of accomplishing that, rather than on a monthly basis when a printed statement is delivered to our home by mail with information that is after the fact and the bank transactions are far from our thoughts or concern. Another thing to keep in mind is that a laptop computer can be taken with you wherever you travel, and accessing the Internet with today's high-speed routers makes the experience of paying bills and getting other important information a pleasant one when away from the comfort of your home. When we are on the road for extended periods of time, I call vendors to determine how much I owe them or, where the opportunity is available, I access my account on the creditor's website and then pay my bill from the data of those sources.

Unfortunately, as time goes by we may not have the wherewithal to continue handling our own finances efficiently. I can best explain the importance of computerized banking for some people by using an example of when we cared for a relative that was disabled and not capable of handling her finances. She lived in Florida; we were located in New York, so tending to her financial needs in person was not feasible. Putting the relative in a nursing home was not an option, so we arranged for in-home care with a group of girls to attend to her needs. They rotated shifts and made sure that the necessary care was provided around the clock. Now the question of paying household bills and the caretakers' fees became a problem as we were not nearby to monitor firsthand what was going on in Florida. What we did is open a bank account for her and link it to our checking account. By doing this, we were able to keep track on our PC of the amount of funds that were necessary every month to pay bills and would transfer the necessary sums by pressing a few keys on our computer. In addition to making cash transfers easy, we were able to see the back and front of checks that the caretaker responsible for paying bills issued for the benefit of our relative. Of course, we made several visits a year to Florida to spend time with her and to keep in touch with the girls in the network that were caring for our loved one. In our case, a computer made a difficult situation manageable and she was able to spend her remaining days on earth in her home, as she had wished.

I know that most seniors use direct bank deposits for their monthly social security checks. Many may even use the direct deposit method for their pension income. But what about other income that is received through the mail and requires preparing a deposit slip and a visit to the local bank, such as dividends earned, annuity checks, interest income, bank transfers, and any other repetitive sums that are received on a regular basis in the form of a check that must be deposited or mailed to the recipients bank? I'd like to list some of the advantages of direct deposits for those who are skeptical about losing control of their deposits if they don't receive the piece of paper, and that's all that it is, a piece of paper:

- There are no checks to get lost or stolen.
- Payments reach accounts on the day they are issued—even if you are out of town, sick, or unable to get to your bank.
- Many banks offer free or lower-cost checking to customers with direct deposits because it saves them the cost of processing paper checks.
- Direct deposits can help prevent you from bouncing checks as the deposits are recorded on the day issued.
- It saves trips to the bank and helps avoid the usual long lines at the teller's window.
- For seniors that are disabled or unable to get to a bank to make deposits, establishing a direct system is a "God-send."
- With the use of a PC, you can determine if the deposits were recorded on time and plan payments accordingly.
- Guess what? You don't have to keep a checkbook balance; the information is at your fingertips at the keyboard.

Online banking can be a senior citizen's best friend; after trying it, you'll wonder how you lived without it for so long and maintained your sanity. With online banking, most of your financial life is in one neat "virtual" place with access 24/7 from the comfort of your home. This is especially convenient for those who can no longer drive, are disabled, or have arthritic fingers and find it difficult to write checks legibly. Bills can be paid day or night with just a few clicks on a keyboard, and reviewing your account statement to determine if bills were paid and to keep apprised of account balances becomes routine and sets the stage for proper budgeting of retirement funds. If you are comfortable with e-bill payments, many companies offer the option of having you sign up for their automatic deductions from your bank account of current bills such as telephone, electric, insurance, association fees, garbage removal, etc. This puts you in a position of supervising your bill payments instead of getting involved with their payments. With online banking, including direct deposits in your life, determining how stable your finances are for retirement becomes a "no brainer." With a little ingenuity, eliminating or reducing expenses that are no longer necessary and forecasting how much money we should transfer into our checking accounts to live comfortable is reduced to a manageable task that most people are able to handle with ease. If a person is not comfortable about doing the arithmetic, they have the information readily available from their computers to seek out a financial adviser and discuss budgeting based on the data that has been accumulated over the years.

A successful and fulfilling retirement means different things to different folks. It may mean going from a full-time career into part-time work or spending more time with family and friends, or starting a garden or making regular visits to tennis courts or golf courses. Once the decision is made as to what may make you happy in retirement, it's important to know how to get there financially. The first step is to write your objectives down, listing the most important goals first without considering the cost. Try to concentrate on the top five important things you would like to do, such as travel to the Italian Lakes in Northern Italy or biking through the United States. Be specific when making your list, for instance, volunteer one day a week at the local hospital or fund raising for cancer research with Sloan Kettering. The more specific you are the easier it will be to determine what it will cost when you begin budgeting for your golden years. If you haven't determined what your goals are, start outlining how you would like to enjoy your retirement in a general way. Whatever your situation, make a list and after giving it some thought, start developing specific things you would like to be involved with when the time comes for you to retire.

Listing your assets and anticipated income is the next important step in determining how you will live, not within your dreams, but within your budget. It's easy enough to ascertain where our assets are and the income that is received from pensions, IRAs, interest, dividends, and nontraditional sources. With the information that is readily available if we have a PC and the use of online banking that I mentioned previously, gathering information to formulate a realistic budget becomes easier. An important consideration when developing a budget is when to start collecting Social Security and how that decision will determine the amount of money that you will be receiving for the rest of your life. It would be nice if we saved enough money to retire in comfort without considering Social Security benefits, but unfortunately most people must consider that income to make their retirement plans a reality and to have some degree of financial freedom. The longer people are able to wait to claim Social Security benefits, the greater the amount for them and their families. An example is: A widow or widower whose spouse claims benefits at full retirement age or older gets 100-percent of the benefits. If the benefits are claimed sooner they are penalized by not receiving credits that are available to those who wait and their payments are decreased considerably. A good place to determine benefits is at WWW.AARP.com and accessing "AARP's Social Security Benefits Calculator," the information will help in determining the best time to claim benefits to maximize and coincide with your plans. Whether a person is married, single, widowed, or divorced, it usually pays to wait, if possible, before claiming benefits.

To get the most out of retirement, and life in general, people should try to be as healthy as possible. No one enjoys doctors' visits, but a little bit of preventive maintenance can go a long way in life, especially during retirement. Having regular medical and dental checkups and following doctors' advice should become routine in our lives as we get older. Regular checkups and living a healthier life will go a long way to stretching Social Security benefits and annuity income that are based on longevity; the longer you live the more dough you get, which in turn will assure retirees more financial freedom and a better life. Of course, we can't predict what our health will be at any point in time, but taking precautionary steps certainly won't do anyone any harm, and in many cases may prevent serious illnesses from developing and changing the quality of our lives in our senior years. A simple annual flu shot and an extended pneumonia shot will go a long way in keeping those diseases from entering peoples' lives and possibly changing their futures into something they certainly didn't plan for when anticipating a good life during retirement. Paramount to maintaining good health is building a network of good doctors that have passed the test of time where our medical needs are concerned. We should develop relationships with doctors that are associated with the top hospitals in our area. Never, never choose a doctor or hospital based solely on the fact that they are conveniently located close to your home. I have known people who have done just that and didn't live to regret it (pun intended). In my experience, I've found that choosing a top hospital first and then getting recommendations from them usually resulted in our having doctors that have been with us for many years, who in turn have recommended other doctors associated with the top hospitals and who have cared for our medical needs far beyond our expectations. My wife and I over the years have accumulated a list of doctors that cover almost all the specialties: internists, cardiologists, dermatologists, oncologists, urologists, optometrists, and gynecologists. What made our experience even more complicated was the fact that we are snowbirds and required doctors in New York and Florida. To round out our medical list we had to locate dentists that were up-to-date with their treatments and the latest dental technology. It seems that Barbara and I spend an inordinate amount of time at the dentist trying to prolong the life or our rapidly decaying teeth with filings, root canals, bridges, caps, and implants. Having dentists with up-to-date equipment resulted in our spending less time in the dreaded treatment chairs, as X-rays and most other procedures take a lot less time. Unfortunately most dentist visits aren't covered by Medicare or supplements, so getting your teeth shipshape when you might have dental coverage prior to retirement is wise. If unable to acquire dental coverage during retirement, it is imperative to include the estimated cost of dental care when developing a budget, as it's one of the most expensive costs that we have to deal with in our battle to retain the white pearls in our mouth during our senior years.

Getting rid of debt before retiring makes budgeting a lot easier and certainly reduces stress that retirees do not need in their golden years. An example of how dangerous debt can be during retirement is illustrated by using a $500-a-month car payment. The payment is fixed while the income to pay for it may not be. If income is from interest or dividends, then any reduction in the rate of their return can cause the debt to possibly go unpaid or to be paid out of principal, which in turn can be the beginning of the depletion of assets that are the basis of the income that is necessary for financial security during retirement. Many people pay off most of their debts before retiring even if it means remaining in the workforce longer than planned. We all have experienced the interest rates in our savings accounts going below one percent, while many of us have been affected by public corporations reducing or eliminating their dividends. The two lessons that we should learn are to stay as debt free as possible prior to retirement, and not to rely on the stability of bank interest or dividend payments when developing a budget. Social Security benefits, annuities, reliable bond interest, and Treasuries are much more stable choices unless you plan on using principal to supplement other revenue.

One of the first things we learn in life is that our decisions, good or bad, stay with us for a long time. Poor decisions not only seem to stick around forever, but seem to be difficult to overcome. As odd as it may seem, most people decide to retire based on their age, which is a poor decision, when they should really decide when the time is right based on how much money they have and the ability of their assets to support them comfortably through retirement, which could be 10, 20, or even 30-years. Retirement is about independence, not age, and money is what determines the amount of independence a person will have. Now here comes the tricky part. When should people start to switch their saving and investments to conservative income producing ones? And what options do they have? We all know that risk is an integral part of investing. When we were in our thirties and forties we could afford to take greater risks in the hope of receiving greater returns. If we lost money, we had decades to try to recover. But when we approach our 50s and 60s, we need to aggressively shift out of potentially volatile investments and into more conservative income producing ones. Large losses during retirement can be devastating to our pockets and stressful to our health at a point in time when we do not have the stamina or quickness of mind to sustain such unwelcomed events. Consider the arithmetic of a major loss. Let's say you have a $1 million dollar portfolio and lose 50% percent of it, reducing your holdings to half that amount. If you subsequently regain 50%, your portfolio value will be worth $750,000. To become whole would require a 100% percent increase, therefore, the greater the loss, the more difficult it will become to get back to where you started, especially when nearing retirement.

The 2008-2009 market crash caught many people that were planning retirement "flat footed." Many of the 78 million boomers approaching retirement got caught up in the **"make a quick buck in the stock market"** frenzy, along with everyone else that didn't learn from the 2000-2003 stock market crash. Most of their stock holdings were in growth securities instead of more conservative investments, resulting in many of them having to postpone their retirement plans and continue working. It's easy in hindsight to discuss how people should have conducted themselves financially after a crisis. But what steps should people take and where should they place their funds when preparing for retirement? I can only discuss how we planned for our retirement and sustained only minor reductions in our portfolios during the aforementioned stock market crashes.

Being a Certified Public Accountant set the stage for my being a little more conservative than most. Till age 50 most of my investments were in aggressive blue chip stocks that paid dividends. I very rarely invested in stocks unless they had a history of paying dividends consistently. After age 50, I used a formula that I learned through my dealings in the financial community, and that is to invest your age in quality bonds, including municipal bonds and the balance in conservative dividend-paying blue chip stocks. So at age 50, my portfolio included that percentage of bonds and 50% in dividend-paying conservative blue chip stocks. As time progressed, my holdings in bonds continued to match my age; at age 60, I decided to invest almost all of my portfolios in bonds, as my retirement time was nearing and I was more concerned about income flow than asset growth.

Sounds good? Well, not so good; my 401K plan and our IRAs had their ups and downs like everyone else, but we stayed our course without panicking and were fortunate enough to reach retirement with a degree of financial security. You might ask what bonds we decided to invest in. Many years ago, I fell in love with the income flow from tax-free Closed End Municipal Bond Funds for my regular investment portfolio and blue chip corporate debt for our IRAs and my 401K plan. In addition to what I thought were relatively safe investments, the income from the municipal bonds were tax free and the interest from the corporate debt that accrued in our retirement accounts was not taxed until we began our monthly required distributions at 70 and 1/2 years of age. My plan may seem too good to be true, so a brief rundown of what these types of investments are about is in order.

Closed End Municipal Bond Funds—Municipal bonds, also called munis, are bonds issued by a state, city, or other local governments, and are traded on the three major stock exchanges, just like regular stocks. Issuers usually include cities, counties, redevelopment agencies, school districts, and any other government entity within a state that is authorized to borrow money in that fashion. Municipal bonds may be general obligations of the issuer secured by specified revenues or can be bonds for specific projects within the states, such as construction of bridges and tunnels. Interest income received by the holders of the bonds is often exempt from federal income tax and from the income tax of the state in which it is issued if the holder is a resident of that state. The bonds usually pay interest semi-annually until maturity then the face amount of the bond is paid to the holder. A taxable equivalent of a bond yielding 5% for someone in the 31% tax bracket is 7.2% and higher if the bond is for the state that the holder is domiciled. Tax-free munis pay an interest rate higher than T-Notes and T-Bills because they are considered to have a greater risk of failure. While unusual, it's possible for the issuer to go broke and declare bankruptcy. To reduce the risk, many investors buy municipal bond funds that pool together portfolios of bonds from different sources within a state or by combining munis from different states into a national fund. Many funds can have 20 or more different bonds in their portfolios, which satisfy many investors who like diversification and safety all wrapped up into one neat package. Some funds are actually insured as to principal, but since the AIG Insurance Company's fiasco there are fewer insurance companies willing to cover municipal bonds or any other types of investments.

Closed-end funds issue a set number of shares that trade on the stock exchanges like any other stock, and are subject to fluctuations from the net asset value (NAV) of the bonds within the fund, resulting in the funds selling at a discount or premium. Most funds pay interest or dividends monthly, which can be reinvested at the market price without a commission or the money can be sent directly to checking accounts for instant use. When the fund is selling at a discount and income is reinvested, the new shares are purchased at the discounted price, which increases the return on investments; conversely, when they are purchased at a premium, the rate of return on the purchased shares decreases.

One of the reasons I was attracted to this type of investment was the safety in the diversification that pooling of many government bonds offered. Another great feature is the ability to automatically reinvest income that is not needed or to have the income deposited into my checking account every month. In the 15-plus years that I have been involved with these funds there has never been a missed or late payment. Currently the yield on many of my funds are paying between 5% and 7% tax free, which is a hell of a lot more than banks are paying, and in my opinion a lot safer, considering that currently there are three major banks that might be forced into bankruptcy or receivership. There are many places to research Closed-end funds; my favorite is WWW.Morningstar.com. To show how readily available information is, a copy of one of my positions with Morningstar's investment data follows:

BlackRock Munivest MVF |

Last Price	Day Change		Last Closing Share Price				1-Year	Market	Total Leverage
$9.93	0.03|0.30%		9.90	Day Range	52-WK Range	Z-Statistic	Value	Ratio
As of Tue 4/27/2011 4:00 PM EST USD				9.91-10.00	8.52-10.44	-0.99	618.5 mil	40.45 %

Last Actual NAV	Last NAV Date	Current Discount	6-Month Avg Discount	3-Year Avg Discount	Total Dist. Rate (Share Price)
9.84	09/23/2011	+0.91%	+1.76 %	-1.00 %	7.14 %
As of 09/26/2011					

CEF Price MVF

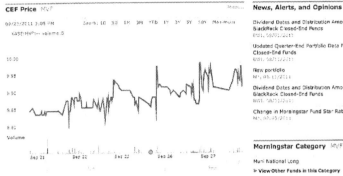

09/23/2011 3:05 PM   Zoom: 1D 5D 1M 3M YTD 1Y 3Y 5Y 10Y Maximum
KASE:MVF-- volume:0

News, Alerts, and Opinions

Dividend Dates and Distribution Amounts Announced for Certain BlackRock Closed-End Funds
BWL, 09/01/2011

Updated Quarter-End Portfolio Data Now Available for BlackRock Closed-End Funds
BWL, 08/31/2011

New portfolio
MT, 08/31/2011

Dividend Dates and Distribution Amounts Announced for Certain BlackRock Closed-End Funds
BWL, 08/01/2011

Change in Morningstar Fund Star Rating
MT, 02/05/2011

Morningstar Category MVF

Muni National Long
> View Other Funds in this Category

Benchmark MVF

Fund Benchmark	—
Morningstar Benchmark	BarCap Municipal TR USD

Investment Objective Summary MVF

The Fund seeks current income exempt from regular Federal income tax through investment in investment grade municipal bonds

Key Statistics MVF

Assets

Total Assets USD	1,037.5 mil
Net Assets USD	517.9 mil
Market Value USD	618.5 mil

Leverage

1940 Act Leverage Ratio	28.29 %
Non-1940 Act Leverage Ratio	22.15 %

Frequency

NAV Update Frequency	DAY
Distribution Payment Frequency	M

Expenses

Total Expense Ratio Reported	1.22 %
Total Expense Ratio Adjusted	1.03 %

Liquidity

Daily Shares Traded	—
Average Daily Shares Traded	0.09 mil
Average Daily Value Traded USD	0.87 mil
Number of Outstanding Common Shares	62.60 mil

Style Map MVF

	Avg Eff Duration	0.00 Yrs
Quality High	Avg Eff Maturity	0.00 Yrs
Med	Avg Credit Quality	Not Rated
Low		

Ltd Mod Ext
Interest-Rate Sensitivity

Valuation Statistics MVF

	09-26-2011	3-Year Low	3-Year High
Price USD	9.90	3.98	10.71
NAV USD	9.83	6.77	10.03
Discount	+0.10%	-27.00%	+8.13%
Z-Statistic (6 Mo)	-0.76	—	—
Z-Statistic (3 Yr)	0.21	—	—

The NAV is at last-previous days NAV. not check below is and frequency.

Asset Allocation MVF

Type	% Net	% Short	% Long
Cash	2.75	0.00	2.75
US Stock	0.00	0.00	0.00
Non US Stock	0.00	—	0.00

Corporate Debt—I'm not suggesting that buying corporate bonds is for everyone, I'm just reflecting what kind of securities made me feel comfortable while returning attractive interest into my retirement accounts. The bonds that I have invested in are called **Exchange-Traded Debt Securities** and are traded on the stock exchanges rather than in the bond markets. The securities include debentures, notes, and bonds and resemble preferred stocks in their basic features. In liquidation they rank junior to a company's secured debt, are equal to other unsecured debt, and are senior to a company's preferred and common stocks. These debts are generally issued in $25 denominations and could have maturity dates of 30 years or more. A nice feature is that the securities are normally redeemable at the issuer's option on or after five years from the date of issue at par. I was pleasantly surprised when one of my positions that I was receiving more than 6% interest was called at face value, which resulted in a nice profit on top of the interest that I had already received for many years, as I purchased the position at a discount. Most of the debt securities pay quarterly interest distributions. Some of the corporations listed are AT&T Inc., Comcast Corp., Ford Motors Credit, MetLife Inc., Sears Roebuck Acceptance, and my Favorite, General Electric Capital. The above corporations pay from 5% to 7% annually, and if the securities are in IRAs or other pension funds, the interest accumulates tax free until distributions are taken. As can be seen by the corporations listed, the bonds are primarily backed by each company's reputation as a leader in the financial community. A useful website to research these securities is WWW.QuantumOnline.com. A description of one of my holdings with Quantum Online's financial information follows:

General Electric Capital Corp., 6.625% Public Income Notes PINES due 6/28/2032

Ticker Symbol: GEA   CUSIP: 369622527   Exchange: NYSE
Security Type: Exchange-Traded Debt Security

QUANTUMONLINE.COM SECURITY DESCRIPTION: General Electric Capital Corp., 6.625% Public Income NotES (PINES), issued in $25 denominations, redeemable at the issuer's option on or after 6/28/2007 at $25 per share plus accrued and unpaid interest, maturing 6/28/2032, distributions of 6.625% ($1.65625) per annum are paid quarterly on 3/28, 6/28, 9/28 & 12/28 to holders of record one business day prior to the payment date while the securities remain in global security form (note that the ex-dividend date is at least 2 business days prior to the record date). Distributions paid by these debt securities are interest and as such are NOT eligible for the 15% tax rate on dividends and is also NOT eligible for the dividend received deduction for corporate holders. Units are expected to trade flat, which means accrued interest will be reflected in the trading price and the purchasers will not pay and the sellers will not receive any accrued and unpaid interest. The PINES are senior, unsecured obligations of the company and will rank equally with all existing and future unsecured and unsubordinated indebtedness of the company. See the IPO prospectus for further information on the debt securities by clicking on the 'Link to IPO Prospectus' provided below.

Stock Exchange	Cpn Rate Ann Amt	LiqPref CallPrice	Call Date Matur Date	Moodys/S&P Dated	Distribution Dates	15% Tax Rate
NYSE Chart	6.63% $1.65625	$25.00 $25.00	6/28/2007 6/28/2032	Aa2 / AA+ 8/27/11	3/28, 6/28, 9/28 & 12/28 Click for MW ExDiv Date Click for Values ExDiv Date	No

Goto Parent Company's Record (GE)

IPO - 6/20/2002 - 40.00 Million Notes @ $25.00/note.   Link to IPO Prospectus
Market Value $ 1 Billion
Click for current GEA price quote from the NYSE

Company's Online Information Links

HOME PAGE: http://www.ge.com/

Company's Investor Relations Information   Goto Investor Relations Information

Company's Online News Releases   Goto News Releases

Online Company Profile   Goto Online Profile

Company's Online SEC EDGAR Filings

Company's SEC EDGAR Filings   Goto SEC Filings

Company's Email Address Links

Email Address   ir.contacts@corporate.ge.com

Preparing for retirement is about accumulating wealth through savings and investment performance. But in retirement, our primary goal becomes more complex, and continuing growth without depleting the core of our holdings becomes our objective. Making sure that we have a steady stream of income to cover our lifestyle without tapping into the principal is paramount to a financially successful retirement. To help accomplish this, hiring an experienced financial advisor is imperative to assist with retirement financial planning; not to do so could be a major financial catastrophe and could mean the difference between retirement bliss and retirement grief.

Few of us head into retirement expecting bad things to happen with our financial planning. But bad unforeseen things invariably do happen. In our case, we were lucky to learn from a bitter experience of friends. They are snowbirds and during a winter storm in New York, their pipes burst due to the failure of their heating system. They had oil-hot-water-baseboard heat with a computerized oil replenishment system. The system failed and the replacement of the precious oil never happened. To make a long story short, the basement flooded and the leaks from the upper pipes just about destroyed everything in their house. To make matters worse, this happened when they were spending quality time in Florida, far away from the cold wintry New York weather, and caused them to return to their home under the worst possible conditions, in freezing weather no less. It took two years of living in hotels before the house was restored and their furnishings replaced. Their story sent us into a panic; we have the same type of heating system, baseboard hot water, except our furnace is gas operated, even so the possibility of broken pipes haunted me until I researched the subject to determine how I could overcome such an event.

The crux of the problem boils down to getting things done prior to retirement when you have the time, and money is usually more readily available. We were already retired when we began our preventive maintenance journey—fortunately, before we had a disaster. First, we decided that our hot water gas furnace was getting on in years, so we replaced it and the hot water heater at the same time. Next, we had to figure out how we could shut off the water coming into our house when we were away for the winter months. We had friends that lived in upstate New York's Snowbelt that simply turned off their water when they left home for extended periods of time. Most have hot air heat, which reduces the number of pipes at risk of bursting, but I was intrigued with the possibility of turning off the water coming into my house, which kept me digging for an answer to alleviate the possibility of our having a similar disaster as our friends. Our plumber supplied us with the perfect solution. First thing to do was winterize the hot water baseboard heating system with antifreeze, just like it's done in automobiles. So if the heating pipes burst for some reason, the worst-case scenario would be 15-gallons of antifreeze leaking into the house instead of an ocean of water from our incoming fresh water system. The next thing we did was install an accustat; this is an electronic device that notifies us in Florida via land-line telephone with a backup radio phone that we installed in our attic, if the temperature in our house drops below 50-degrees. If it does, we immediately call our house sitter to investigate. Then the final and most important steps were, we turned off the water to the house and set the heating thermostat to 60-degrees and our hot water heater to vacation. The antifreeze that was put into the hot water heating system circulates and is self-contained; the same as in a car engine, and keeps the house above freezing, which gives us an amazing degree of comfort when we're away from our New York home in the freezing-snowy months.

While we were on a preventive maintenance kick, we decided to replace our 25-year-old roof before leaks from it became a problem. While we were at it, we had several oak trees that were over 80-feet high and a little too close to our house removed and many others trimmed; luckily for us, two of the larger oak trees were infested with carpenter ants and were probably waiting for just the right inopportune time to fall on our house. If we were smart, we would have done all of the above before retiring, but being human, we waited for a **sign;** fortunately, the **sign** was not our reality, but the reality of our dear friends. These turned out to be major expenses that should have been considered prior to retiring, as the cost was something that we hadn't anticipated and put quite a dent in our retirement funds.

Chapter Seven – Preparing a Will and other Important Documents

Preparing a Will

Those of us who had the courage when they were younger to deal with documents that concerned death, probably already have a will. But there are many who wait until they are sick or are threatened with the possibility of death before they put pen to paper and outline what they want to happen to their assets after their demise. There are no laws that state that you have to make a will or estate plans, but there are laws that dictate what will happen to your assets if you do not take advantage of your right to determine the distribution of your wealth in the form of a will.

If you do not have a will, your state of residence will determine who will get your assets. Many states have different formulas, but generally, your wealth will be split between close relatives, including the cousin that you hate. If you have no close relatives then your estate may go to a relative that you didn't know existed. If you have no living relatives then the state becomes your long lost "uncle" and becomes the recipient of your hard-earned assets. It is a mistake to think that you will save money by not having a will or trust set up to protect your wealth after your demise. It is always more costly to rely on the good intentions of a state since it may not be able to easily determine who all your heirs are and will have to spend an inordinate amount of your money to find heirs and satisfy the intentions of the state laws. While the search for relatives goes on, money that is usually needed by the immediate family is tied up until the legalities of the state laws are satisfied. Through the state-made will process, everything may be held in abeyance while attempts are made to find heirs, post bonds, marshal assets, and prepare the necessary accounting documents that are required by the state to move forward with the lawful distribution of the estate's assets. Let's not forget federal and state estate taxes that might have to be paid at the top tax brackets if there is no will.

In addition to the distribution of assets, there are many other problems of not having a will. One example is, a widowed grandmother dies in a car crash with her only living adult relative, her daughter, and has no will. Her daughter has two minor children whose lives, according to law, will be dictated by the state until they reach maturity. The state will appoint a person or institution to care for the children and to manage the grandparent's wealth. When the grandchildren reach legal age, usually 18, any assets that remain will be distributed to them. I'm sure that no one wants the states to determine how their wealth is disbursed or how minor children are cared for until their maturity. Fortunately, there is an alternative to the state-made will, which simply requires preparing a will of your own—hopefully, while you are still young and healthy. With a valid will, trust, or other arrangements, such as electing beneficiaries in life insurance policies and retirement plans, you decide who receives the fruits of your labor and not the state.

With the help of a competent attorney specializing in estate planning, a will can be prepared to satisfy a person's after-death wishes. A major consideration to discuss with your lawyer is the amount of taxes that must be paid upon your death and how to provide for the cash to meet those obligations. Gift and estate taxes are not usually a primary concern at the beginning of the preparation of a will, but after all the bequests are made, the subject becomes the second most important one, as no one wants to pay more than their fair share of taxes. Remember there are no laws against legal tax avoidance, especially if directed by competent and honest advisers.

Preparing Living Wills and Other Advance Notices

- **Living Wills**—These legal documents spell out the types of medical treatments and life-sustaining measures a person wants or doesn't want, such as mechanical breathing (respiration and ventilation), tube feeding, or resuscitation. A living will describes a person's preferences regarding treatments if faced with a serious accident or illness. The document speaks for you when you are unable to speak for yourself.

- **Medical or Health Care Power of Attorney (POA)**—The medical POA is a legal document that designates an individual, referred to as a health care agent or proxy, who will make medical decisions for a person if they are unable to do so. This POA should not be confused with a person who has the POA to make financial decisions. The medical POA will be guided by the living will but has the authority to interpret a person's wishes in situations that aren't covered in a living will. Choosing this person is possibly the most important part of the planning process; it should be a person that is trusted, has your interests at heart, understands your wishes, and will act in accordance with your advance written directives. The person should be mature and levelheaded, and comfortable dealing with death-related issues and conversations. Never, never pick someone out of feelings of guilt or obligation. Many people prefer not to have the same person as financial and medical POAs.

- **Do not Resuscitate (DNR) Order**—This is a very controversial topic within families. When the time comes to "pull the plug," there are always family members that refuse to be instrumental in ending a loved one's life. Therefore, it's important to discuss with family members your wishes and let them understand your values, such as how important it is for you to be independent and self-sufficient, and what you feel would make your life not worth living. Let them know under what circumstances you want your life extended or terminated. Let them know if you want painkillers to ease your pain and discomfort if you are terminally ill. Explaining some of the terms that apply to DNR might be helpful at this point:

- **Resuscitation**—This procedure restarts the heart when it has stopped beating by CPR or a device that delivers an electric shock to stimulate the heart. Many people are uncomfortable with having these procedures attempted, especially if they are very old, terminally ill, or have religious concerns.
- **Mechanical Ventilation**—Takes over breathing when a person is unable to do so. It's important that you stipulate how long you want to continue being on this life support.
- **Nutritional and Hydration Assistance**—Supplies the body with nutrients and fluids intravenously or via a tube in the stomach. It should be made clear how long you might want to remain on this type of support.
- **Dialysis**—Removes waste from your blood and manages fluid levels if your kidneys no longer function. Again, it should be made clear how long this procedure should be used.

Injury, illness, and death, at any age, aren't easy subjects to talk about openly, but planning ahead will insure that your medical wishes will be followed, and will also relieve your family of the burden of trying to guess what your wishes were. Let them know that you have written advance directives and explain to them in detail what you want to happen when the time comes.

When all of the essential documents are completed and your family is aware of your wishes, the only thing left for you to do is to make a detailed list of where all of your documents are and the names and telephone numbers of your contact people. I use an **Important Information** schedule listing, which includes the following:

- My name, address, social security number, and date of birth.
- Where my safety deposit box is located and who has the keys and authority to access it.

- Where the original and copies of my wills and living wills are located.
- Names, addresses, and telephone numbers of my executors and trustees.
- Names, addresses, telephone numbers, and personal contacts at my brokerage accounts.
- Names, addresses, telephone numbers, and personal contacts at my checking and savings accounts.
- Name, address, and telephone number of the attorney that I wish to handle my estate.
- Name, address, and telephone number of the accountants that I wish to prepare documents and file tax returns that are required by law.
- Name, address, and telephone numbers of my doctors.
- Name, address, telephone number, and policy numbers of life insurance companies and my contacts, detailing the value of the insurance policies and the beneficiaries.
- Obituary information that I want used; this relieves a lot of tension for family members.
- Burial instruction and place of internment.

With all of the above accomplished, life after your death will become much easier for those remaining and will give them much more time to figure out how to dispose of your assets. . .

Chapter Eight – Getting Rid of Stuff

I saved writing about the most distasteful chore of becoming a senior citizen for last, and that is getting rid of **stuff.**

Over our lifetimes, we accumulate an amazing amount of **stuff.** It seems that we are pack rats by nature and find it very difficult to get rid of our bountiful accumulation of **stuff.** Everyone is different when it comes to getting rid of things, so I'll relate how I began getting rid of my possessions over the past few years, with **some** degree of success:

- **Old Tax Returns**—It took me months to go through all the tax returns that I filed since I was married in 1960. My files included cancelled checks, charitable receipts, proof of payments, diaries, and stock receipts. My filing cabinets were bulging with ancient history that I so foolishly accumulated in the event that I might somehow have to refer to information some time in the future. I now only have the last seven years' tax returns and have thrown out unnecessary paper work pertaining to those years. It took weeks to shred the old documents, reminiscing about those precious years as I placed each piece of my past into the recycling bags.

- **Old Photos**—In addition to the multitude of photo albums that we have, we managed to accumulate hundreds of pictures of family and friends that ended up in several cardboard boxes in our basement. What to do with these precious gems? Well, Barbara and I spent several weeks sorting through them, reminiscing while placing them in separate piles for our two children, ten nephew and nieces and our other relatives. We delivered the photos, neatly boxed and wrapped in Xmas paper to them, and presented the gifts at Christmas time. A big hit were the baby pictures of my nieces and nephews that they had never seen along with pictures of their parents when they were in their prime of life.

- **Old Videos**—What to do with the hundreds of super 8 films and video tapes that accumulated over the years and were placed in a sacred place never to be viewed again? It took us months to review reels of film and tapes. Sorting them by the person we wished to receive our gems took longer than we anticipated, but was worth the effort. The only problem remaining was how to present our relatives with so many pieces of history? Barbara had a brainstorm; a young neighbor had the right equipment and volunteered to transfer the reels and tapes onto DVDs. We worked out financial arrangements and within a couple of months, he finished the job to perfection. After the enormous undertaking was over, we presented our relatives with the discs as Xmas presents. Their reaction was overwhelming and they rewarded us with lots of hugs and kisses and many phone calls of appreciation after they viewed precious family moments that were caught on film.

- **Clothing**—How do I begin to explain the amount of suits, jackets, slacks, shirts, ties, dresses and shoes that accumulated over the years? The big question was, which do we get rid of? It was a lot easier for me to dispose of my collection, as it seemed that most of my clothing didn't fit my ancient body. But Barbara still had her girlish figure and parting with her garments was a traumatic experience for her. Many a blouse and dress that went into the donation pile ended up back in her closet or in the new space that miraculously appeared in my emptied closets that she insisted had to be filled with her clothing. Most of my stuff went to the homeless shelter at the Salvation Army and was received with lots of gratitude. Barbara's small pile of stuff went to the Lupus Society to be sold at their various outlets to assist in their research programs.

- **Books, Books, Books, and more Books**—I couldn't believe the amount of books that we collected over our 40-years of marriage. Barbara made a habit of recycling many of her books to her friends, but I never could part with a book once it was in my possession. As I wrote previously, most of my books were on the topic of "Christopher Columbus and the Age of Discovery." I was fortunate to place much, but not all, of my collections of over 400 books and documents at the Columbus Foundation in New York City where it currently resides in the Mike Bivona Library. Giving away my gems was one of my saddest experiences, but it was a better choice than having them disbursed to unknown places after my demise.

Chapter Nine-What Have We Learned?

It is easy to look back to determine what we should have done differently to make our retirement and life an easier and more productive journey. Hindsight is wonderful; it allows us to put ourselves at perfect places in a perfect world. But life is not perfect and we have all made decisions that, if given a chance, we would have made differently. I can't speak for others, but I can draw from our experiences about the things we should have done to make our lives and those of our loved ones more comfortable.

The three most important segments of our existence that affected our retirement were **health**, **attitude** and **finances**. Barbara and I, after long discussions and debates, agreed that if we could relive our younger days that we certainly would have done many things differently. At this time in our lives, the most important thing is staying healthy, so we can get the most out of life and be there for the people who mean so much to us. We asked ourselves what we should have done differently to accomplish this. There is no doubt that we should have been more proactive when it came to:

1. **Having annual medical check-ups.** I'm sure that we all did the same thing in our younger days when we felt invincible. The only time we visited a doctor's office was when we didn't

feel well. Barbara and I began having annual check-ups after we both had life-threatening illnesses. I'm sure that if I made earlier visits to doctors that my open heart surgery at age 59 may have been avoided or postponed to a time when alternative methods, such as artery stents or improved medications, were developed that could have been a lot less intrusive and dangerous. I don't know if Barbara's aneurysm operation could have been avoided, but the problem may have been detected sooner and handled accordingly, maybe under less critical and life threatening circumstances. Now that we are wiser, we practice preventive medical care. We have flu and pneumonia shots regularly and take cholesterol and other tests that may detect abnormalities, frequently, before they become serious and possibly life-threatening.

2. **Developing the right attitude.** As our Tango mentor impressed on us when we visited Buenos Aires to learn the Argentine Tango, "The right attitude in dancing and life is the essence of our existence." When we were young we let many unimportant things dictate our actions and the level of stress we put ourselves under. The pressure of our jobs always played a central role in how we behaved while working and in our homes. It would have been nice if we learned to let important and unimportant things that created stress in our lives roll off our shoulders and dealt with them as if they were natural and normal events and soon would pass. Looking back it seems as if the little unhappy events created as much stress as the major ones, both having the same effect on us. I think if we would have taken dance lessons and had exercise programs when we were younger, that we would have worked off lots of unwelcomed stress on the dance floor and gym, and would have developed a healthier attitude towards life with a lot less stress.

3. **Financial Considerations.** Barbara and I were born during the Great Depression. Although we were both too young to remember that period, we were brought up in families that carried with them memories of those hard times and they passed their concerns on to us. So, what does that have to do with financial matters during retirement? Well, the lesson I learned from the many financial recessions and near depressions

that I've witnessed is that I should have paid more attention to what people who experienced the Great Depression said. Some of the advice that my parents drilled into me was: "A fool and his gold are soon parted," "A penny saved is a penny earned," "There is no such thing as becoming rich overnight," "Remember that someone trying to sell you something is doing so for his benefit, not yours," and "If it seems too good to be true then it's probably not true." The cautious advice I received goes on and on. What it took me to learn when I was in my 50s would have saved me lots of money and grief if I applied the same strategy when I was in my 30s. As mentioned previously, investing your age, let's say 30% in safe bonds at age 30, and 40% at age 40, and the remainder, 70% and 60% in high quality dividend paying stocks, would have avoided many sleepless nights and would have done wonders for my retirement funds. Many times when I tried to make a "killing" or a "quick buck" I ended up losing money, which was always followed by unwelcomed stress for me and my family.

I hope in some way that my writing based on our experiences will help future retirees smooth their paths into a more stable and secure retirement, free of unnecessary stress and hopefully with more than enough money to make their journey into retirement one that they hoped for.